A Wesleyan Theology
of the Eucharist

A Wesleyan Theology of the Eucharist

The Presence of God for Christian Life and Ministry

General Editor
Jason E. Vickers

A Wesleyan Theology of the Eucharist: The Presence of God for Christian Life and Ministry

The General Board of Higher Education and Ministry leads and serves The United Methodist Church in the recruitment, preparation, nurture, education, and support of Christian leaders— lay and clergy—for the work of making disciples of Jesus Christ for the transformation of the world. The General Board of Higher Education and Ministry of The United Methodist Church serves as an advocate for the intellectual life of the church. The Board's mission embodies the Wesleyan tradition of commitment to the education of laypersons and ordained persons by providing access to higher education for all persons.

Contents

Introduction

For John and Charles Wesley, few things were more important for both theology and ministry than attentiveness to the Lord's Supper. John Wesley insisted that the people called Methodists partake of Holy Communion as often as possible.[1] Charles Wesley wrote and published an entire hymn collection devoted to the Lord's Supper.[2]

Down through the centuries, the Wesleyan commitment to the centrality of the Eucharist for Christian life and practice has waxed and waned. To be sure, most Wesleyan churches acknowledge the importance of the sacraments. Yet, many do not partake of Holy Communion on a frequent basis. In some cases, Communion is celebrated once per month; in other cases, once per quarter or less.

Most recently, a growing number of Wesleyan theologians have been seeking to recover the importance of Holy Communion for theology and ministry. This volume seeks to bring the work of some of these theologians together in one place in a systematic and coherent way.

In part 1, leading Wesleyan theologians reflect on the Eucharist in connection with each of the major areas of Christian theology, including the doctrine of the Trinity (Geoffrey Wainwight), creation (Daniel Castelo), sin (Andrew Sung Park), Jesus Christ (John Drury), the Holy Spirit (Jason Vickers), the church (William Abraham), salvation (Sarah Lancaster), and eschatology or the doctrine of last things (Brent Peterson).

In part 2, a second group of distinguished Wesleyan scholars reflect on the relationship between the Eucharist and various aspects of Christian life and ministry, including worship (Robin Knowles Wallace), preaching (Richard Eslinger), evangelism (Elaine Heath), formation (Paul Chilcote), ethics (Rebekah Miles), the use of money (Ed Phillips), pastoral care (Ed Wimberly), prayer (E. Bryon (Ron) Anderson), and ecumenism (Karen Westerfield Tucker).

Finally, with respect to the organization and contents of the volume, the two-part division should not be taken to imply that part 1 does not contain insights with respect to the work of ministry or that part 2 is lacking in deep theological reflection. From beginning to end, readers will discover a treasure trove of theological insights and applications for Christian life and ministry.

---

1   John Wesley, "The Duty of Constant Communion," *in The Works of John Wesley*, vol. 3, ed. Albert C. Outler (Nashville: Abingdon Press, 1986), 427–39.
2   John and Charles Wesley, *Hymns on the Lord's Supper* (Bristol: Farley, 1745).

PART I

Theology and Eucharist

ONE

The Trinity and Eucharist

Geoffrey Wainwright

One of the most important tasks of (reflective) theology is to mediate between *doctrine*, or the official teaching of the church, and *liturgy*, or the formal worship of the church. Characteristically, there is a two-way movement between doctrine and liturgy, where each draws on and contributes to the other. Historically, it is sometimes the *lex credendi* or "rule of faith" that has set the pace for the *lex orandi* or "rule of prayer"; at other times, the *lex orandi* has taken the lead, to be followed by the *lex credendi*. Ideally, there should be an excellent match between liturgy and doctrine, and it is partly the job of reflective theology to help ensure the correspondence between the pair. Both teachers and preachers should thereby be assisted in their respective and related services to the believing community's encounter with God, and indeed the composers of prayers and of hymns for the worshiping body should benefit also.

Our assigned topic on this occasion is The Trinity (doctrine) and The Eucharist (liturgy). We shall chiefly examine this interactive pair in the ecclesiastical context of Methodism (broadly understood), both as to our beginnings in and under the Wesleys and then in the more recent circumstances of the ecumenical and the liturgical movements of the twentieth century, which continue into the present. To begin with, however, we go much further back in history, namely to the fourth century, where the Trinitarian shape of both doctrine and liturgy was classically and lastingly elaborated. In fact, we will shed light on one figure who had responsibility, as a bishop, in both liturgy and doctrine, and who (providentially) was gifted with a mind capable of theological reflection, namely Bishop Basil of Caesarea, author of a decisive treatise for the integrity of both faith and worship.

The Trinity in Patristic Liturgy and Doctrine

St. Basil wrote on the Holy Spirit around the year 373, during perhaps the third generation of the Arian controversies.[1] He had faced accusations

---

1 Basil's Greek text, with facing-page French translation, can be found in the amply annotated edition of Benoît Pruche, *Basile de Césarée: Sur le Saint-Esprit, Sources chrétiennes 17 bis* (Paris: Éditions du Cerf, 1968). An English translation

by Arianizers of innovation when he concluded his church's prayers with a "co-ordinated" doxology in terms of an address to the Father "with" (*meta*) the Son "together with" (*sun*) the Holy Spirit. Part of his reply consisted in citing examples from his predecessors of similar usage but also, and more important for our purposes, in demonstrating the propriety of addressing worship to the Second and Third Persons on account of their divine status as proven by delicate exegesis from Scripture. Basil also needed to show that the more usual practice of concluding praise and prayer to the Father "through" (*dia*) Christ "in" (*en*) the Spirit did not entail any subordination of the latter two.

Basil's work, together with those of the two Cappadocian Gregories, helped to solidify the full Trinitarianism that would receive conciliar statement in the Nicene-Constantinopolitan Creed of 381. The most significant "liturgical" legacy of Basil's treatise was the continuance throughout corporate Christian worship of *both* types of address: the co-ordinate address to all Three Persons of the Trinity in the high doxological ascription of all glory and honor to God and the mediatorial formulation of prayer when it comes to more particular matters of thanks and petition. Basil's underlying "theological" achievement was to justify the two types by making the one appropriate to God "contemplated in himself," where the three Persons are "co-inherent," and the other appropriate to that same God when considered in his "economy" where the three Persons "co-operate" for the sake of the creatures: all good gifts originate from the Father and reach us through the Son in the Spirit; correspondingly, thanks and petition arise in the Spirit and are transported by the Son to the Father as the ultimate source and goal of salvation. While there are, to be sure, mixed and borderline cases in the course of liturgical and doctrinal history, the dual pattern has been broadly maintained.

John Wesley's Teaching on the Trinity

Now John Wesley was a thoroughgoing Trinitarian as to both doctrine and liturgy, and he could give detailed theological expositions of the Trinitarian pattern in appropriate ecclesiastical and pastoral circumstances. In his Letter to a Roman Catholic, written from Dublin in July 1749 in an effort to allay Catholic opposition to the evangelistic work of the Methodists in

---

of Basil's treatise figures in the Popular Patristics series: *Stephen Hildebrand, St. Basil the Great: On the Holy Spirit* (Yonkers, NY: St. Vladimir's Seminary Press, 2011).

Ireland, Wesley begins with the "tenderest regard" in which he must hold his addressee on account of being creatures of the same God and both being redeemed by God's own Son and "studying to have a conscience void of offence towards God and towards man." In the two main sections of the Letter, Wesley then sets out "the belief of a true Protestant" and "the practice of a true Protestant," making the most of the commonalities between Protestants and Catholics. The content of the faith (*fides quae creditur*) is presented in terms of an exposition of the Nicene-Constantinopolitan Creed, and Wesley expands on the Creed in order to bring out the Chalcedonian teaching concerning the person and natures of Christ and the traditional understanding of Christ's "threefold office" as prophet, priest, and king. As to "the infinite and eternal Spirit of God, equal with the Father and the Son," this Third Person is believed to be "not only perfectly holy in himself," but—along the *via salutis*—"the immediate cause of all holiness in us." Ecclesiologically, the church extends "to all nations and all ages," and its members "have fellowship with God the Father, Son, and Holy Ghost." The attitude or virtue of faith (*fides qua creditur*) gets embodied in love towards both God and neighbor: "works of piety" (the true believer "worships God in spirit and in truth, in every thing gives him thanks, calls upon him with his heart as well as his lips, at all times and in all places, honours his holy Name and his Word, and serves him truly all the days of his life") and, of course, "works of mercy" ("and do all as unto the Lord, as a sacrifice unto God, acceptable in Christ Jesus"). Together these constitute "the old religion," "true, primitive Christianity."[2]

Wesley's most sustained exposition of Christian worship as Trinitarian is found in his sermon on "Spiritual Worship."[3] The text is 1 John 5:20: "This is the true God, and eternal life," which stands for the whole epistle, read by Wesley as a "tract" aimed at "the happy and holy communion which the faithful have with God the Father, and Holy Ghost." The epistle, or tract, is structured thus, Wesley discerns: first as to communion with the three divine Persons severally, "the Father" (in 1:5–10), "the Son" (in chaps. 2 and 3), and "the Spirit" (in chap. 4); second, conjointly, as to "the testimony of the Father, Son, and Holy Ghost, on which faith in Christ, the being born of God, love to God and his children, the keeping his commandments, and

---

2   John Wesley's "Letter to a Roman Catholic" may be conveniently located in Albert C. Outler's anthology, *John Wesley* (New York: Oxford University Press, 1964), 492–99.

3   John Wesley, "Spiritual Worship," in *The Works of John Wesley: Sermons*, vol. 3, ed. Albert C. Outler (Nashville: Abingdon Press, 1986), 88–102.

victory over the world, are founded" (in 5:1–12); and finally the "recapitul-
tion," where "eternal life" is to be found in "the true God," "the Son who is
come," whom we know "by the Holy Ghost."

One-third of Wesley's sermon is, in fact, devoted to demonstrating how
the Scriptures take Jesus Christ as this "true God," not only by directly
attributing divinity to him as in John 1:1-2 and giving him the title "Lord"
but also by ascribing to him "all the attributes and all the works of God":
he is creator, supporter, preserver, author, governor and end of all things,
and "the redeemer of all the children of men." This Jesus is "the author of
eternal salvation to all them that obey him" [Wesley is citing Heb 5:9], and
"this eternal life commences when it pleases the Father to reveal his Son in
our hearts; when we first know Christ, being enabled to 'call him Lord by
the Holy Ghost' [1 Cor 12:3]; when we can testify, our conscience bearing
witness in the Holy Ghost, 'the life which I now live I live by faith in the
Son of God, who loved me, and gave himself for me' [Gal 2:20]." Thereby we
reach the "spiritual worship," which Wesley adumbrated at the start as "the
happy and holy communion which the faithful have with God the Father,
Son, and Holy Ghost."

The same soteriological thrust, with consequences for Christian worship, is found in the conclusion of Wesley's sermon "On the Trinity":

> The knowledge of the Three-One God is interwoven with all true Christian
> faith, with all vital religion. . . . I know not how anyone can be a Christian
> believer till "he hath" (as St. John speaks) "the witness in himself" [1 John
> 5:10], till "the Spirit of God witnesses with his spirit that he is a child of God"
> [Rom 8:16]—that is, in effect, that God the Father has accepted him through
> the merits of God the Son—and having this witness he honours the Son and
> the blessed Spirit "even as he honours the Father" [John 5:23].[4]

In Wesley's sermon "The Duty of Constant Communion," God is called
our Maker and Redeemer, our Mediator and Governor. The Lord's Supper
is both "a command of God" and "a mercy from God to man":

---

4   Wesley, "On the Trinity," *The Works of John Wesley*, vol. 2, ed. Outler. 373–86. In
    that sermon Wesley disclaims any too intimate knowledge of the inner consti-
    tution of the Godhead: "I believe this **fact**—that God is Three and One. But the
    manner, how, I do not comprehend" (384). Elsewhere, however, he warns against
    deistic or socinian tendencies in the thought of his time: "The quaint device
    of styling them three offices rather than persons gives up the whole doctrine"
    (letter of August 3, 1771, to Jane Catherine Marsh). For more on Wesley's opera-
    tion as a reflective theologian on Trinitarian matters, see Geoffrey Wainwright,
    "Why Wesley Was a Trinitarian," in *Methodists in Dialogue* (Nashville: Abingdon
    Press [Kingswood Books], 1995), 261–74.

As God, whose mercy is over all his works, and particularly over the children of men, knew there was but one way to be happy like himself, namely, by being like him in holiness; as he knew we could do nothing toward this of ourselves, he has given us certain means of obtaining his help. One of these is the Lord's Supper, which of his infinite mercy he hath given for this very end: that through this means we may be assisted to attain those blessings which he hath prepared for us; that we may obtain holiness on earth and everlasting glory in heaven.[5]

The eschatological prospect of communion with the Holy Trinity forms the peroration of Wesley's sermon "The New Creation": "To crown all, there will be a deep, an intimate, an uninterrupted union with God; a constant communion with the Father and his Son Jesus Christ, through the Spirit; a continual enjoyment of the Three-One God, and of all creatures in him!"[6]

"The Sunday Service of the Methodists"

Now what practical provisions did Wesley make to enable a Eucharistic encounter between the Trinitarian faithful and the Triune God, in which they might worship God, thank God for God's gifts, and entreat God's continuing grace? On home ground, the liturgy would be that of "The Order of the Administration of the Lord's Supper, or Holy Communion" in the 1662 Book of Common Prayer. At the start, the beautiful collect for purity is discreetly Trinitarian in content and mediatorial in structure: "Almighty God, unto whom all hearts be open, all desires known, and from whom no secrets are hid: Cleanse the thoughts of our hearts by the inspiration of thy Holy Spirit, that we may perfectly love thee, and worthily magnify thy holy Name; through Christ our Lord. Amen."

After the reading of the Scriptures, the Nicene-Constantinopolitan Creed "shall be sung or said." The Exhortation to Communion then includes these words:

---

5   Wesley, "The Duty of Constant Communion," *The Works of John Wesley*, vol. 3, ed. Outler, 427–39.

6   Wesley, "The New Creation," *The Works of John Wesley*, vol. 2, ed. Outler, 500–10, in particular 510. Further evidence of Wesley's Trinitarian understanding of worship may be found by following up those twenty or so passages in Wesley's Sermons where he quotes or alludes to John 4:23-24: "The hour cometh, and now is, when the true worshippers shall worship the Father in spirit and in truth; for the Father seeketh such to worship him. God is Spirit; and they that worship him must worship him in spirit and in truth." See Geoffrey Wainwright, "Worship according to Wesley," *Australian Journal of Liturgy* 3, no. 1 (May 1991), 5–20, in particular 7–9 ("Worship in Spirit and in Truth").

> And above all things ye must give humble and hearty thanks to God, the Father, the Son, and the Holy Ghost, for the redemption of the world by the death and passion of our Saviour Christ, both God and man. . . . To him therefore, with the Father and the Holy Ghost, let us give (as we are most bounden) continual thanks; submitting ourselves wholly to his holy will and pleasure, and studying to serve him in true holiness and righteousness all the days of our life. Amen.

When, therefore, we come to the high doxological moment of the triple Sanctus, the Trinitarian resonances are not far to seek. And in the two (alternative) post-Communion prayers, the conclusions run "through Jesus Christ our Lord; by whom, and with whom, in the unity of the Holy Ghost, all honour and glory be unto thee, O Father almighty, world without end. Amen"; and "And we most humbly beseech thee, O heavenly Father, so to assist us with thy grace, that we may continue in that holy fellowship, and do all such good works as thou hast prepared for us to walk in; through Jesus Christ our Lord, to whom, with thee and the Holy Ghost, be all honour and glory, world without end. Amen."

Then the Greater Gloria "shall be said or sung"—again, a high doxological moment, with the address of worship to the "Lord God, heavenly King, God the Father Almighty"; central petitions to the "Lord, the only-begotten Son Jesus Christ" for mercy and forgiveness of sins; and the triple conclusion: "Thou only art holy; thou only art the Lord; thou only, O Christ, with the Holy Ghost, art most high in the glory of God the Father. Amen." And at the end of the service the people are dismissed with the final "blessing of God Almighty, the Father, the Son, and the Holy Ghost."

Of the liturgical changes that Wesley made in assembling *The Sunday Service of the Methodists in North America* few, if any, were of doctrinal significance in the matters of the Eucharist and the Trinity. It was "probably to avoid redundancy and to answer complaints regarding the length of the Sunday liturgy" that "the Nicene Creed was removed from the order for Communion since that office was generally preceded by Morning Prayer that contained the Apostles' Creed"—and, on occasion, the Trinitarian *Te Deum Laudamus*; and if Wesley omitted the Athanasian Creed (*Quicunque Vult*) that was appointed for periodic recitation in Morning Prayer in the Book of Common Prayer (BCP), perhaps it was that Wesley shared the view of some contemporaries that "the Athanasian Creed with its so-called 'damnatory clauses' might not be appropriate for liturgical use."[7] Certainly

---

7   See Karen B. Westerfield Tucker, "Early Methodist Liturgical Practices and the Book of Common Prayer," in *The Oxford Handbook of Methodist Studies*, ed. William J. Abraham and James E. Kirby (New York and Oxford: Oxford University Press, 2009), 296–98.

we find no quibble in Wesley with the substance of any of the three creeds. The most significant point in Wesley's letter of September 10, 1784, to "Our Brethren in America" was perhaps the christological connection between Sunday and the Holy Communion: "I also advise the elders to administer the Supper of the Lord on every Lord's Day."[8]

Hymns on the Lord's Supper

Before leaving the Wesleyan beginnings we must, of course, look in the hymnody for the substantive connections established there between the Trinity and the Eucharist. Our attention will be concentrated on *The Hymns on the Lord's Supper*, published in 1745 under the joint names of the brothers John and Charles, but we must at least mention such a collection as Charles's "Hymns on the Trinity" (1767), where the quadripartite structure—"The Divinity of Christ," "The Divinity of the Holy Ghost," "The Plurality and Trinity of Persons," "The Trinity in Unity"—matches the treatise of William Jones of Nayland, *The Catholic Doctrine of the Trinity, proved by an hundred short and clear arguments, expressed in terms of the Holy Scripture* (1756), which was written precisely to combat resurgent Arianism and emergent Unitarianism.[9]

In the original eighteenth-century Methodist context of reviving eucharistic observance and participation, the Wesleyan *Hymns on the Lord's Supper* served at least three purposes: catechetical, liturgical, and devotional. First, the hymns taught the significance and benefits of the Lord's Supper. Second, they will have contributed to the repertoire for singing at the time of the Communion itself, which we know took place particularly when there were large numbers of communicants. Third, they provided a resource for meditative preparation before, and recollection after, the sacrament.

---

8   For eucharistic observance among Methodists in Britain, see John C. Bowmer, *The Sacrament of the Lord's Supper in Early Methodism* (London: Dacre Press, 1951), and again Bowmer, The Lord's Supper in Methodism 1791–1960 (London: Epworth Press, 1961); and in the United States, see Karen B. Westerfield Tucker, *American Methodist Worship* (New York: Oxford University Press, 2001), especially chaps. 1, 2, and 5.

9   The Hymns on the Lord's Supper figure in George Osborn, ed., *The Poetical Works of John and Charles Wesley*, vol. 3 (1869) (London: Wesleyan-Methodist Conference Office), 181–342; and the Hymns on the Trinity, in vol. 7 (1870), 201–98. A facsimile reprint of Hymns on the Lord's Supper was produced by The Charles Wesley Society (Madison, NJ: 1995), to which I contributed an introduction (v–xiv). The mid-twentieth-century revival of interest in the *Hymns on the Lord's Supper* owed much to the study of J. Ernest Rattenbury, *The Eucharistic Hymns of John and Charles Wesley* (London: Epworth Press, 1948).

Already in 'The Christian Sacrament and Sacrifice, Extracted from Dr. Brevint, which the Wesleys set as a preface to *The Hymns on the Lord's Supper* we find at the very beginning: "At the holy Table the people meet to worship God, and God is present to meet and bless His people. . . . So that the holy Sacrament, is a great mystery, consisting of both Sacrament and Sacrifice; that is, of the religious service which the people owe to God, and of the full salvation which God hath promised to his people" (I.1). The text quickly moves to a Trinitarian account of Christ's sacrifice, echoing Hebrews 9:14 ("How much more shall the blood of Christ, who through the eternal Spirit offered himself without spot to God, purge your conscience from dead works to serve the living God"): "The Sacrifice of Christ being appointed by the Father for a propitiation that should continue to all ages; and withal being everlasting by the privilege of its own order, which is an unchangeable Priesthood; and by His worth who offered it, that is, the Blessed Son of God; and by the power of the Eternam Spirit, through whom it was offered: it must in all respects stand eternal, the same yesterday, today, and for ever" (II.7).

That is predominantly the picture conveyed in the hymns when they expound the Sacrament as now presented before the Father in commemoration of Christ's unique sacrifice ("The Holy Eucharist as it implies a Sacrifice"; Hymns 116–127), to which is joined, by the Spirit's grace, "The Sacrifice of our Persons" (Hymns 128–157). On account of the pneumatological connection with the "epiclesis" of the Eastern liturgies, particular mention may be made of "Come, Holy Ghost, set to Thy seal" (Hymn 7); "Come, Thou everlasting Spirit" (Hymn 16, which borrows from the fourth-century liturgy of *Apostolic Constitutions VIII* the biblical image of the Holy Spirit as the "true Recorder" of Christ's passion, the "witness of his Dying," and now the "Remembrancer Divine"); and "Come, Holy Ghost, Thine influence shed" (Hymn 72), which attributes to the Spirit the consecration of the eucharistic elements and their sacramental efficacy:

> Come, Holy Ghost, thine Influence shed,
> And realize the Sign,
> Thy life infuse into the Bread,
> Thy power into the Wine.
> Effectual let the Tokens prove,
> And made by heavenly Art
> Fit Channels to convey Thy love
> To every Faithful Heart.

Fuller citation (at least in part) may be offered here of three further hymns because of their close resemblance to two liturgical items in the Book of Common Prayer's Order of Communion: the Sanctus and the Greater Gloria:

> Father, Son, and Holy Ghost,
> One in Three, and Three in One,
> As by the celestial host
> Let Thy will on earth be done,
> Praise by all to Thee be given,
> Gracious Lord of earth and heaven.
> *(Hymn 155)*
>   * * * *

> Lord and God of heavenly powers,
> Theirs—yet O! benignly ours,
> Glorious King, let earth proclaim,
> Worms attempt to chant Thy name.

> Thee to laud in songs Divine
> Angels and archangels join;
> We with them our voices raise,
> Echoing Thy eternal praise:

> "Holy, Holy, Holy Lord,
> Live by heaven and earth adored!"
> Full of Thee, they ever cry,
> Glory be to God most High!"
> *(Hymn 161)*
>   * * * *

> Glory be to God on high,
> God whose glory fills the sky:
> Peace on earth to man forgiven,
> Man the well-beloved of Heaven!

> Sovereign Father, Heavenly King!
> Thee we now presume to sing;
> Glad Thine attributes confess;
> Glorious all and numberless.

> Hail! By all Thy works adored,
> Hail! The everlasting Lord!
> Thee with thankful hearts we prove
> Lord of Power, and God of Love!

Christ our Lord and God we own,
Christ the Father's only Son!
Lamb of God for sinners slain,
Saviour of offending man!

Bow Thine ear, in mercy bow,
Hear, the World's Atonement Thou!
Jesu, in Thy name we pray,
Take, O, take our sins away.

Powerful Advocate with God,
Justify us by Thy blood!
Bow Thine ear, in mercy bow,
Hear, the World's Atonement Thou!

Hear; for Thou, O Christ, alone
With Thy glorious Sire art One!
One the Holy Ghost with Thee,
One supreme Eternal Three.
      (Hymn 163)

Now, however, we must advance our story beyond the original Wesleyan times. Historians report that "during the first part of the nineteenth century, published ritual texts for the Lord's Supper used by Methodists on both sides of the Atlantic were drawn directly from the BCP, from Wesley's abridgment of it, or from a revision of Wesley's."[10] And indeed that remained largely true of the bigger Methodist denominations in both Britain and America throughout the nineteenth century and the first half of the twentieth.[11] As to the *Hymns on the Lord's Supper*, eight were included in the large and influential *Collection of Hymns for the Use of the People Called Methodists*, but their relocation in a different framework rendered their eucharistic reference less obvious. Varied selections of anywhere between a dozen and twenty of the Wesleyan eucharistic hymns appeared in the hymnals of the Methodist Episcopal Church and the Methodist Episcopal Church, South throughout the nineteenth century. By the time of the 1905 joint *Hymnal* of the Methodist Episcopal Church and the Methodist Episcopal

---

10   See Westerfield Tucker, as in n. 5, 306–7.
11   See the studies named in n. 8, although the British Methodist *Book of Offices* (1936) contained also a second order of Communion that was meant to cater to the tastes of those who had come from "freer" styles of Methodism into the Methodist ecclesial union of 1932 (see Bowmer, *The Lord's Supper in Methodism 1791–1960*, 44–46).

Church, South, however, their number had sunk to two (HLS 157, and the first stanza of 155), and the 1935 *Hymnal* took away even what its immediate predecessor had left. The 1966 *Hymnal* of the Methodist Church climbed from zero to four (HLS 40, 57, 96, 165), but the 1989 *Hymnal* of The United Methodist Church sank back to two (HLS 29, "O Thou who this mysterious bread didst in Emmaus break"; and HLS 57, "O the depth of Love divine"). The history on the other side of the Atlantic ran rather similarly in the nineteenth century, while in the twentieth century the earlier numerical record was there more happily maintained, and the successive British Methodist hymnals of 1904, 1933, and 1983 each included a variable selection of about fifteen items from the *Hymns on the Lord's Supper*.

Our account having reached (however sketchily) the latter half of the twentieth century, it is time to look at the situation of "The Trinity and the Eucharist" in Methodism amid the new circumstances introduced by the confluence of the broader ecumenical and liturgical movements in which our ecclesial tradition has played an active part. A good place to begin might be the bilateral dialogue between the World Methodist Council and the Roman Catholic Church. Already in its first report ("The Denver Report, 1971"), the Joint Commission reported:

> The hymns of Charles Wesley, a rich source of Methodist spirituality, find echoes and recognition in the Catholic soul. This is not least true of the eucharistic hymns, which we saw as giving a basis and hope for discussion of doctrinal differences about the nature of the Real Presence and the sense of the "sacrificial" character of the Eucharist. Methodists on their side were candid in considering Roman Catholic questions on how far the Wesleys remain a decisive influence in contemporary Methodism." (para. 9)

> [Yet] there are signs that Methodists on their part are re-capturing through the liturgical movement an appreciation of the sacraments such as is enshrined for example in Charles Wesley's eucharistic hymns." (para. 19)

We shall postpone for the moment the treatment of our interactive theme of Trinity and Eucharist in the Methodist/Roman Catholic dialogue in order to look first at the broader multilateral scene, and particularly the epoch-making text *Baptism, Eucharist and Ministry*, issuing from the meeting of the Faith and Order Commission of the World Council of Churches at Lima (Peru) in 1982.[12]

---

12   *Baptism, Eucharist, and Ministry*, Faith and Order Paper No. 111 (Geneva: World Council of Churches, 1982).

Faith and Order

In the Lima text itself, "The Meaning of the Eucharist" is, in fact, expounded according to a five-part "creedal" structure:

A. The Eucharist as Thanksgiving to the Father (3–4)
B. The Eucharist as Anamnesis or Memorial of Christ (5–13)
C. The Eucharist as Invocation of the Spirit (14–18)
D. The Eucharist as Communion of the Faithful (19–21)
E. The Eucharist as Meal of the Kingdom (22–26)

The Trinitarian pattern could hardly be more obvious. It is already adumbrated in paragraph 4 at the end of Thanksgiving to the Father: "The eucharist thus signifies what the world is to become: an offering and hymn of praise to the Creator, a universal communion in the body of Christ, a kingdom of justice, love and peace in the Holy Spirit." Paragraph 14 spells the Trinity out more directly as the origin and content of the Eucharist:

> The presence of Christ is clearly the centre of the eucharist, and the prom-
> ise contained in the words of institution is therefore fundamental to the
> celebration. Yet it is the Father who is the primary origin and final fulfill-
> ment of the eucharistic event. The incarnate Son of God by and in whom
> it is accomplished is its living centre. The Holy Spirit is the immeasurable
> strength of love which makes it possible and continues to make it effective.
> The bond between the eucharistic celebration and the mystery of the Tri-
> une God reveals the role of the Holy Spirit as that of the One who makes
> the historical words of Jesus present and alive. Being assured by Jesus'
> promise in the words of institution that it will be answered, the Church
> prays to the Father for the gift of the Holy Spirit in order that the eucha-
> ristic event may be a reality: the real presence of the crucified and risen
> Christ giving his life for all humanity.

In their extremely positive response to Faith and Order's *Baptism, Eucharist and Ministry* (BEM) the Council of Bishops of the United Methodist Church pointed to a "remarkable recovery" of the Wesleyan Eucharistic tradition and a "vigorous renewal of liturgical theology and practice," and the bishops endorsed the Lima text's use of *anamnesis* and *epiklesis* to expound the Eucharist in ways that matched original Methodist teaching, declaring that "as Wesleyans we are accustomed to the language of sacrifice, and we find BEM's statements to be in accord with the Church's Tradition and with ours." The bishops approved the Lima text's characterization of the Eucharist as "work of the Triune God":

BEM carefully shows how the eucharist, considered in its wholeness, expresses the historic faith in the unity of God's activity by the three persons. Thus it brings together the dimensions which, if kept separate, distort Christian faith: that is, eternity and time, spirit and matter, redemption and creation. BEM deftly unites the truths and testimonies of the New Testament and the ecumenical creeds. . . .

In terms of the congregation's appropriation of the reality of Christ's presence, the *anamnesis* (memorial, remembrance, representation) means that past, present and future coincide in the sacramental event. All that Jesus Christ means in his person and redemptive work is brought forth from history to our present experience, which is also a foretaste of the future fulfillment of God's unobstructed reign. And this presence is made to be a reality for us by the working of God's Spirit, whom we "call down" (*epiklesis*) by invocation both upon the gifts and upon the people. All this we find explicitly taught by John and Charles Wesley, who knew and respected the apostolic, patristic and reformed faith of the Church.[13]

Together to Holiness

Returning to the Methodist/Roman Catholic international dialogue, we find the following summary by the Joint Commission in its thematic synthesis of the first eight rounds (forty years!) of reports:

> Methodists and Catholics are already agreed that when the Eucharist is celebrated, we hear afresh the Word of God spoken to us; we enter together more deeply into the saving mystery of Christ; we encounter Christ anew in a way which ensures the living presence of Christ at the heart of the Church; we are anointed by the transforming love which is God's Holy Spirit and become more truly the Body of Christ; we are sent forth together in Christ to share more deeply in God's work in our world; and we share together a foretaste of the heavenly banquet. As we celebrate the Eucharist, called together by the Father, the Risen Lord makes us more fully what he wills his Church to be, by the power of the Holy Spirit. Together these affirmations already provide a rich foundation from which we can face the remaining issues in the hope that one day Catholics and Methodists will be able to gather together in full communion around the table of the Lord.[14]

13   See Max Thurian, ed., *Churches Respond to BEM: Official Responses to the "Baptism, Eucharist and Ministry" Text*, vol. 2, Faith and Order Paper No. 132 (Geneva: World Council of Churches, 1986), 187–89.

14   *Synthesis: Together to Holiness. Forty Years of Methodist and Roman Catholic Dialogue* [preface dated Easter 2010], para. 107.

The ninth report of the Joint Commission bore the title *Encountering Christ the Saviour: Church and Sacraments*. Trinitarian patterns in liturgy and doctrine there play a large part in the effort to bring Methodists and Catholics ever closer together in understanding the sacrificial dimension of the Eucharist (especially para. 99–134). There one finds it written, for instance:

> The sacrificial self-giving of Christ is something "made flesh" once-for-all in human history on the cross, but the innermost reality of Christ's "Grand Oblation" [a phrase from *The Hymns on the Lord's Supper*] is an eternal mystery at the very heart of the Holy Trinity. God the Father eternally begets the Son—who is true God from true God—and the Son eternally responds to the Father in total self-giving. Jesus' death on Calvary can be understood as the "sacrament"—the making tangibly, visibly available to all humanity for our salvation—of this eternal self-giving of God the Son to God the Father in the love of the Holy Spirit, and of the Father's ready welcome and acceptance of that self-giving. (para. 103)

> God the Son, made flesh and living among us, comes in the Eucharist to unite us with himself so that we can become one with him in his eternal giving of himself to the Father, and share the eternal welcome his Father gives him. (para. 105)

> By the power of the Holy Spirit, the whole of God's saving action in Christ becomes present here and now for us. (para. 107)

> At the heart of our common understanding of the eucharistic sacrifice is the intimate union between Christ and his Church, between the high priest and his priestly people. It is the risen and ascended Christ himself, by the power of the Holy Spirit, who unites his once-for-all yet eternal self-giving and ours as one single offering, pleaded and presented to the Father and accepted by him. We come to the Eucharist to enter into Christ's self-gift to the Father, and are taken "through him, with him and in him," in the unity of the Holy Spirit, to the Father. (para. 134)

This Holy Mystery

Now what do we find specifically in the doctrinal teaching and the authorized liturgical use of The United Methodist Church? We may properly turn to a text that was "overwhelmingly approved" by the General Conference of 2004: *This Holy Mystery: A United Methodist Understanding of Holy*

Communion.[15] Confidence was able to be placed in "Our Doctrinal Heritage" as contained in *The Book of Discipline*:

> United Methodists share a common heritage with Christians of every age and nation. This heritage is grounded in the apostolic witness to Jesus Christ as Savior and Lord, which is the source and measure of all valid Christian teaching. . . . With Christians of other communions we confess belief in the triune God—Father, Son, and Holy Spirit. This confession embraces the biblical witness to God's activity in creation, encompasses God's gracious self-involvement in the dramas of history, and anticipates the consummation of God's reign.

This salvation-historical perspective governs the exposition of "The Meaning of Holy Communion":

> Holy Communion is Eucharist, an act of thanksgiving. The early Christians "broke bread in their homes and ate together with glad and sincere hearts, praising God and enjoying the favor of all the people" (Acts 2:46-47a, NIV). As we commune together, we express joyful thanks for God's mighty acts throughout history—for creation, covenant, redemption, sanctification. The Great Thanksgiving ("A Service of Word and Table I," *The United Methodist Hymnal*, pages 9–10) is a recitation of this salvation history, culminating in the work of Jesus Christ and the ongoing work of the Holy Spirit. It conveys our gratitude for the goodness of God and God's unconditional love for us. . . . Holy Communion is a vehicle of God's grace through the action of the Holy Spirit (Acts 1:8), whose work is described in John 14:26: "But the Advocate, the Holy Spirit, whom the Father will send in my name, will teach you everything, and remind you of all that I have said to you." The *epiclesis* (biblical Greek meaning "calling upon") is the part of the Great Thanksgiving that calls down the Spirit: "Pour out your Holy Spirit on us gathered here, and on these gifts of bread and wine." The Church asks God to "make them be for us the body and blood of Christ that we may be for the world the body of Christ, redeemed by his blood. By your Spirit make us one with Christ, one with each other, and one in ministry to all the world" (*The United Methodist Hymnal*, 10).

And again, liturgically, the Great Thanksgiving displays the Trinitarian pattern that we have been tracing:

> The Trinitarian structure is evident in the Great Thanksgiving in the Word and Table services of *The United Methodist Hymnal* (pp. 6–16). Following the

---

15 The text of *This Holy Mystery* is generally accessible in the "commentary and study guide" prepared by Gayle Carlton Felton (Nashville: Discipleship Resources, 2005). The passages about to be quoted figure there on pp. 59, 17–18, and 36 respectively.

introductory exchange between presiding minister and people in the Great Thanksgiving, prayer is addressed to "Father [God] Almighty, creator of heaven and earth." Following the Sanctus (Holy, holy, holy . . .), the work of the second person of the Trinity is proclaimed: "and blessed is your Son [Child] Jesus Christ." The presence and work of the Holy Spirit are invoked in the portion beginning "Pour out your Holy Spirit on us gathered here and on these gifts. . . ," words historically known as the *epiclesis*. Throughout the great Thanksgiving the congregation prays actively but silently and speaks its responses aloud at designated points in the service.

Whereupon *This Holy Mystery* immediately cites Hymn 72 from the Wesleyan *Hymns on the Lord's Supper*: "Come, Holy Ghost, Thine influence shed, And realize [make real] the sign. . . ."[16]

His Presence Makes the Feast

In 1975 the Methodist Church of Great Britain issued a new *Methodist Service Book*, which included two orders for Holy Communion, with the one remaining close to the BCP/Wesleyan line and the other showing more influence from the twentieth-century liturgical movement. That second tendency was prolonged in the *Methodist Worship Book* of 1999, which provided fuller seasonal variants for the entire eucharistic service. Both books declare that "these forms are not intended to curb creative freedom, but rather to provide norms for its guidance."

The British *Methodist Worship Book* of 1999 includes these paragraphs in its introduction to the "Orders of Service for Holy Communion" (pp. 114–15):

> Many of the themes of John and Charles Wesley's *Hymns on the Lord's Supper* (1745) are reflected in present-day ecumenical understanding of this sacrament. In communion with the people of God in heaven and on earth, we give thanks for God's mighty acts in creation and redemption, represented supremely in the life, death and resurrection of Jesus Christ. In this means of grace, the Church joyfully celebrates the presence of Christ in its midst, calls to mind his sacrifice and, in the power of the Holy Spirit, is united with him as the Body of Christ. At the Lord's Table, Christ's disciples share bread and wine, the tokens of his dying love and the food for their earthly pilgrimage, which are also a foretaste of the heavenly banquet, prepared for

---

16   The supplementary hymnic resources—*The Faith We Sing* (2000) and *Worship and Song* (2011)—each reintroduced one Wesleyan Eucharistic Hymn: "Victim Divine, thy grace we claim" (HLS 116) in the first case, and "Author of Life Divine, who hast a table spread" (HLS 40) in the second case.

all people. Those who gather around the table of the Lord are empowered for mission: apostles, sent out in the power of the Spirit, to live and work to God's praise and glory. One of the keynotes of the Methodist revival was John Wesley's emphasis on "The Duty of Constant Communion" and it is still the duty and privilege of members of the Methodist Church to share in this sacrament. The Methodist Conference has encouraged local churches to admit baptized children to communion. Those who are communicants and belong to other Churches whose discipline so permits are also welcome as communicants in the Methodist Church.

The shape of the Lord's Supper follows the record in Scripture of Jesus' characteristic sharing with his disciples, especially after the final meal on the night before the crucifixion. His seven actions with the bread and wine (four with the bread, three with the wine) were taken up in the Church's tradition as a fourfold shape: Taking, Giving Thanks, Breaking and Sharing. In the great Thanksgiving, the service of praise offered by God's people on earth is joined with the praises of the heavenly host, praising God, Father, Son and Holy Spirit. This Eucharistic Prayer (the word "Eucharist", derived from a Greek word which means "Thanksgiving," is increasingly accepted by Christians of all traditions as one of the names for this sacrament) is Trinitarian both in its structure and in its focus.

In 2003, a report on the doctrine, understandings, and practices of the Lord's Supper was presented to the British Methodist Conference under the title *His Presence Makes the Feast* (an echo from *Hymns on the Lord's Supper*, 81). The report draws favorably from the Faith and Order "Lima text," making a paraphrase thus: "The unity and communion of the whole Church and of each member of it, one with another, and of all with the Father through the Son in the Spirit is at the heart of Holy Communion. Therefore Holy Communion both creates and expresses the one communion and fellowship of all Christians" (para. 155). Paragraph 14 of Lima's *Eucharist* with its hearty Trinitarianism is directly quoted in paragraph 183 of the British report of 2003: "The Lima text saw invocation of the Spirit as one of the five themes of Holy Communion, arguing that 'though the presence of Christ is clearly the centre of the Eucharist', it is 'the Father who is the primary origin and final fulfilment of the Eucharistic event' and the Holy Spirit 'is the immeasurable strength of love which makes it possible and continues to make it effective.'"

In its paragraph 152, the 2003 report cites the First Epistle of St. John in the sense we have already seen John Wesley expounding it: "In the

First Letter of John believers share in the communion that exists between the Father and the Son." And as to sacrifice: "It is perfectly reasonable to regard Holy Communion as one of the actions of the Christian community in which a sacrifice of praise is offered to the Father through the Son. Holy Communion is a sacrifice of praise because it is a means of offering praise to God through Christ" (para. 163). Pneumatologically, the *Hymns on the Lord's Supper* are quoted for "Come, thou everlasting Spirit" (HLS 16, cited in para. 182), "the Divine Remembrancer" of that hymn having already been invoked in paragraph 180; and "Come, Holy Ghost, thine influence shed" (HLS 72) is also cited in paragraph 182. It is noted that "the Wesleys gave importance to the relationship between Eucharist and eschatology. The feast of Christ truly present with his people is a foretaste of the final ingathering of God's holy people drawn from every nation into a kingdom of justice and righteousness"; and "The Sacrament, a Pledge of Heaven" (HLS 93) is quoted for such lines as "The wine which doth His passion show, / We soon with Him shall drink it new, / In yonder dazzling courts above" (HLS 93).[17]

Just as happened in connection with the United Methodist Church's 2004 report *This Holy Mystery*, so the responses to *His Presence Makes the Feast* persuaded the British Methodist Conference that serious teaching was called for among the members of the British Church. A result can be found in the attractively printed and illustrated booklet *Share This Feast: Reflecting on Holy Communion.*[18]

To conclude our present theme of "The Trinity and the Eucharist"— while also pointing forward to some perhaps more pastoral aspects of the theological task—it might be hard to better the very first paragraph of *Share This Feast: Reflecting on Holy Communion*:

> Celebrating Holy Communion is always about participating in community. We gather together with other Christians, in the name of a God whose very nature is loving community—the Trinity. Communion is not something we

---

17 *In His Presence Makes the Feast*, para. 98 reads: "The most monumental piece of original twentieth-century Methodist writing on Holy Communion was undoubtedly Geoffrey Wainwright (1939–) in his *Eucharist and Eschatology* (Epworth Press 1971; reissue Epworth Press 2003), in which he could claim that 'not until the Wesleys' *Hymns on the Lord's Supper* (1745) did the Western Church achieve again the richness and appreciation of Holy Communion as a sign of the future banquet of the heavenly kingdom.'" Expanded editions of *Eucharist and Eschatology* appeared in the United States in 1981 (New York: Oxford University Press) and in 2003 (Akron, OH: Order of St. Luke Publications).

18 *Share This Feast: Reflecting on Holy Communion* (2006, with an endorsement by the Archbishop of Canterbury; ISBN 1-85852-322-2; EAN 978-1-85852-322-4).

can celebrate alone, and, though it always takes place in an actual human community, it isn't a feast that we create. It is something God offers and invites us to. We take our place alongside other people we know, whom we love and maybe struggle with, and in company with all faithful disciples, present and past, who celebrate across the world and before the face of God in heaven. We share as the "Body of Christ," the community of his followers.

TWO

Creation and Eucharist

Daniel Castelo

Author of Life Divine

Who hast a Table spread

Furnished with Mystic Wine

And everlasting Bread,

Preserve the Life Thyself hast given

And feed, and train us up for Heaven[1]

W hat all is involved with the notion of creation? The matter may be assumed to be self-evident to many, that creation is an obvious cate-gory with easily apprehensible implications. In the wake of environmental concerns, it may be the case that creation becomes synonymous with ecol-ogy, and undoubtedly, there is a point to be made with the link. Neverthe-less, it is important to note that creation is thoroughly a *theological* category. The affirmation of a "creation" inherently suggests the existence of a "cre-ator" who in turn participates in the act of "creating." Therefore, to speak of "creation" is already to imply an agent, an act, and an outcome. Simply put, a creator creates a creation. In this sense, Christians confess that creation is a product of the triune God's activity of bringing about something that is not God.

These are all startling claims that hint at realities and logics that simply go beyond all of us. For instance, what is the difference, if any, between "creating" and "making"? In our common speech practices, we may assume these terms to be synonymous, but theologically they are worlds apart. If one attends to the history of metaphysical reasoning within Christianity,

---

1   John and Charles Wesley, *Hymns on the Lord's Supper,* "Hymn 40," st. 1 (Madison, NJ: facsimile reprint by Charles Wesley Society, 1995), 30 (spelling modified for this chapter).

one would note that creating something suggests bringing something to be that was not before; this claim is a radical notion at the ontological level, and for this reason it can mean something altogether different from the idea of making. Herbert McCabe helps indicate the point: "To make is to actualize a potentiality. *To create is to produce the potentiality as well as the actuality.*"[2] Creating in this sense is truly a remarkable, and in some sense, an unfathomable act; the move suggests bringing to be something that was not before in any kind of potential way. Since we as humans are implicated in such reasoning, and given that we cannot empirically verify or participate in such activity as defined presently, we have to admit humbly that we do not have a clue about all that is involved with the notion of creation. We are, to use Dietrich Bonhoeffer's phrase, "in the middle" of such arrangements.[3] At our core, we are creatures, and we cannot transcend our identities as creatures when we move to speak of creation.

Despite these challenges, Christians have managed to confess a number of claims related to creation over the centuries, the most prominent being that God brought to be a creation out of nothing (*creatio ex nihilo*).[4] This phrase came about as a result of resisting some unhelpful cosmological alternatives; it was meant to "clear the table," so to speak, in how one relates immateriality and materiality or, to use Christian terms, the Creator-creation interface. Rather than competing realities, as they seem to be in sundry ancient cosmologies, immateriality and materiality were placed in a "before and after" relationship by Christians: first there was God, and then this God created that which was not-God. Once this understanding was formulized and developed, it was certainly controversial by the standards of the day given its scope and audacity. "Creation out of nothing" continues

---

2   Herbert McCabe, OP, *God and Evil in the Theology of St. Thomas Aquinas* (New York: Continuum, 2010), 104 (italics in original).

3   Dietrich Bonhoeffer, *Creation and Fall*, Dietrich Bonhoeffer Works, vol. 3 (Minneapolis: Fortress, 2004), 28.

4   It should be noted that confusion has resulted from how to think of the "nothing" in *creatio ex nihilo*; let us be clear from the beginning in terms of this chapter's perspective: the affirmation of *nihilo* is simply a cipher, a conceptual placeholder for God. In other words, a better phrasing would be "creation out of nothing apart from God." What is being suggested here is not emanationism but true difference that comes to be simply at the divine initiative. A helpful summary is the following clarification by Paul Copan and William Lane Craig: "So when we describe what creation out of nothing means, we affirm that without God's initiating creation, only God exists. . . . Thus, creation out of nothing affirms that the universe is contingent on God, not just in having its (continued) existence in being (ontological dependence) but also in having its temporal origination from nothing preexistent, but simply by the will and word of God *(ex nihilo)*" (*Creation out of Nothing* [Grand Rapids: Baker, 2004], 15).

to be one of the most distinctive features of a Christian cosmology, and when pressed, it is one of the most basic—and nevertheless challenging—tenets of the faith.

In that Christians confess that creation is an indicator of God's gracious activity, one can make links between this action and another—and more pointed—manner of God's self-presentation, namely God's self-offering in the Eucharist. The link holding the two is no doubt the Word of God, which brought the cosmos to be and which subsumed itself incarnationally within the boundaries and conditions of a post-lapsarian situation. This pivotal moment in the universe's history, the Incarnation of the Son of God, makes possible the suggestion that creation and Eucharist are both indicators of the divine gratuity. In this sense, much is at stake theologically with how one goes about relating creation and Eucharist. What follows presses this link and proceeds as a self-understood Wesleyan treatment of these themes, first in terms of what the act of creating potentially says about the triune God of Christian confession and subsequently in relation to what this gesture says about God's purposes within the creation itself.

What Does Creation Say about God?

Let us begin with the first point. What does creation say about God? In Spanish, we have a saying apropos to the matter: *"Todas las cosas se parecen a su dueño"* ("All things resemble their owner"). Creation is God's and properly no one else's, for God, and only God, brought it to be. In this gesture of God creating that which is not-God, inevitably something of God's "Godness" is extended to and perdures within the creation. This claim is not only secured through the traditional notion of *imago Dei* language found in Genesis 1, but it goes deeper still when God evaluates the whole of creation as "good" and "very good." If God is the ultimate good, the *summum bonum*, then anything that is good is such because of the definitive divine imprint upon it. The Christian theo-logic of the Creator-creation distinction would irreparably break down if the goodness of creation were somehow secured in another way than by the divine gratuity. All that is, in that it is, is from God; being is a kind of goodness, and so all that is good, in that it is good, is from God as well.

I have purposefully begun with the question of goodness not simply on biblical grounds but also in light of what is at stake in narrating the divine character. Creation, in that God brought it to be, says something about God. Now, what can become intricately tricky, much like the negotiation of the distinctions between "creating" and "making," alluded to above, is the basic question: What precisely does creation say about God? The matter becomes one of divine characterization or divine attribution.

Divine attribution is a significantly risky activity. I already alluded to the little we can definitely say about the act of creating, since we ourselves are in the middle of created arrangements. Nevertheless, such limits rarely, if ever, deter us from proceeding, and we often do so with self-granted authority and expertise. The same is applicable to divine attribution specifically and God-talk more generally: we often talk about who God is and what God is like without taking into consideration the contingencies of human knowing and the limits of language as well as the conceptual complexity involved in specifying divine action. Let me take a contrasting example as a way of moving forward with a Wesleyan take on these matters.

The typical answer given by many Christians today when they are posed with the question, "What is the first thing that comes to your mind when asked, 'God is (blank)?'" is that "God is sovereign." Now, "sovereign" could mean any number of things. Within the economy of salvation, one could specify that God is sovereign over sin and the principalities and powers of evil. One could tie "sovereignty" not only with "governance" but also with "victory" and suggest Christ's resurrection as an overcoming of sin, thereby making him Lord of (and so sovereign over) all. Within the economy of creation, however, something very different may come to the fore; without the notions of sin and redemption at play, sovereignty could suggest any number of things. Positively, it could suggest that God is properly the Creator of all things, and so all things are God's, as mentioned earlier. Negatively though, the privileging of God's sovereignty could perpetuate patterns and tendencies of increased speculation and abstraction. One finds this readily not so much in accounts of creation but in ones related to election and predestination, but oftentimes the sensibilities fostered in these accounts are extended to creation as a supposed implication or result.

A long history of debate exists regarding divine sovereignty. In fact, Randy Maddox goes so far as to make the point that "no issue concerning God's nature received more attention from Wesley than that of Divine sovereignty."[5] The difficulty with divine sovereignty is partially tied to its conceptual migration from being a moral/relational to a power/capacity attribute. In other words, divine sovereignty (properly an exemplification of the former category) oftentimes gets bundled in haste with God's power

---

5   Randy L. Maddox, *Responsible Grace* (Nashville: Abingdon Press [Kingswood Books], 1994), 54.

and God's foreknowledge (instantiations of the latter category). This shift from moral/relational to power/capacity attributes is a devastating mistake in Christian dogmatics, especially when the latter category is understood to retain more appeal and explanatory prowess than the former. Let us press the point a bit more.

What is fascinating about God's power and God's foreknowledge for the present task is not so much what they say with regard to predestination, election, and creation but rather what little they truly say about God. Given that divine power and divine foreknowledge are not so much character-attributes as capacity-attributes, they suggest what God can (or cannot) do and know, but in and of themselves they say nothing about the moral framing of these and so nothing about the divine character per se. To have a capacity for something is one thing; when, how, and to what degree a capacity is exercised are questions that require a broader framework of meaning that in turn can make these capacity-attributes "do work" within theological speech. Without moral framing, capacity and power considerations have little value in God-talk.

One could respond and say that such a claim diminishes the importance of a venerable tradition of divine attribution, namely the "omni" attributes, particularly omnipotence and omniscience. Many find these "omni" attributes appealing and so desirable in God-talk, and the particularization of these may seem threatening. But that form of privileging is precisely what has to be called into question if (1) the theological integrity of the Creation-creator interface is to be vibrant and (2) (as we will note shortly) the dogmatic link between creation and redemption is to be made. According to Maddox's reading, Wesley had the good sense to see the point: "Central to [Wesley's] various discussions of this issue was the insistence that Divine sovereignty not be understood in isolation from God's other attributes. In particular, it must never be understood in abstraction from God's justice or love."[6] Implied within this makeshift account of divine simplicity is the claim—one that is among other things quite Wesleyan[7] – that God's moral/relational attributes are to be privileged in Christian God-talk over God's power/capacity attributes.

---

6   Ibid.
7   At the beginning of Maddox's account, he remarks, "The final dimension of God's infinitude is omnipotence. If Wesley had a characteristic emphasis here, it was that we cannot properly understand God's power apart from God's moral attributes. . . . The importance of God's moral attributes is that they define God's character. Theoretically, a divine Being could be eternal, omnipresent, omniscient, and omnipotent, while being indifferent to humanity, or even maleficent" (Responsible Grace, 53).

In the case of the "omni" attributes, they are inherently apophatic: at day's end, they do not say anything generative about God; rather, they aim to show how God is not limited by the strictures associated with creaturely existence. "Omnipotence" is another way of saying "God is not incapacitated in the ways humans are" and "omniscience" suggests "God is not ignorant in the ways humans are." But when attempted to be positively understood, the "omni" attributes are unintelligible: to harken back to both the humility and ignorance at play with talk of creation, it is worth asking: What does it mean to say that God is "all-powerful" or "all-knowing"? Can our minds fathom these capacities positively and generatively at all? More to the point: Why do these attributes often get emphasized and in turn over-determine attributes like divine sovereignty? What does such a penchant for categorical totalization say about our historical and theological *Sitz im leben*? And perhaps most detrimental of all, what kinds of theological sensibilities (both intellectual and moral) are fostered by such privileging?

My concern resonates with the following possibility: by privileging these capacity-attributes (which at their core are apophatic claims), one heightens the burden to remark something generatively positive about them, and in doing so potentially blurs the distinction between Creator and creation from the divine side of the dyad. Simply put, if the Creator God is "all-knowing" and "all-powerful," then one wonders how much space is available for creation to exercise any kind of knowing or power that does not in some way rival or compete with God. Or to phrase it another way, the privileging of God's capacity-attributes within the perspectival orientation of the economy of creation leaves open the question of the divine gratuity in the act of creating itself so that what results potentially is a contentious, agonistic relation between Creator and creation.[8] Again, Maddox is helpful on this score in his reading of the Wesleyan corpus: "Whenever [Wesley] developed this point [of divine omnipotence] . . . it became clear that his

8   At this point, Rowan Williams makes the suggestive point that "creation is not an exercise of divine *power*, odd though that certainly sounds. Power is exercised *by* x *over* y; but creation is not power, because it is not exercised *on* anything" (*On Christian Theology* [Oxford: Blackwell, 2000], 68). Additionally, I follow the point of Kathryn Tanner that the relation between creatures and God has to be ultimately noncompetitive, and this claim is made possible by another one, namely a vision of God's transcendence in which God is the source of all that a creature is in its goodness (*Jesus, Humanity and the Trinity* [Minneapolis: Fortress, 2001], 2–3). Only through these two basic claims, namely God's transcendence and the noncompetitive nature of the Creator-creature interface, can a dogmatically sustainable account of synergy ensue, and synergy is something that Wesleyans would wish to preserve (in spite of the easily distortable nature of such a claim; more on this below).

distinctive concern was that God's power not be defined or defended in any way that undercuts human responsibility."[9] Put colloquially, that God creates something which is not-God assumes that God gives that which is not-God the proverbial "space to be."[10] In this sense, God's act of creation demonstrates God to be hospitable, which is one way of expressing the divine gratuity.

The Wesleyan Tendency in Divine Attribution

Rather than divine sovereignty, Methodists and Wesleyans are prone to emphasize explicitly another feature of God's character, namely that God is loving. Usually, this tendency takes shape within claims made in the elaboration of features of the economy of salvation. For instance the most famous Christian verse in Scripture, John 3:16—one stemming from Wesley's "canon within the canon," the Johannine witness—would suggest as much. But when speaking of the economy of creation, one can see the claim performing distinct moves that I would argue can be made on Wesleyan grounds; and yet these traditionally have not been extended within this theological subtradition, because of a certain privileging within Wesleyan theology itself. Therefore, the constructive side of this point involves excavating and unearthing what a loving God could suggest of the divine character in terms of the doctrine of creation with an eye to eucharistic practice and ministry.

It is true that saying "God is love" is equally dangerous to saying "God is sovereign" if not more so in our contemporary environs. Whereas divine sovereignty tends to be quickly aligned with power/capacity attributes that are more befitting of Enlightenment theism than the biblical presentation of the triune God, "God is love" (particularly in a therapeutic culture like ours) can devolve into sentimentalism rather quickly. With the sentimentalizing of the phrase "God is love" come unfortunate theological consequences: sin tends to be deemphasized and made illegitimate as a theological concern, "the fear of the Lord" is largely missing as a mark of Christian wisdom, and God is anthropomorphized so as to become the tolerant, politically correct, and nonjudgmental modern-day ideal of a respectable and engaged citizen.

---

9 Maddox, *Responsible Grace*, 54.

10 And the God of Christian confession logically does this by virtue of this One being triune; this is so because the Trinity brought about the creation relationally and continues to be related to it via the missions of the Son and the Spirit. See Colin Gunton, *The Triune Creator* (Grand Rapids: Eerdmans, 1998), 10 and (with development of an Irenaean point) 54.

These are real dangers that face Christianity in the contemporary West, and they are often at play in contemporary God-talk, including speech related to the divine love.

Nevertheless, a clear advantage presents itself with an emphasis upon the divine love within speech related to the economy of creation, and that is its ability to address one of the most perplexing questions of all in philosophical thought: Why is there something rather than nothing? Or if theologically framed, the question would run: Why did God create after all? Traditionally, and not just in our therapeutic age, an oft-repeated claim by Christians to this all-important question has been: because God is love. The triune God created not out of deficiency but out of fullness; God's act of creating was *ek-static*, pointing outward the superabundance of God's very self as a fellowship constituted by free and loving relationality. If God is love, then creation is an act of God's loving fullness, a gesture on God's part of giving space to that which is not-God to simply be.

In spite of the emphasis on the divine love within Wesleyan/Methodist circles, few have made the point to connect this emphasis to the doctrine of creation; in fact, some have lamented that Wesleyan theology lacks an explicit doctrine of creation. Edgardo Colón-Emeric believes that "Wesley's lack of sufficient attentiveness to the difference between first perfection and second perfection leaves him incapable of affirming the goodness of nature as it exists today."[11] This neglect is in some ways understandable given the life of the man: Wesley's work as a revivalist preacher had him emphasizing the "new birth" or "new creation" more so than—to state it awkwardly—the "old birth" or "old creation" given his role in establishing a renewal movement within the Church of England. In emphasizing the new birth, Wesley spoke of being awakened from the effects of the perpetually enacted "art of forgetting God," one that contributes to our dissipated selves.[12] The language is important to note: an awakening presupposes a slumber; the conceptual progression is narrated as one of rupture or crisis rather than continuity or a flourishing of what was always possible and meant to be. Such neglect of an explicitly extended doctrine of creation has led to difficulties over the years for Wesleyan theology in that it has been easy for those involved in such a task to employ all too readily Protestant soteriological accounts to make the Wesleyan revivalist logic work. Wesley himself contributed to the cause with his continual use of the language of original

---

11   Edgardo Colón-Emeric, *Wesley, Aquinas and Christian Perfection* (Waco: Baylor University Press, 2009), 150.

12   See John Wesley, "On Dissipation" in *The Works of John Wesley*: Sermons, vol. 3, ed. Albert C. Outler (Nashville: Abingdon Press, 1986), 115–25.

sin, justification, affirmation of a hypothetical "natural state," and so forth.

Thankfully, this situation of neglect is being remedied as indicated by the recent ecumenical document "Heaven and Earth Are Full of Your Glory: A United Methodist and Roman Catholic Statement on the Eucharist and Ecology."[13] By focusing on the Eucharist, the document recognizes that in this liturgical act believers "offer thanks to the Father for the goodness of all the things that he has made" (ibid., 1). The document proceeds by recognizing one of the basic claims mentioned above: "Creation is God's rst gift. Creation is the first sign of God's glory and God's love" (ibid., 8). The document also sustains the missing claim that Colón-Emeric found to be important: "Gratitude toward God for the gift of creation opens the way for a renewed understanding and appropriation of the work of redemption, and of the unity of God's work of creation and redemption. We believe in one God, who both creates and redeems" (ibid., 11). God's works are indeed mighty, and they involve both creation and salvation; these are in turn rec-ognized within doxological mode and space by the worshiping faithful in such acts as the celebration of the Lord's Supper.

This remedying helps solidify the divine gratuity in all its dimensions within the creaturely amphitheater of God's self-presentation. In that the God we confess and worship is the triune Creator "who out of the super-abundance of divine love . . . freely bestows being on that which is not God" (ibid., 19). Wesleyans and Methodists have something significant to contribute in discussions related to divine characterization and attribution. Although the tradition has neglected the merits of the "old creation" in light of a revivalist penchant to emphasize "new creation," the unity of divine purpose requires this correction. Truth be told, the tradition demands it since Wesleyans and Methodists are prone to emphasize a vital and explicit role for creaturehood within salvation history.

What Does God's Work within Creation Say about the Creaturely Realm?

If the locus of creation says some definitive things about God, what do God's work and character within the created order say about the creaturely realm of which we are a part? This query, as said before, can pivot off a Wesleyan account of the Eucharist, for it is in doxological mode and space

---

13   The document can be found at http://www.usccb.org/beliefs-and-teachings/ dialogue-with-others/ecumenical/methodist/upload/Heaven-and-Earth-are-Full-of-Your-Glory.pdf.

where the creation and Creator-proper are jointly at work in some way.

For all that one can say about how indistinctive Wesley's theology of the Eucharist is,[14] its framing as a "means of grace" is vital if for no other reason than its positive localization of creaturehood within the economy of salvation, and so the economy of sanctification. This appeal to the creaturely domain is significantly qualified to be sure, but it nevertheless is vital. According to the Wesleyan vision, creatures can be mechanisms through which the Creator shines. Put another way, we can be sanctified from an interplay of "from above" and "from below" aspects of the spiritual life and not reductively simply in terms of the former. Creatures have a role to play in their own healing, and this is so, again, because of the divine gratuity.

This dynamic is at play in various ways as a consequence of Wesley's theology of the Eucharist. I will mention two prominent features that are consonant with what has been developed so far. A distinctive characteristic of Wesley's eucharistic theology is that Christ is truly present at the table. Such a claim puts Methodist and Wesleyan fellowships in the company of Catholics, Anglicans, and the Orthodox and distinguishes them from most Protestant fellowships. As Steve Long has recently noted, Wesleyans and Methodists can affirm real presence without subscribing to the conceptual apparatus of transubstantiation.[15] But if real presence is affirmed, then an account of mediation is required, one in which God's presence can be present and available through the creaturely realm. Such a notion does not mean giving unwarranted dignity to the creation so that such mediation somehow takes away from God's glory; for again, that kind of thinking operates from a competitive construal of the Creator-creation interface. Rather the logic would be that because of its origins in the Creator, the creation can act in conformity to the Creator's purposes in whatever ways the Creator ultimately deems as fitting. What this means is that God makes Godself available through the created order, and as such this domain is sacramental in some sense. To recall "Heaven and Earth Are Full of Your Glory": "Our encounter with the mystery of our origins, of the origin of all creation in God, invites us to a recognition and continued awareness of the sacramentality of the world."[16]

Another matter implied by Wesley's eucharistic theology is the notion of synergy. The term *synergy* tends to be a linguistic taboo in theological circles, beckoning concerns related to the Pelagian controversy and the subsequent Protestant self-justifying mantra of "salvation by faith, not

---

14   "Indistinctive" in the sense of its heavy reliance on Daniel Brevint's treatise On the Christian Sacrament and Sacrifice (1672).

15   D. Stephen Long, *Keeping Faith* (Eugene, OR: Cascade, 2012), 66.

16   "Heaven and Earth Are Full of Your Glory," 9.

works." Nevertheless, extremes (and extremist thinking) notwithstanding, Christian theologians and traditions have readily tried to steer clear of a mechanistic account of creation, one in which God saves and heals us apart from us; quite the contrary, much is at stake to involve the creation some way in soteriological depictions.[17] The question becomes how to do so in such a fashion that God is given a preeminent role while at the same time recognizing that we as creatures are very much involved in such processes. Again, competitive accounts of the Creation-creation interface complicate (and at some point make impossible) such a move.

What is needed as an alternative is a set of substantiating claims, for no single term (including *causality*, *agency*, and to some extent *synergy*) can do all that is required.[18] In a Wesleyan framing, these claims would relate precisely to what we have been considering thus far: an account of the divine character and gratuity, God's transcendence and nevertheless very intimate tie to the created order, the giftedness and capacities of the creaturely realm, and so forth. To stay with the last major point: humans can confess, bless, and praise God, and such acts are immeasurably significant in part because of their synergistic indeterminacy.[19] In other words, one of the positive outcomes of the Creator giving the creation "space to be" is that the creation can in turn proclaim and celebrate its Creator truly and genuinely from its side of the interface.[20] And in participating in these doxological movements and practices, the creation can take part in God's mission of healing and sanctifying the world.

At Eucharist the celebrants and communicants take up and ingest God's self-offering, and they do so with their entire selves. They offer back to

---

17   See for instance the *Catechism of the Catholic Church*, 1847, and its quote of Augustine: "'God created us without us: but he did not will to save us without us.' To receive his mercy, we must admit our faults."

18   I entertain features of this vision in conversation with John Webster in "Holiness Simpliciter: A Wesleyan Engagement and Proposal in Light of John Webster's Trinitarian Dogmatics of Holiness" *Wesleyan Theological Journal* 47, no. 2 (2012): 147–64.

19   What I mean by "synergistic indeterminacy" is that God's role and the human role are both vitally important in such acts, but it is unclear and unnecessary to specify precisely how this is so apart from an orientational intuition of God's prevenience and the epistemological and praxis-oriented modality of worship. I extend this category further in *Revisioning Pentecostal Ethics—The Epicletic Community* (Cleveland, TN: CPT Press, 2012).

20   In eucharistic tone, Alexander Schmemann can say, "The whole creation depends on food. But the unique position of man in the universe is that he alone is to *bless* God for the food and the life he receives from Him. He alone is to respond to God's blessing with his blessing" (*For the Life of the World* [Crestwood: St. Vladimir's Seminary Press, 2002], 14–15).

God what God has given, and they do so with what they can, namely their whole being. Such is a model of Christian existence, one that can account for such complicated considerations as "agency" and "causality" but also "affections" and "holy tempers." The point registers the ongoing value of the Latin tag *lex orandi, lex credenda*. At the Table, creatures come ready to receive God's gifts, and in doing so, they offer themselves back to God in gratitude and praise. The image of the Table is apropos for Christian life as a whole and suggests a further alteration of the phrase mentioned above, namely *lex orandi, lex vivendi*. Christian existence is eucharistic throughout, making our lives one long epiclesis, a creaturely confession and self-offering that can take place because of God's initial blessing and self-offering.

Concluding Remarks on Ministry

These claims related to the divine gratuity and the creaturely significance and role within the economy of healing suggest sundry possibilities for the practice of Christian ministry. Most pertinently, they help make sense of the sheer materiality of salvation inherent to Wesleyan theological sensibilities. The triune God of Christian confession does not work over and against creation but does so through and in it because it is properly God's. Therefore, those who follow the Wesleyan spirit in terms of works of mercy, the practice of constant Communion, Christian conferencing, and so forth do so out of the basic theological commitment that in such acts God makes Godself known as creation's Creator and Healer. It is because Wesleyans and Methodists envision, worship, and participate in God in distinct ways that such activity maintains its robust theological character. Part of this characterization would include that this creation, God's creation, is grace-laden and grace-saturated, and so, in some sense, it is good as its Creator is good. That God's grace permeates the creation does not suggest that God is doing something contrary to God's character in relating to that which is thoroughly and irreparably marked by its anti-God disposition; quite the contrary, the way God continues to work in God's own handiwork through activities leading to its healing, restoration, and fullness suggests that the divine gratuity continues to drive the possibility of speaking of creation's goodness in post-Fall conditions. What is good is good because of God's goodness, and the task of practitioners of Christian ministry is to identify, join, and extend such goodness out of the particularity of their eucharistic lives.

Such theological claims form the bedrock of the nature and mission of the church, the eucharistic fellowship. As a creaturely reality marked by

creaturely embodiment, the church is simply that material expression that exerts its God-given powers of directedness to its source and end within the self-conscious modality of worship. As such, the claims that the church is, among other things, "one holy catholic and apostolic" are ones made first and foremost on the basis of the divine gratuity within the economy of salvation *and* creation. If ecclesiology is driven by God's self-presentation within the divine economy, then both the Table in question as well as those surrounding it can truly occasion moments of Spirit-related surprise. If the church is where the Spirit is, as Irenaeus suggested so many centuries ago, then the economy of salvation mandates an account of the economy of creation; the "new creation" is unintelligible apart from the "old creation." And these sundry points lead to the legitimacy of a pneumatically prompted humility, one that inspires the confession that we are all both a dignified and a needy people, and that by God's grace, we can help one another along to see more readily with that which is both the source of our dignity and the end of our hunger and thirst.

THREE

Sin, Han, and Eucharist

Andrew Sung Park

The Eucharist is a sacrament. The Latin term *sacramentum* means a sacred pledge of sincerity or fidelity. In Greek, it is *mysterion*—translated "mystery." The Eucharist has been one of the most exalted mysteries of the church. Augustine's most important phrases on the sacrament are "visible form" and "invisible grace."[1] The meaning of the Eucharist (the Greek *eucharistia*) is "thanksgiving." It is a heavenly banquet that has been extended to us all.

We have celebrated the Eucharist as the rite to forgive sins and a means of grace to sanctify. This chapter is written to reflect on the meaning of the Eucharist and its significance for the sinned-against, the brokenhearted, the wounded, and the sick. It has been our church custom to omit the sinned-against from the benefits of the Eucharist. Do we have any biblical and historical grounds of caring about them through the Eucharist? From a Wesleyan perspective, I will explore a more holistic meaning of the Eucharist by examining the concept of *han* (woundedness in Korean) of the sinned-against in its relation with sin.

Han

What is han? Han is an intricate and complex concept to define. However, han can be described as a buried wound generated by unjust psychosomatic, social, political, economic, and cultural repression and oppression.[2] It entrenches itself in the soul of the victims of sin and crime, demonstrated by diverse reactions such as those of the survivors of the Nazi holocaust,

---

1   For Augustine, sacraments are visible signs. He further distinguishes the visible sacrament itself, the *sacramentum* (sign: the outward and visible), from the *res* (reality: the inward fruits). In the twelfth century, Peter Lombard refined Augustine's distinctions into three by adding the *sacramentum et res* (both sign and reality, the two combined). (James F. White, *Introduction to Christian Worship*, 3rd ed. [Nashville: Abingdon Press, 2001], 184–85.)

2   Han is a term that Korean *minjung* (downtrodden) theologians began to employ in the 1970s. See Yong Bock Kim, ed., *Minjung Theology* (Singapore: The Christian Conference of Asia, 1981).

the Palestinians in the occupied land, the racially discriminated-against, bat-
tered wives, the molested, the abused, and the exploited. In essence, han is a
physical, mental, and spiritual hurt due to a terrible injustice, eliciting deep
brokenheartedness, internalized agony, a writhing of all the organs, the in-
tense rending of the soul, and the sense of helplessness and hopelessness.

Such a hidden wound has lasting effects on abused children. When a
child is badly hurt or terrified, that pain not only produces a traumatic
memory but also changes the developing brain, according to Dr. Jerald Kay,
chair of the psychiatry department at Wright State University's School of
Medicine.[3] Their data show that abused children are inclined to suffer from
depression, drug abuse, and other chronic ailments as adults. Supported
by the research of Paul Plotsky of Emory University, Dr. Kay says, "People
who have been abused have parts of their brains that are different sizes
than other people. And those different parts of their brains will function in
different ways."[4] With animal studies to lead them, scientists found strong
tendencies in those abused as children toward a more active amygdala (the
fear center of the brain) and a smaller connection between the left and right
hemispheres, which enables the more rational right brain to better control
feelings and anger. Abused children see far more threatening worlds than
those who weren't abused, becoming hypersensitive or withdrawing and
growing numb.[5] Childhood traumas cut into the child's sense of control
and abuse victims will go to incomprehensible lengths to recover control.
They often blame themselves rather than their offenders for their abuse. For
Paul Plotsky, this requires an explanation.[6]

Han and Sin

On Sundays, pastors stand before a congregation and deliver a message
of salvation coming from Jesus Christ. The major theme of most Christian
sermons is salvation from the power of sin. In the pews, however, we find
all kinds of people from various walks of life. There are some offenders or
sinners (exploiters, aggressors, abusers, and rapists), some victims (the exploited, injured, abused, and raped), and their family members waiting for
an appropriate message.

In Christian theology, we usually use one category to diagnose the

---

3   Kevin Lamb, "Lasting Effects of Abuse," *Dayton Daily News*, 25 June 2002, C1.
4   Ibid.
5   Ibid., C3.
6   Ibid., C1.

wrong of the world: sin. We have drawn the chart of salvation for sinners and have left out the sinned-against from the blueprint of salvation in our theology. The victims of sins or crimes usually go to see professional counselors, psychotherapists, or psychiatrists. When pastors as counselors consult with them, they would rather use psychology or/and psychotherapy than theology to deal with their problems. It is time for the church to name and face this issue. Naming a problem is the beginning of its solution.

When sin is committed, the victim of sin comes to develop han, if the injury that is caused by the sin is not healed. The victim bears heartbreaking agony and humiliation under oppression, exploitation, abuse, mistreatment, or violation. As their situations do not allow them to change, they further deepen their han. Sin causes han and han produces sin.[7] Sin is of injurers; han is of the injured. The sin of injurers may cause a chain reaction via the han of the injured. Sometimes han causes han. Furthermore, unattended or unhealed han gives rise to evil. This evil can regenerate han and sin. Also, sin and han collaborate to engender evil. They overlap in many tragic areas of life.

Although for expediency we have divided the sin of injurers and the han of the injured, most people experience both sin and han. This does not mean that we belittle the difference of han between the injured and the injurers, we but point out the complex entanglement of sin and han. Many people who are injured in one aspect of life are injurers in another. The notion of han may help us transcend a one-dimensional approach to the problem of the world from the doctrine of sin. With the oppressor-oriented doctrine of sin alone, the Christian doctrines of sin and salvation are helplessly trapped in notions of ego from which they must be liberated. To consider a Christian doctrinal theology for victims, we need to find the subject in the Bible. So, we will turn to the Bible to see whether it addresses the contents of han.

Biblical Han

The Bible is full of stories of distraught people. Jesus came into the world to set free the downtrodden from their grief and burden and forgive the sins of transgressors. Between the downtrodden and transgressors, Jesus was primarily concerned about the downtrodden: "Those who are well have no need of a physician, but those who are sick" (Mark 2:17).[8] Accordingly,

---

7   Although tragedies and natural catastrophes can create han, our focus will be on han caused by human actions.

8   Unless otherwise noted, all scripture is NRSV in this chapter.

the main subject of the Bible was to care for the afflicted, particularly the unjustly injured. This section shows how prevalently the notion of han is present in the Bible.

Cain and Abel

The story of Cain and Abel is a story of han. The two brothers give offerings to God. Cain's offering is rejected, while Abel's is accepted. The text is silent on the purposes of their offerings and on the reason for the rejection and acceptance. God's response, however, ignites Cain's anger. Out of his deep jealousy and frustration, Cain strikes his own brother in the field. The dying Abel looks at his brother Cain. Abel's eyes ask, "Why are you killing me?" Cain watches this horrible scene of his brother's last moment. The murdered cannot speak! Only Abel's blood cries out to God from the ground (Gen 4:10). The crying-out blood is the voice of han.

Job

The Book of Job is written to contradict the retributive or the Deuteronomistic theology that regards suffering as God's punishment for sin and as an instructive tool. Job undergoes a series of unspeakable human tragedies. All Job had is destroyed, his sons and daughters are killed, and he is physically afflicted by sores.

Worse, his three friends come to visit him and urge him to reveal and repent of his sin. Their theology represents the orthodox retributive theology. Eliphaz accuses Job of culpability. Job rejects the charge and begs for compassion. Bildad indicts him of hypocrisy. Job insists that he has committed no sin and that God is unfair to destroy the righteous and the wicked together (9:21-22). Zophar rebukes Job as a liar and a hypocrite. Job rejects his rebuke as banality. Lastly, Elihu appears and pours out his anger at Job for his self-justification. His argument is that God is just and uses suffering as a medium to refine humans, and in Job's case his iniquity caused his affliction (36:21).[9]

At the end, God speaks to Job out of the whirlwind. It is strange that God does not reveal the fact that Job's suffering was just a trial initiated by Satan with God's own consent. This is the han of many suffering victims. They do not know why God does not make God's hidden purposes known.

---

9   Most scholars believe that someone later inserted the speeches of Elihu between the Dialogues and God's answer. This is why God refers only to the three friends and mentions no name of Elihu (Solomon B. Freehof, *Book of Job: A Commentary* [New York: Union of American Hebrew Congregations, 1958], 235).

In his reply to God's speech, Job acknowledges divine all-powerfulness and confesses his ignorance. Although Job obtains no satisfactory explanation for his predicament, he is satisfied with personally seeing God.

Overall, the Book of Job can correct the preoccupation of traditional theologies with the justification or salvation of the sinner (oppressor). Job shifts our focus from a sinner's salvation to the healing of the han-ridden. Emphasizing the forgiveness of sinners or wrongdoers and their justification, traditional theologies have neglected the liberation or healing of suffering Jobs.

In the end of this epic, God expresses God's anger to Job's three friends, for they have afflicted Job with their own one-sided theology of retribution. God speaks to Eliphaz: "My wrath is kindled against you and against your two friends; for you have not spoken of me what is right, as my servant Job has" (42:7b). As judgment, God demands of them burnt offerings and their apology to Job. They forced the innocent victim to repent of his sin and be saved. Job needed comfort and healing from the han of great tragedies, but they demanded his immediate confession of sin.

In pulpits we have preached the one-sided theology of a sin-repentance formula for everyone, including the sinned-against and the wounded: "Repent of your sin and be saved." Toward victims, we have done wrong. The God of Job is angry at this one-dimensional sin-repentance formula the church has applied to the victims of sin, overlooking their han. It is overdue for us to provide a sensible theology of caring about the victims of sin and tragedy. Our present one-dimensional theology is under God's wrath. Theologians owe burnt offerings to God and their apology to modern-day Jobs.

Jesus: A Person of Han

Jesus, a carpenter's son, was one of the common people in Palestine. He interpreted the Hebrew Scriptures from a commoner's perspective. To locate han in the New Testament, it is necessary for us to walk with Jesus in Palestine and see how Jesus attends to the people of han. He himself was a man of han. Innocent, yet he was condemned, rejected, despised, and handed over to be crucified by his own people.

In his hometown, Nazareth, Jesus declared the purpose of his mission: to bring good news to the poor, to proclaim release to the captives and recovery of sight to the blind, to let the oppressed go free, to proclaim the year of God's favor (Luke 4:18-19). He knew the agony of the downtrodden. He knew there were many people who sat in darkness and the shadow of death (Matt 4:16). Jesus diagnosed his time and people, and a goal of his ministry was to release the downtrodden from their bondage.

The Afflicted: *The* Theme of the New Testament

The primary reason of Jesus' coming into the world was to bring good news to the afflicted and the sinned-against. Jesus said, "Those who are well have no need of a physician, but those who are sick; I have come to call not the righteous but sinners" (Mark 2:17).

There were two types of sinners in Jewish society at that time. One was a publicly recognized criminal against civil laws. The other was a person in a lowly and socially unacceptable occupation.[10] We can differentiate the latter type of so-called sinner into two categories. One is the sinner of dishonorable and despised occupations. Some examples were herders, tax collectors, and publicans.[11] These were sinners because of the unclean or ill-smelling nature of their jobs (e.g., butchers, tanners, coppersmiths). They were alienated and could not partake in worship.[12]

The other is the sinner of low status such as the sick or the poor. The sick could not fulfill the duties of the law. As we have seen in the Book of Job, the theology that treated sickness as the consequence of sin was widespread in Judaism (Ps 73; John 9; Mark 2:5). Thus, the blind, the lepers, the mentally disturbed, and the hemorrhagic were particularly regarded as either unclean or cursed by God.[13] The sick were not transgressors, but those who were condemned by the religious leaders.

Jesus' followers in general were the disreputable, the uneducated, and

---

10 Joachim Jeremias, *Jerusalem in the Time of Jesus* (Philadelphia: Fortress Press, 1969), cited in Byung-mu Ahn, "Jesus and the Minjung," in *Minjung Theology,* ed. Commission on Theological Concerns of the Christian Conference of Asia (Maryknoll, NY: Orbis, 1983), 143.

11 Herders were believed to drive their herds on to others' land and steal the produce of the herd. The publicans were particularly outlawed. They were *toll* collectors (*môk'sâ*), different from *tax* collectors (*gabbâyâ*). While tax collectors as state officials took in the direct taxes, the toll collectors were subtenants of the rich toll farmers, who had to extract the agreed amount plus their additional profit. They often capitalized on public ignorance of the scale of tolls to bring money into their pockets during the tax season (Luke 3:12-13). The civil rights of the publicans were denied, and they were deprived of their rights to be witnesses. (Joachim Jeremias, *New Testament Theology* [New York: Charles Scribner's Sons, 1971], 109–10, quoted in Byung-mu Ahn, "Jesus and the Minjung," in *Minjung Theology,* 143.)

12 Byung-mu Ahn, "Jesus and the Minjung," in *Minjung Theology,* 144.

13 Ibid., 144.

the ignorant, whose religious ignorance and moral behavior were problematic to their access to salvation, according to the public view of the time.[14] They were publicans and sinners (Mark 2:16), prostitutes (Matt 21:32), or the sick. They were simply called "sinners" (Mark 2:17; Luke 7:37, 39).

Jesus came into the world to take their infirmities and bear their grief (compare Matt 8:17). He had compassion for the crowds, "because they were harassed and helpless" (Matt 9:36). He proclaimed the good news for these heavy-laden. In Jesus' eyes, the righteous were the actual sinners who needed to repent of their sin of self-righteousness, religious persecution, and ostentation. In contrast to the religious leaders and scribes, Jesus invited the han-ridden—the despised, the sick, and the poor—to his rest: "Come to me, all you that are weary and are carrying heavy burdens, and I will give you rest" (Matt 11:28). Their burden was double: public contempt and the hopelessness of attaining God's salvation.[15] They were not in fact sinners, but were the sinned-against and marginalized by the oppressive religious leaders and their legal system.

This implies that these so-called "sinners" needed solace, healing, and liberation, not repentance. Jesus used all his measures, including miracles, to heal the wounded from their suffering, oppression, and affliction. Contrary to our present theology that is basically engaged with sinners' sin and salvation, Jesus' teaching centered on comforting the sinned-against, healing the wounded, giving voice to the voiceless, that is, liberating them from their han while confronting their oppressors. Jesus was the friend of the han-ridden.

Someone has said that to be current, pastors need to preach on the pain of their audiences. Likewise, pastors need to be aware of people's sin and their han to address the themes of repentance and healing. Sin may be forgiven by the repentance of sinners, whereas han can be resolved by the healing of the sinned-against. As we understand the reality of sin and han interwoven at the individual and collective levels, the fullness of Christian salvation and healing will be more real and concrete in the world of the sinned-against and the sinned.

It is time for us to deal with the reality of han in the world. Most violence and crime are the results of the vicious cycle of sin and han. Unresolved han or superficial treatments of han continually produce sin, violence, and tragedies and thus perpetuate the eruption of han by triggering another han.

---

14   Jeremias, *New Testament Theology*, 112.
15   Ibid., 113.

The Eucharist for Healing

When we reflect on the Eucharist from the perspective of han and from a Wesleyan point of view, we have an opportunity to gain a more holistic understanding. The Wesleyan understanding of the Eucharist involves Jesus' real presence that brings redemption and healing to participants. In light of the spirit of the Wesleyan Lord's Supper, we can deepen the Eucharist's pertinent meanings for the present and coming generations of Wesleyans.

The following section deals with three points. First, the Eucharist signifies the healing of the wounded (han-ridden) in addition to the forgiveness of sinners. Second, the Eucharist can be a means of grace for the physical healing of the sick (han-ridden). Third, the Eucharist can be a means of grace for social holiness. The practical implementation of these points may be to incorporate a healing prayer for the wounded in a communion worship service.

The Healing of the Brokenhearted (Han-ridden)

For John Wesley, Christ is really present in the Eucharist, not in his human nature, but in his divine nature. The divine nature of Christ by the operation of his Spirit carries the benefits of his death to grace-seeking receivers.[16] By saying this, he disagreed with the Roman Catholic doctrine of transubstantiation. Through his real presence in the Eucharist, Jesus forgives our sins and heals our broken hearts:

> The whole body of Christians being agreed, that Christ had ordained certain outward means, for conveying his grace into the souls of men. Their constant practice set this beyond all dispute.[17]

> Is not the eating of that bread, and the drinking of that cup, the outward, visible means, whereby God conveys into our souls all that spiritual grace, that righteousness, and peace, and joy in the Holy Ghost, which were purchased by the body of Christ once broken and the blood of Christ once shed for us? Let all, therefore, who truly desire the grace of God, eat of that bread, and drink of that cup.[18]

---

16 John Wesley, *The Letters of John Wesley,* ed. John Telford, 8 vols. (London: Epworth, 1931), I:118 and quoted in Luke Tyerman, *The Life and Times of the Rev. John Wesley,* M.A., 3 vols. (London: Hodder & Stoughton, 1878), I:82.

17 Albert Outler and Richard P. Heitzenrater, eds., *John Wesley's Sermons: an Anthology* (Nashville: Abingdon Press, 1991), 158. [text of the 1872 edition]

18 Ibid., 165.

John Wesley holds that in the Eucharist the Holy Spirit will infuse righteousness, peace, and joy into our souls. This signifies that the Eucharist bears the fruits of the Holy Spirit, bringing inner healing to us.

Furthermore, Christ's Passion discloses God's love that heals the brokenheartedness of the sinned-against and transforms sinners. Christ's presence is never passive or nostalgic. It is active and transformative. Jesus particularly gives his body and blood to the sinned-against and feeds them with his bread and wine so that they may receive his wholesome and indestructible life. The Eucharist empowers participants to bind up their han of brokenheartedness first and then the broken world.

By selecting Isaiah 61:1 to read, Jesus declares his mission statement in Luke 4:16-18:

> "The Spirit of the Lord is upon me, because he has anointed me to bring good news to the poor. He has sent me to proclaim release to the captives and recovery of sight to the blind, to let the oppressed go free."[19]

When Jesus is present, the poor will hear the good news, the brokenhearted will be bound up, the captives will be set free. The real presence of Jesus in the Eucharist will embody His mission of the healing of these wounded.

So far, we have used the Eucharist as a means of grace for the sign of God's forgiveness of our sin and our sanctification in The United Methodist Church. So we have "Confession and Pardon" in our Eucharist order. Since Jesus bears our griefs and carries our sorrows (Isa 53:4) and through his woundedness, we are healed (1 Pet 2:24), it will be appropriate that we include a healing prayer for the sinned-against or victims in our Wesleyan services of the Eucharist. Most of us are both sinners and the sinned-against.

The Healing of the Sick

Can the Eucharist be a means of physical healing? Is it biblical and Wesleyan? Paul directly relates the Eucharist with the health of recipients: "Whoever, therefore, eats the bread or drinks the cup of the Lord in an unworthy manner will be answerable for the body and blood of the Lord. . . . For this reason many of you are weak and ill, and some have died" (1 Cor 11:27-30). Does it imply that the Eucharist in a worthy manner may reverse weakness and illness? Jesus promises his presence in those recipients of the

---

19   "Moreover the light of the moon will be like the light of the sun, and the light of the sun will be sevenfold, like the light of seven days, on the day when the Lord binds up the injuries of his people, and heals the wounds inflicted by his blow" (Isa 30:26).

Eucharist: "For my flesh is true food and my blood is true drink. Those who eat my flesh and drink my blood abide in me, and I in them" (John 6:55-56). Through the real presence of Jesus, he would restore the weak and the sick to their health. There are a number of cases of the restoration of health through the Eucharist.

Even Wesley uses an allegory of the physical healing of the blind for the wondrous work of the Eucharist.

> I come then to GOD's Altar, with a full persuasion that these words, This is my Body, promise me more than a figure; that this holy Banquet is not a bare memorial only, but may actually convey as many blessings to me, as it brings curses on the profane receiver. Indeed, in what manner this is done, I know not; it is enough for me to admire. One thing I know (as said the blind man of our Lord), He laid clay upon mine eyes, and behold I see. He hath blessed, and given me this Bread, and my soul receiveth comfort. I know that clay hath nothing in itself, which could have wrought such a miracle. And I know that this Bread hath nothing in itself, which can impart grace, holiness, and salvation. But I know also, that it is the ordinary way of GOD to produce His greatest works at the presence, though not by the power, of the most useless instruments.[20]

Wesley points out the miraculous power of insignificant matter, either clay or bread, that can impart salvation and holiness only when Jesus is present in it. This implies that either clay or bread can heal a blind person through Jesus' real presence.

Here Wesley accentuates the meaning of the Eucharist beyond the memorial motif. It is significant that Wesley connects the Eucharist with the healing of the blind man. Wesley's heart in front of the bread and wine of the Eucharist was the same as that of the blind, being grateful for the clay that was laid upon his eyes. He allegorizes the story of the blind for the opening of his spiritual eyes. To him, the presence of Jesus in the bread can work miracles—physical and spiritual.

Thus, it will not be inappropriate for us to bring forth the healing aspect of the Eucharist by paying attention to the divine touch of healing for the sick. In addition to its redemption for sinners, the Eucharist offers healing for the sick. So it is time for the church to include some liturgical prayers for the healing of the sick in the Eucharist service.

---

20   John and Charles Wesley's *Hymns on the Lord's Supper*, 1745, with parts of Daniel Brevint's *Christian Sacrament*, 1673; transcribed from the 1951 reprint of the selection issued in 1936 by the Methodist Sacramental Fellowship. http://www.canamus.org/Enchiridion/Xtrs/brevint.htm.

A Means of Grace for Social Holiness

Leonardo and Clodovis Boff begin their *Introducing Liberation Theology* with the following story:

> A woman of forty, but who looks as old as seventy, went up to the priest after Mass and said sorrowfully: "Father, I went to communion without going to confess first." "How come, my daughter?" asked the priest.
>
> "I arrived rather later after you had begun the offertory. For three days I have had only water and nothing to eat; I am dying of hunger. When I saw you handing out the hosts, those pieces of white bread, I went to communion just out of hunger for that little bit of bread." The priest's eyes filled with tears.[21]

What does it mean for us to share the Eucharist in such a hungry world? The Eucharist signifies that the eucharistic table is entwined with the common table of people. Thus, sharing the Eucharist means that the hungry and the rich are one family. The term *family* in Chinese means those who eat together. The eucharistic table makes all of us a heavenly and earthly family. It proclaims our commensality until he comes. Participating in the Eucharist is not only for our holiness but also for "social wholeness" that is connected with social holiness.

Rolland and Heidi Baker are missionaries to Mozambique. Their own story of the multiplication of bread and drink dramatically bridges the Eucharist and its commensality. In late 1995, Rolland Baker was personally hugely influenced at the Toronto Airport Christian Fellowship. The Holy Spirit hit him with massive conviction and an overwhelming joy in the truth of the gospel. Greatly amazed by Rolland Baker's rejuvenation, Heidi Baker decided to visit the Toronto Airport Christian Fellowship as well. In one of the early meetings she attended there, she experienced something extraordinary:

> One night I was groaning in intercession for the children of Mozambique. There were thousands coming towards me and I was crying, "No, Lord, there are too many!" Then I had a dramatic, clear vision of Jesus. I was with Him, and thousands and thousands of children surrounded us. I saw His shining face and His intense, burning eyes of love. I also saw His body. It was bruised and broken, and His side was pierced. He said, "Look into my eyes. You give them something to eat." Then He took a piece of His broken body and handed

---

21 Leonardo Boff and Clodovis Boff, *Introducing Liberation Theology* (Maryknoll, NY: Orbis Books, 1987), 1.

it to me. It became bread in my hands, and I began to give it to the children. It multiplied in my hands. Then again the Lord said, "Look into my eyes. You give them something to drink." He gave me a cup of blood and water, which flowed from His side. I knew it was a cup of bitterness and joy. I drank it and then began to give it to the children to drink. The cup did not go dry. By this point I was crying uncontrollably. I was completely undone by His fiery eyes of love. I realized what it had cost Him to provide such spiritual and physical food for us all. The Lord spoke to my heart and said, "There will always be enough, because I died."[22]

At the Toronto Airport Christian Fellowship, Heidi Baker experienced other significant occurrences in addition to this, and these have profoundly affected all that they do in their ministry. Since this particular vision they have never declined any abandoned children on the street, and God has supplied their daily provisions. Many months later in Mozambique, Heidi Baker faced hunger herself:

Our daughter, Crystalyn, began to cry because she was so hungry. I thought I was going to snap. We didn't have any big pans for cooking. We weren't prepared in any way to feed all those children. A precious woman from the U.S. embassy came over with food. "I brought you chili and rice for your family!" she announced sweetly, with just enough for the four of us. We hadn't eaten in days. I opened a door and showed her all our children. "I have a big family!" I pointed out tiredly but in complete and desperate earnest. My friend got serious. "There's not enough! I need to go home and cook some more!" But I just asked her to pray over the food. Now she was upset. "Don't do this!" she begged. But she prayed, quickly. I got out the plastic plates we used for street outreaches, and also a small pot of cornmeal I had. We began serving, and right from the start I gave everyone a full bowl. I was dazed and overwhelmed. I barely understood at the time what a wonderful thing was happening. But all our children ate, the staff ate, my friend ate and even our family of four ate. Everyone had enough. Since then we have never said no to an orphaned, abandoned or dying child. Now we feed and take care of more than one thousand children. They eat and drink all they want of the Lord's goodness.[23]

It is necessary for us to connect the Eucharist and feeding the hungry. When we partake of the Eucharist, we commit ourselves to proclaiming the Good News of Jesus Christ until he comes. For Jesus, Eucharist was his last

---

22   Heidi Baker and Rolland Baker. *Always Enough: God's Miraculous Provision among the Poorest Children on Earth* (Grand Rapids: Chosen Books, 2002), 529–32. Kindle Edition.

23   Ibid., 532–37.

supper. The Eucharist denotes that we are one body of Jesus Christ. "For as often as you eat this bread and drink the cup, you proclaim the Lord's death until he comes" (1 Cor 11:26). We proclaim his good news until all of us eat together around his table. There will be always bread and wine around his table. The Eucharist is the extension of Jesus' body and blood that is his love. Thus, the Eucharist must be for us the embodiment of the bread and wine of his love as we proclaim our common table before Christ, implementing Wesley's vision of the "social holiness."

Conclusion

As stated earlier, to be current, pastors need to address the pain in their congregations. Likewise, pastors need to be aware of the issues of sin and han in order to address the pressing themes of repentance and healing. Sin and han are different but related. Sin may be forgiven through repentance, whereas han can be resolved through the healing of brokenheartedness. As we understand the reality of sin and han as they intersect in the lives of people and groups of people, the fullness of the gospel of Jesus Christ will reach out to more suffering people in the world.

We have reviewed the Bible and its theology from the perspective of the sinned-against in light of han. The Bible is for both sinners and the sinned-against. However, the Bible, particularly the New Testament, turns its attention to the community of faith that was persecuted and sinned-against. If we aspire to keep the balance between the care of sinners and the sinned-against, it is critical to understand the Bible more from the perspectives of the sinned-against. The notion of han may contribute to such an effort to see biblical truth from such perspectives, complementing the doctrine of sin. This notion may free people from the unilateral interpretation of the sin-penalty scheme and provide an alternative theological mode of interpretation for victims. Imposing the sin-penalty formula upon the victims of sin is a grave injustice. By naming the reality of the suffering of victims, we can begin to heal rather than overlook or judge them. Such a move will start off a new journey to a theology of holistic salvation and healing.

Particularly, the concept of han can shed light on the meaning of the Eucharist for the victims of sin. The latter part of this chapter discussed three points: the Eucharist is also for the inner healing of the wounded, the Eucharist is a means of grace for the physical healing of the sick, and the Eucharist is a means of grace for social holiness. In addition to "Confession and Pardon" for sinners in the Eucharist, if we incorporate a "healing prayer" for the wounded, the sick, the brokenhearted, and the abused in a eucharistic service, this will effectuate our restoration of health and our social holiness. Here is an example of such a healing prayer, which also can serve to celebrate the wholeness we can find in God and the spirit of this chapter:

> *Loving God,*
>
> *We are truly thankful for this invitation to the Table of your heavenly banquet. We know that your healing is available to us through this bread of your flesh and this wine of your blood. Thank you, Jesus, for bearing our griefs and carrying our sorrows (Isa 53:4). Through your stripes, we are healed (1 Pet 2:24). Abide in us and restore our physical bodies, our minds, and our spirits by feeding us with your healing bread and wine as we partake of this Eucharist. In the name of Jesus. Amen.*

FOUR

Christology and Eucharist

John L. Drury

How do Christology and the Eucharist intersect? And how might one navigate that intersection? With regard to the first question, I believe the intersection to be rich and complex. Christology and Eucharist are not two county roads meeting at a stop sign, but two interstates forming a multilevel cloverleaf. In fact, the intersection is so complex that many if not most of the historic Eucharistic controversies can be traced to Christology— not to different Christologies, but to the selection of different aspects of Christology as determinative for understanding the Eucharist. Because of the sheer complexity of this intersection, my second question concerning its navigation comes to the fore. So, after some detailed mapping, I will argue that the trick to navigating the intersection of Christology and the Eucharist is to put eucharistic practice (rather than theory) in the driver's seat. At least in this case, putting practice first is the better part of wisdom.

This chapter falls into three sections following a standard christological narrative: the Incarnation, Crucifixion, and Resurrection. The first and briefest treats the intersection between Eucharist and Christ's person. The second concerns the intersection between Eucharist and Christ's work—his life of love unto death. The third and longest deals with the intersection between Eucharist and Christ's resurrection—his life of love beyond death. The thesis mentioned above will emerge again and again throughout each of these three sections.

Eucharist and Christ's Person

For the sake of clarity, I will adopt the scholastic distinction between Christ's person and his work. I begin, again in scholastic fashion, with Christ's person. It seems to me that there are three points of contact between Christ's person and the Eucharist. Each generates a dialectic that must be carefully navigated to avoid reductionism. The first is the *Chalcedonian* juxtaposition between the unity of Christ's person and the duality of his natures. Those who accent the duality of natures (such as the Tome of Leo) tend to be concerned with delineating the distinction between the sign and thing-signified in the Eucharist. Those who accent the unity of Christ's person (such as Cyril) tend to emphasize the unity of the liturgy without reference to such hairsplitting. Both sides of this dialectic are valid; the problem is the reduction to one without the other.

The second point of contact between Christ's person and the Eucharist concerns the *direction* of the union of deity and humanity. In Christ there is both a downward vector, namely, the Incarnation of the Word, and an upward vector, namely, the Word's assumption of human flesh. A tendency to lead with one or the other direction correlates with two ways of conceiving the presence of Christ at the Table. The downward vector befits talk of Christ's bodily condescension to us at Table. The upward vector befits talk of our spiritual ascension to Christ at the right hand of the Father.

The third point of contact between Christ's person and the Eucharist concerns the *deification* of Christ's humanity. In what sense and in what manner is Christ's human nature deified? If one answers this in a stable way, or to put it another way, if one speaks of the deification of the human as an accomplished fact, then a similar stability emerges with reference to the Eucharist: the conversion of the elements produces a permanent state of being. But if one answers in a progressive way, that is, if one speaks of deification as an ongoing process, then a much looser association between Christ's body and the elements emerges.

In each of these points the pattern is clear: accent in christological dialectic correlates with accent in eucharistic conception. This should not surprise us, for the mystery of the Eucharist is not ultimately separable from the mystery of Christ himself. And the ultimate unity of these mysteries implies a lesson: beware of disrupting the dialectic of our Lord's person, for reductionism with regard to his Supper lies crouching at the door. Stated positively: keeping the christological dialectical alive is crucial to retaining the full meaning of the Eucharist.

Eucharist and Christ's Work

The intersection between Christology and Eucharist includes reflection on Christ's work. The intersection is even more complex here, for the work of Christ has so many aspects. One traditional way of organizing the manifold significance of Christ's saving activity is the *threefold office*. Much of what Christ does for us can be placed under the titles prophet, priest, or king. And so the relation between Christ's work and the Eucharist naturally fits within this framework.

However, to get at this relation, a third dimension must be introduced: *time*. The temporal structure of the Table has been much discussed, especially when clarifying its connection to Christ's work. Much light is shed on the Eucharist when we attend to all three tenses of each office of Christ. As the chart shows, this coordination of tenses and offices highlights nine distinct ways of conceiving the Eucharist. Obviously, I cannot explore all nine; rather, I'll identify two examples where this coordination helps us to ward off reductionism.

	PAST	PRESENT	FUTURE
PROPHET	command	proclamation	expectation
PRIEST	remembrance	representation	participation
KING	constitution	renewal	anticipation

First example: some of us were reared in traditions that reduced the meaning of the Lord's Supper to its past prophetic aspect, which is to say, Christ as true prophet has *commanded* us to do this thing, so we better get on with it. The risk of this reduction is not only its poverty of meaning but also its susceptibility to alternative reductions. So, once exposed to the richness of another account—say, for instance, the future priestly aspect of participation in the worship of heaven—we quickly trade one reduction for another, rejecting all other aspects. The wiser route is to expand our notion of Christ's work and with it our understanding of the Eucharist.

Second example: there is an odd, almost ironic, correlation of past priestly with present royal on the one hand and past royal with present priestly on the other. See the four boxes on the bottom left-hand corner of the chart. Those who seek to protect the singularity of Christ's sacrifice on the cross tend to reduce the priestly aspect of the Eucharist to its past tense (as a *remembrance*) and not in any sense a re-presentation. And yet this past reduction of the priestly makes room for an understanding of the Lord's Supper as a covenant *renewal* service, a declaration of allegiance to Christ the King, an act of recommitment, even an occasion for revival.

The inverse correlation occurs as well. Those who assert that "Eucharist makes the church" highlight the past-tense royal work of Christ. By instituting the Eucharist, Christ *constitutes* his church, establishing the apostolic community as his body on earth. Though not fully excluded, talk of remembrance and renewal is, from this vantage point, often dismissed as mere memorialism. And yet this past reduction of the royal office makes possible a rich account of present-tense priestly *representation*, for a body so constituted may and must be presented before the Father with thanksgiving.

In each case, an act of reduction is accompanied by insight into the meaning of the Eucharist in relation to other aspects of Christ's work. This should give us hope for an even greater inclusion of aspects without a tradition being forced to abandon its historic point of entry. So the warning against reduction need not entail a "view from nowhere," but rather a simple call to abandon an unhealthy attachment to any one aspect of the Eucharist.

With these words of advice I am once again moving towards my thoughts on how to best navigate the intersection of Christology and Eucharist. So let me turn to what one of my colleagues calls the "patronizing practical platitudes" that so often conclude dogmatic essays. What I have been doing throughout this chapter, and wish to recommend explicitly now, is a *deflationary strategy of inclusion*. The intersection between Christology and Eucharist is so rich and complex that we ought to include as many aspects as possible. However, our eucharistic theories consistently reduce the mystery of Christ's person and/or work to one or a cluster of its aspects. I do not hold out hope for some theoretical resolution. Rather, I deflate the importance of such theoretical accounts, regarding them as secondary and dependent on the living practice of the Eucharist. As I am sure you can all attest, a robust eucharistic piety can embrace the dialectics of Christ's person and work in a way that no theory can. The primacy of practice does not solve every problem—our doctrinal differences still divide us, and so we've got our theoretical work cut out for us. But the primacy of practice can dissolve many of our problems, making them less important and lowering the stakes. I think the model here is the E section of the Baptism, Eucharist, and Ministry paper (BEM),[1] which wisely does not offer an inclusive theory of the Eucharist, but deploys a wealth of Trinitarian and christological tropes to make explicit the multivalent meaning of the Eucharist that is in fact embedded in our overlapping practices. The act of mutual recognition there inscribed is far more significant than any forthcoming theoretical breakthrough. Perhaps more attention is due to this and other acts of practice-oriented theologizing.

---

1   *Baptism, Eucharist, and Ministry*, Faith and Order Paper No. 111 (Geneva: World Council of Churches, 1982).

Eucharist and Christ's Resurrection

So far my mapping of the intersection of Christology and Eucharist has emphasized the complexity of this relation. I do not wish to diminish this emphasis one bit. However, a question does emerge: What holds it all together? Are we still talking about one practice. the Eucharist? And are we still talking about one person: Jesus Christ? Or does the primacy of practice eventuate in a diffusion of dogma? These questions bring us to the third and final intersection of Christology and Eucharist: resurrection. For it is the risen Christ, and he alone, who holds together the surfeit of practical and doxastic commitments regarding both Christology and Eucharist.

It is immediately necessary to underscore that it is not the Resurrection as such that holds together the many aspects of Christology and Eucharist. The singular event of Christ's resurrection is just that: an event. Events as such do not hold together commitments. Perhaps one could transmute the event into a concept. But even if such a concept would succeed at this task, doing so would transgress the primacy of practice asserted above. And, more important, it would usurp the rightful claimant to this role: Jesus Christ himself. Jesus Christ, who was raised from the dead, is uncontained by any conceptual apparatus concerning Christology and Eucharist. Jesus Christ, who is risen from the dead, is unperturbed by the apparent contradictions in our conversations about him and his Table. Jesus Christ, who will live unto eternity, is unthreatened by the excess of language thrown at his feet as he presides at his Table. For the risen Christ himself holds together Christology and Eucharist.

I will develop this claim by first highlighting the centrality and pervasiveness of this connection as it appears in the New Testament and inquire as to why it has been marginalized and minimized in the subsequent Christian tradition. Then I will supply a brief dogmatic sketch of the risen Christ's relationship to the Eucharist. I intend these two moves to work together to articulate a true if inadequate testimony to the risen Christ in his relationship to the Eucharist.

One of the great ironies of the Christian tradition is that reflection on the Lord's Supper has centered exegetically on the event of the Last Supper. This irony runs in two directions. On the one hand, the Last Supper is so-called because it is the last in a series of meals shared with disciples, crowds, sinners, and others. Meals play a central role in the ministry of Jesus. And so a singular focus on the Last Supper in abstraction from his whole life of table fellowship is misleading at best. On the other hand, the Last Supper is so-called only in a certain sense. It is the Last Supper prior to our Lord's death. And since his death is the culmination of his life of love for us, this Supper is fittingly called his Last. And yet it is not his only Last Supper.

It is the Last Supper only with regard to the series of meals occurring in his life of love unto death. But there is another series of meals: those that occur in his life of love beyond death. Upon being raised from the dead, the risen Jesus ate with his disciples yet again. Both Luke and John bear explicit witness to the role of table fellowship in the appearances of the risen Jesus. Now this series of suppers also came to a close (according to Luke, after forty days). So there was in fact a Last Supper among the series of meals the risen Christ shared with his disciples. Yet that is not the final Last Supper. There is at least one more: the banquet that shall accompany the consummation of Christ and his church. So, in a sense, there are three Last Suppers: the first occurring the night that he was betrayed, the second occurring during the forty days, and the last occurring at the end of time. And so there is a great irony in our myopic focus on the Last Supper: for its very name points both backward and forward to the full meaning of Christ's table fellowship with us.

As a thought experiment, let us consider the second of the three meals, the one that gives meaning to the rest. We are not denying the fullness sketched above, but simply seeking its center. Surely the Last Supper is a contender for this role. The narration of a final meal in the Gospels and the reference to the night of betrayal in Paul's first letter to the Corinthians are more than sufficient evidence of its importance.

However, the Easter meals are no mere afterthought. They are perhaps just as central, at least when it comes to understanding the early Christian practice of breaking bread together. For this practice was bound up with the practice of gathering on the first day of the week. And the first day of the week was the day of gathering precisely because it was the day on which the Lord rose from the dead. The fact that breaking bread together and gathering on the first day of the week are intertwined from the earliest days of Christianity stands as a testament to the deep connection between eucharistic practice and the presence of the risen Christ.

Now the church has had good reasons for centering its eucharistic reflection on the Last Supper. At the very least, the association of the Last Supper with Passover invited all kinds of deep insights. Furthermore, the meaning of Christ's death is the great puzzle of Christian thinking. So it needs all the help it can get. A Passover-inflected common meal fits the bill perfectly. In a way, the meal was making sense of the death as much as the other way around. But once reflection on Christ's death developed, the dialectic turned around so that it became the center from which to understand the Lord's Supper theologically.

This was not wrong. Insofar as the early Christians conceived the practice of breaking bread together as a remembrance of Christ's dying passion for us, the meal shared on the night he was betrayed is a natural prototype. But it is one-sided. To the extent that they also conceived this practice as a recognition, a celebration, of Christ's living presence with us, the meal shared on the day he rose from the dead is the most fitting prototype.

I have no interest in offering a one-sided overcorrection. Both crucifixion and resurrection ought to be central in our reflection upon the practice of the Lord's Supper. The primacy of practice can cope with such a multicentered model of reflection. More to the point, these are not two competing centers. For the practice of the Eucharist has one center: Christ himself, the crucified and risen one. I am seeking to highlight the importance of Christ's resurrection precisely in order to highlight the importance of Christ himself, who must be alive to occupy the living center of a living practice.

So, without further ado, allow me to conclude by offering a brief dogmatic sketch of the risen Christ's relationship to the Eucharist. I do not intend to supplant any of the inclusionary moves made above. This is but one more deflated account, offered as a testimony to one indispensable but by no means exhaustive aspect of eucharistic practice. Its truth consists solely in its witness to the risen Jesus who in himself is the center and substance of all Christian practices and who alone holds together Christology and Eucharist.

Let us begin with the event of Easter. The one event of Easter occurs under three aspects. First, Easter is the event in which Jesus Christ was raised from the dead. Second, Easter is the event in which Jesus Christ in his risenness reveals himself to his own. Third, Easter is the event in which Jesus Christ lives and reigns unto eternity. Analogously to the doctrine of the Trinity, these three aspects are one yet distinct, ordered yet equal. This formal analogy is fitting because in this event occurs a material analogy to the Trinity: Jesus Christ was raised by God the Father; Jesus Christ arose and reveals himself to be the Son of God; Jesus Christ lives unto eternity in the power of the Holy Spirit. And these three are one.

These three aspects of Christ's resurrection correspond well with the threefold structure of breaking bread together: *eucharistia*, *anamnesis*, and *epiklesis*. First of all, we break bread together as *eucharistia*, as an act of thanksgiving to God the Father as the giver of all good gifts. Secondly, we break bread together as *anamnesis*, as an act of remembering Jesus Christ as the one who was and is and will be for us. Thirdly, we break bread together as *epiklesis*, as an act of invoking the Holy Spirit to move us and all things toward their eternal end. As with the threefold structure of the Easter event, this too is analogous both formally and materially to the doctrine of the Trinity. And yet it shares more than this structural similarity. For our practice of breaking bread is itself embedded within the reality of the risen Christ. To show what I mean, let's take each correlated aspect in turn.

First, thanksgiving is our mode of participation in Christ's own self-receiving risenness. By breaking bread together eucharistically, we not only give thanks to God the Father for all he has done for us in Christ but also join the risen Christ in his continual thanksgiving to his Father for raising him from the dead. First and foremost, resurrection is an act of God the Father received by the one who was crucified, dead, and buried. Jesus Christ was raised by God the Father. I think it is a mistake to ever speak of Christ raising himself. I explore the reasons for this view elsewhere. Suffice it to say that this is the consistent witness of Paul's letters and the sermons of Acts: that God the Father is the one who raised Jesus from the dead. Furthermore, even in the Gospel of John, Jesus participates in his own resurrection by way of receptivity. He has life in himself from the Father who gave it to him (John 5). He has the authority to lay down his life and to receive it again (John 10). So the event of resurrection begins in receptivity: the Father graciously giving life and the Son graciously receiving life. Jesus Christ receives from God the Father his very own self, his life, his own most being, which had gone the way of all flesh. This receiving corresponds to his eternal generation from the Father, in which the distinction of giver and receiver entails no inequality or diminution of deity. And this receiving in time takes on the form of thanksgiving. For a gracious gift evokes a gracious reception. Jesus Christ graciously receives God the Father's act of raising by thanking God unto eternity. When we break bread together on the day that Christ was raised, we join him in his eternal act of giving thanks to God the Father.

Second, remembering is our mode of participation in Christ's own self-revealing risenness. By breaking bread together anamnetically, we not only remember what Christ in his death has done for us but also recognize Christ himself in his risen presence among us. The immediate intent of resurrection is revelation. God raised Jesus so that Jesus may reveal himself. Although we must be wary of reducing resurrection to a function of revelation, revelation is without a doubt the immediate function of resurrection. This conceptual point comes to expression in the two basic types of Easter stories: empty tomb narratives and appearance narratives. Although this distinction was perhaps overdrawn during the heyday of form criticism, it is nevertheless a genuine difference with theological weight. For the empty

tomb points backward to the once-for-all past act of God the Father in raising the Son Jesus from the dead. This is an act that took place in the mystery
of the triune relations and of which only indirect witness is befitting. But
the appearances point to the again-and-again present act of Jesus Christ in
his self-revealing risenness.

Two recurring themes in the appearance stories are particularly relevant
to our topic: recognition and eating. In both Luke 24 and John 21, Jesus appears to a small band of disciples who do not immediately recognize him.
This theme highlights the self-revealing character of the risen Christ. He
must reveal himself for them to recognize him. And in both cases the confirmation of this recognition is connected to table fellowship. In the case of
Luke 24, the connection could not be any stronger, for it is twice pointed out
that Cleopas and the other disciple recognized him at the breaking of the
bread. When we break bread together on the day the risen Christ appeared
to his own, we recognize him in his self-revealing risen presence.

Third, invoking is our mode of participation in Christ's own self-giving
livingness. By breaking bread together epikletically, we not only seek a
miraculous work upon this meal but rather expect the living Lord Jesus
Christ to draw us into the spontaneity of his pentecostal Spirit. The event
of resurrection culminates in the eternal life of Jesus Christ. He was not
raised back to life just to die again. He arose unto a life with death behind
it. Death is defeated by being defanged; it is no longer the last word, the
last act of a life lived, but a narrated element of a living person's past. Jesus
Christ in his eternal livingness invites us into a life no longer defined
by death. His life, life in him and with him, is life in the Spirit. The New
Testament consistently links the Spirit with Christ's resurrection and life.
Paul's discourse in Romans 8 is the starkest in this regard. But the point is
expressed narratively by both Luke and John, who, despite their different
chronologies, clearly place Christ's giving of the Spirit as the culminating
moment of the event of resurrection. When we break bread together on the
day the risen Christ exhaled his Spirit onto his apostles, we open ourselves
to him in his self-giving spontaneous life in the Spirit.

With this, my reflections come to a close. I am tempted to recapitulate
all the points made above concerning Christ's person and work from the
perspective of Christ's resurrection. But that is a project much too large for
one mere chapter. Furthermore, it may give the false impression of intent to
construct a comprehensive theory of eucharistic practice. But as I have been
asserting throughout this chapter, the complexity of the intersection between Christology and Eucharist is best navigated by a commitment to the
primacy of practice. So we needn't work out every conceptual connection to

attain insight into our practice. Nor do we need to worry about the potential confusion generated by greater and greater complexity. Let theoretical explorations abound! The simplicity of breaking bread together stands strong on its own. For we sit at Christ's Table, not our own. And so the risen Christ himself holds together Christology and Eucharist. And our words are just that: words. We ask and hope that they are faithful words. But they are just words: words about the Word-made-flesh and words about the meal he shares with us. May the words of my mouth and the meditation of my heart be pleasing in your sight, O Lord, my rock and my redeemer.

FIVE

Pneumatology and Eucharist

Jason E. Vickers

When Wesleyans think and talk about the Holy Spirit, we usually focus our attention on the *work* of the Spirit.[1] Characteristically, we ask two questions: (1) *where* is the Spirit at work and (2) *for what purpose* or toward what end is the Spirit at work? I will begin by indicating how Wesleyans have answered these two questions across space and time. More specifically, I will identify some broad patterns in the way Wesleyans think about the location and purpose of the Spirit's work. These patterns will set the stage for a discussion of the work of the Spirit in Holy Eucharist.

Wesleyan Pneumatology: Introducing the Tradition

When it comes to the location of the Spirit's work, Wesleyans accentuate the freedom of the Holy Spirit. We stress that the Spirit is free to be present and at work wherever the Spirit sees fit. In other words, we do not restrict the work of the Spirit to any one place. Rather, we insist that the Spirit is at work in all sorts of places. We believe that the Spirit is at work both within and beyond the sacramental life of the church. We believe that the Spirit is at work in preaching, in the sacraments, in the lives of the ordained and the laity, in Sunday school classrooms, and wherever two or three faithful Christians are gathered. But we also insist that the Holy Spirit is at work in the hearts and minds of unbelievers everywhere, from city streets and nightclubs to corporate boardrooms and prison cells. Put simply, we

---

1 Wesleyans have not been especially concerned with theological reflection on the person of the Holy Spirit. We have not been preoccupied with questions about *who* or *what* the Holy Spirit is, say, relative to God the Father and God the Son. We are not uncertain or ambivalent about the Spirit's identity. Rather, we readily confess that the Holy Spirit is one of the three divine persons of the Holy Trinity. We believe that the distinctions among the three divine persons are real, and we believe that there is also real unity in the Godhead. In other words, we confess that God is mysteriously three *and* one, but most Wesleyans are not especially motivated to speculate further about the manner of the distinctions or the unity.

Wesleyans have an industrial-strength doctrine of the freedom of the Spirit. We really do believe that the Spirit is at work throughout the whole of God's good creation.

At times, the emphasis on the freedom of the Spirit has been controversial. For example, the bitter disagreement between John and Charles Wesley (a disagreement that caused Charles Wesley to withdraw from active participation in the revival) is perhaps best understood as a disagreement over the location of the Spirit's work. On the one hand, Charles Wesley believed that the Spirit works primarily through the sacramental life of the church, which is to say through the Holy Eucharist properly administered by the ordained. Consequently, Charles was not particularly supportive of field preaching or lay preaching. On the other hand, John Wesley agreed that the Spirit was at work in the sacramental life of the church, but he also insisted that the Spirit was free to be at work through means other than Holy Eucharist. As far as he was concerned, there was ample evidence that the Spirit was at work in field preaching and in lay preaching.

This brings us to a second pattern or tendency concerning the location of the Spirit's work. As we have just noted, John and Charles Wesley both affirmed the work of the Spirit in the sacraments. For his part, John Wesley implored the early Methodists to receive Holy Communion as often as possible.[2] Nevertheless, Wesleyans have tended to place an even stronger emphasis on the work of the Holy Spirit in and through preaching. Thus most Wesleyan churches only celebrate Holy Eucharist once a month or in some cases just once per quarter, but preaching takes place on a weekly basis. During revivals and camp meetings, preaching happens at least once per day, whereas Holy Eucharist is often celebrated in a single service. Again, it is not that Wesleyans deny that the Spirit is present and at work in Holy Eucharist. Rather, it is simply that we tend to associate the presence and work of the Holy Spirit even more strongly with preaching.

In addition to preaching, Wesleyans associate the presence and work of the Holy Spirit with the fellowship of believers. This tendency can be seen in the Wesleyan commitment to small groups, ranging from the bands and class meetings in early Methodism to Sunday school and midweek prayer services in the twentieth century.[3] It is also evident in

2   John Wesley, "The Duty of Constant Communion," in *The Works of John Wesley: Sermons*, vol. 3, ed. Albert C. Outler (Nashville: Abingdon Press, 1986), 427–39.

3   Kevin M. Watson, *The Class Meeting: Reclaiming a Forgotten (and Essential) Small Group Experience* (Wilmore, KY: Seedbed Publishing, 2014) and *Pursuing Social Holiness: The Band Meeting in Wesley's Thought and Popular Practice* (New York: Oxford University Press, 2015).

our commitment to conferencing. When Wesleyans get together for fellowship or for conferencing, we believe that the Holy Spirit is present and at work in our midst, binding us together and strengthening us for the work of ministry.

Wesleyans also associate the presence and work of the Holy Spirit with Holy Scripture. We believe that the Spirit inspired the original authors of Holy Scripture, but we also have strong doctrines of illumination and divine speaking. We believe that the Holy Spirit illumines or speaks directly to our hearts and minds when we attend to Holy Scripture in a spirit of humility and prayer. Consequently, we have a long history of stressing the importance of the personal daily devotional reading of Scripture.

In addition to preaching, the fellowship of believers, and Holy Scripture, Wesleyans also closely associate the work of the Spirit with prayer. Until somewhat recently, most Wesleyan churches had midweek prayer services. In camp meetings and revivals, entire services were often dedicated to prayer. For Wesleyans, all true prayer begins with the work of the Holy Spirit.

We could easily add other locations to the list of places and practices that Wesleyans associate with the presence and work of the Spirit. For example, Wesleyans have long associated the presence and work of the Holy Spirit with the practice of anointing the sick with oil for healing.[4] But more than all the places named thus far, the place that we most consistently and strongly associate with the presence and work of the Holy Spirit is undoubtedly the human heart. For Wesleyans, the Holy Spirit may be present and at work through preaching, the fellowship of believers, the reading of Scripture, prayer, healing, and other places besides, but the work of the Spirit begins and ends in the human heart. Even before the Spirit is at work through external means of grace, we believe the Spirit is at work in human hearts, readying them to receive the grace that flows so freely through the sacramental life of the church. Moreover, we believe that the Holy Spirit ultimately longs to be present and at work *within* us, shaping and guiding the inmost thoughts and desires of our hearts. Nothing is more central to Wesleyan sensibilities concerning the presence and work of the Spirit than that. We affirm that the Spirit's presence and work is mediated through external means of grace, but we also stress the need for the Spirit's presence and work ultimately to be internalized in the human heart. From start to finish, Wesleyanism is heart religion.[5]

---

4   See Candy Gunter Brown, "Healing," in *The Cambridge Companion to American Methodism*, ed. Jason E. Vickers (New York: Cambridge University Press, 2013), 227–42.

5   Wesley, "The Circumcision of the Heart," *The Works of John Wesley*, vol. 1, ed. Outler, 398–414.

The strong emphasis on the internalization of the presence and work of the Holy Spirit is a direct result of the way in which Wesleyans tend to conceive the purpose of the Spirit's work. Across space and time, Wesleyans have understood the purpose of the Spirit's work almost exclusively in soteriological terms. We have believed, taught, and confessed that the Holy Spirit (1) convicts us of our sins; (2) opens our eyes to the truth of gospel; (3) enables us to put our whole trust in Jesus Christ for our salvation; (4) assures us that, having put our trust in Christ, we really are sons and daughters of God; and (5) sanctifies us entirely, filling our hearts with love for God and neighbor. Whether through preaching, the sacraments, the fellowship of believers, Bible study, prayer, or some other means, we have stressed that the Holy Spirit is present and at work in human hearts, reconciling us to God the Father through Jesus Christ the Son.

A second purpose of the work of the Holy Spirit is organically related to the first. Heeding the words of Jesus in Holy Scripture, Wesleyans believe that the Holy Spirit is present and at work in our midst, enabling and empowering us to be effective witnesses in Judea, Samaria, and to the ends of the earth (Acts 1:8). In other words, we believe that the Holy Spirit enables and empowers us for the work of ministry, most notably the ministry of proclamation and evangelism. This is, of course, a natural extension of a soteriological conception of the Spirit's presence and work. Having been reconciled to God ourselves, we become means of grace through which the Holy Spirit is present and at work reconciling the world to Christ.

In addition to reconciling us to God and empowering us to bear witness to Christ, Wesleyans also affirm that the Holy Spirit gives a wide array of spiritual gifts to the church so that we lack nothing for building up the body of Christ in the world (1 Cor 12). But we tend to conceptualize spiritual gifts in a way that always relates to the primary purpose of reconciliation. For Wesleyans, spiritual gifts are a means to an end rather than an end in themselves.

Wesleyan Pneumatology: Assessing the Tradition

At this stage, we need to step back and survey the terrain that we have just covered. The Wesleyan theological tradition is easily the most prominent expression of the Pietist revolution within Protestantism. Reflective of this wider revolution, Wesleyans insist that being Christian is about more than believing rightly or being good. It is simply not enough to have right beliefs about God or to be a well-mannered and well-regarded member of society. On the contrary, we believe that becoming and being a Christian requires a deeply personal encounter with the living God. And that personal encounter is something that the Holy Spirit facilitates through various means of grace and ultimately by being present and at work in the inmost recesses of our hearts.

It is hard to overstate the global impact of this way of thinking about the work of the Holy Spirit. The Wesleyan tradition, together with its Pentecostal and charismatic offspring, has been instrumental in spreading the good news of God's free offer of salvation around the globe. Our work in missions and evangelism over the last two hundred years is second to none. And it is easy to see why. The message that the Holy Spirit is not tethered to any one location is an enticing one. It conveys a strong sense that God meets people wherever they are. They don't have to clean up, purchase expensive clothing, and join the church before God will speak to them or be at work in their lives. It is also an empowering message insofar as it stresses that the Holy Spirit stands ready not only to speak *to* all people but also to speak *through* all people. In other words, the Holy Spirit is free to speak through the ordained and through laity, through the educated and the uneducated, through men and women, through people of means, and through the poor. In this sense, Wesleyan pneumatology is thoroughly egalitarian.

The emphasis on the Spirit's presence and work in the human heart is also highly attractive. It conveys to people a strong sense that the Holy Spirit is with them always and everywhere, even before they are aware of the Spirit's presence. The Holy Spirit may be present and at work in preaching the sacraments, in Holy Scripture, in the fellowship of believers, and in many other places, but the Holy Spirit can also be present and at work in our homes, in the workplace, or in prison. Again, this is highly empowering.

So what could possibly be the downside of such a persuasive vision of the presence and work of the Holy Spirit? First and foremost, this way of conceiving the presence and work of the Holy Spirit has at times caused Wesleyans to be unduly preoccupied with taking our spiritual temperature. At its best, the vision of the Holy Spirit articulated above has resulted in an outward evangelistic orientation. Having been changed from within, we are eager to share the gospel with others. But the emphasis on the presence and work of the Holy Spirit in the human heart has led many Wesleyans, including John Wesley himself (!), to get stuck in a spiritual cul-de-sac. We can easily wind up worrying more about the state of our own souls than about the well-being of the world around us. Having proclaimed that the Holy Spirit resides within our hearts, we sometimes associate certain emotional states with the Spirit's presence. When we go through a season in which those emotional states are lacking, it can be very disconcerting.

Indeed, more than a few Wesleyans have experienced deep spiritual angst because they do not sense or feel the presence of the Holy Spirit in a particular way. At its worst, this tendency causes us to spend an inordinate amount of time and energy trying to maintain whatever emotional state we associate with the presence and work of the Holy Spirit. In the process, we too easily forget about everyone but ourselves.

A closely related phenomenon has to do with the relationship between sin and the presence and work of the Holy Spirit. Because the first work of the Holy Spirit has to do with awakening us to the reality of sin and helping us to repent and to ask for forgiveness, it is easy to assume that the Holy Spirit can only be present and at work in our hearts if we are free from sin. Of course, if that were true, then the Holy Spirit would not have been able to be present and at work in our hearts in the first place. Nonetheless, we sometimes tie ourselves in knots worrying about the possibility that the Holy Spirit might depart over the least little slipup. By extension, Wesleyans, including John Wesley, are sometimes given over to paranoia about too much contact with the sinful world around us.[6] When this happens, we wind up focusing more on our own moral rectitude than on the need to reach the lost with the good news of the gospel.

The strong tendency to locate the presence and work of the Holy Spirit within the inner recesses of the human heart can also result in a disembodied understanding of salvation. Wesleyans are fond of recalling Wesley's admonition to Methodist preachers, "You have nothing to do but to save souls."[7] But we must also remember that the One to whom the Spirit bears witness is none other than the Lord who was bodily raised from the dead.[8] Hence salvation cannot finally mean an escape from our bodies or embodied life. On the contrary, the Resurrection affirms the goodness of God's creation and anticipates an embodied future. Because it is Christ who saves us, salvation cannot be limited to the human heart.

To summarize, the singular strength of Wesleyan pneumatology across space and time has been the emphasis on the freedom of the Spirit to be present and at work throughout the world, regardless of whether we are looking for the Spirit in a particular place and regardless of whether we are ready for the presence and work of the Holy Spirit. This emphasis provides a needed check against presumption, manipulation, and abuse.

---

6   Wesley, "On Friendship with the World," *The Works of John Wesley*, vol. 3, ed. Outler, 126–40.

7   Minutes of the Methodist Conferences (London: John Mason, 1862), 1:494.

8   Beth Felker Jones, *Marks of His Wounds: Gender Politics and Bodily Resurrection* (New York: Oxford University Press, 2007).

It also coheres well with the one doctrine that surely has dogmatic status among Wesleyans, namely, that Christ died for all. If Christ died for all, and not just for the educated or wealthy or religiously inclined, then it makes perfect sense that the Holy Spirit would be at work in every corner of the world.

When combined with an emphasis on the human heart as the initial and ultimately most important location of the Spirit's presence and work, the emphasis on the freedom of the Spirit can also become a weakness in two closely related ways. First, Wesleyans can easily become preoccupied with whether or not we sense or feel the Spirit within. When we do not feel the presence of the Spirit within, we can quickly become spiritually anxious, and our anxiety can deepen our preoccupation with the state of our soul before God. Second, an almost obsessive preoccupation with our inner spiritual life can truncate our understanding of salvation, causing us to overlook or forget the embodied dimension of salvation through Jesus Christ.

The best way to prevent these two weaknesses from emerging is to orient Wesleyan pneumatology in a much more consistent and rigorous way to Christology. But this cannot be done in theory alone; it must take place in practice and most especially in Wesleyan worship. As noted above, Wesleyan worship has, historically speaking, revolved around preaching. And herein lies the problem. Wesleyan preaching is not sufficiently Christological. For starters, Wesleyans routinely preach on all sorts of topics that do not bear witness to Jesus in an explicit way. This may very well be justifiable, insofar as preaching is normed by Holy Scripture. The Bible is a very large collection of books that addresses all sorts of topics, many of which are only tangentially related to the person and work of Jesus Christ. To complicate matters further, Wesleyans who follow the lectionary are far more apt to preach on the teachings of Jesus than we are the Incarnation and the Resurrection of Jesus (the exceptions being Christmas and Easter Sundays).

For Christians already prone to taking our spiritual temperature, an emphasis on Jesus' teaching can actually make matters worse. We can easily obsess over whether we are doing the things Jesus commands and whether we are doing them for the right reasons. Before we know it, we are right back to where we started, worrying over whether our failure to realize Jesus' teachings might somehow cause the Holy Spirit to abandon us. This is the Achilles's heel of the Wesleyan tradition; we are constantly tempted to make the presence and work of the Holy Spirit contingent upon the sincerity of our faith or the adequacy of our adherence to Christian moral teaching.[9] To correct this, we need to balance our emphasis on the freedom of the Spirit with an equal emphasis on the fidelity of the risen Lord, to whom the Spirit ever lives to bear witness. And the best way to do that is to strengthen our emphasis on the presence and work of the Spirit in the Eucharist.

Wesleyan Pneumatology: Strengthening the Tradition

The purpose of preaching and the sacraments is ultimately the same, namely, the mediation of God's holiness or presence in world. Having said this, the way in which God's holiness is mediated through preaching and the sacraments differs considerably. The best way I know to demonstrate the differences between preaching and sacraments with respect to the presence and work of the Holy Spirit is to step back and recall the biblical basis for each of these ministries.

The ministry of preaching is biblically undergirded by the prophetic conception of God's holiness. Found initially in the book of Deuteronomy, the prophetic tradition envisions God's holiness as the word of the Lord that comes through the mouths of prophets. Important to note here is the fact that the word of the Lord can come without warning or preparation. It breaks in upon us whenever and wherever it chooses. Also important to note, however, is the final resting place of the word of the Lord. When the word of the Lord comes through the mouths of prophets, it ultimately takes up residence in the human heart, after which the people themselves are declared holy. Having been declared holy, the people must maintain their holiness, which is to say, their purity. Thus the prophetic vision of God's holiness culminates in the ban (the prohibition against marrying or intermingling too extensively with outsiders, i.e., the impure or unholy in our midst).

The biblical basis of the ministry of sacraments is found in the priestly tradition, beginning with the Book of Exodus and continuing in the Book of Leviticus. For the priestly tradition, God's holiness is conceived in terms of God's glory, which descends upon Mount Sinai and ultimately takes up permanent residence in the altar of the Temple. The important thing to note here is that, in the priestly tradition, God's holiness is never fully transferred to the people themselves. Rather, it remains in the Temple where it can always be accessed through carefully orchestrated rituals. This

---

9   Even John Wesley wrestled with this. See Richard P. Heitzenrater, "Great Expectations: Aldersgate and the Evidences of Genuine Christianity," in *Mirror and Memory: Reflections on Early Methodism*, ed. Richard P. Heitzenrater (Nashville: Abingdon Press [Kingswood Books], 1989), 106–49.

enables the people of Israel to interact more freely with their neighbors, as any resulting impurity can be dealt with through the appropriate sacrifice.[10]

My purpose in providing these thumbnail sketches of the biblical bases for preaching and the sacraments is not to advocate for one over against the other. After all, both are clearly biblical. The main point, rather, is to show how these two traditions complement one another. On the one hand, the prophetic tradition captures the sheer *unpredictability* of the word of God. God's word erupts in the mouths of prophets whenever and wherever it will. The prophetic tradition also stresses the need to internalize God's in-breaking word. It is not enough for the word of God to be spoken by a prophet; it must make its way into our hearts. Finally, the prophetic tradition is surely right to emphasize the importance of maintaining the purity of our hearts once God's Word has taken root there.

On the other hand, the priestly tradition bears witness to the abiding nature of the presence of God in the world. It locates God's presence in a place that is permanent and readily accessible to all. In turn, the sheer *reliability* of God's abiding presence enables us to be God's representatives in a sinful world without being overly worried about God withdrawing from us because we come into contact with impurity.

Taken together, the prophetic and priestly traditions in Scripture constitute a dynamic vision of God's holiness in the world. The prophetic tradition emphasizes God's freedom, whereas the priestly tradition stresses God's fidelity; the prophetic tradition accentuates the need to maintain heart purity, whereas the priestly tradition calls us to extend God's holiness out into the world; in the prophetic tradition, God's holiness ultimately resides in human hearts, whereas in the priestly tradition God's holiness remains in the sanctuary to renew and to heal us through ritually orchestrated contact.

What makes the combination of the priestly and prophetic visions of God's holiness so dynamic and powerful is precisely the deep tensions between them. This is not a matter of simple math. When we lose sight of either of these visions, it is not simply that the overall impact is diminished by half. Rather, when one of these visions is obscured, the other can become distorted and even harmful. For instance, when taken by itself, the priestly tradition can be distorted in a way that runs the risk of antinomianism or cheap grace. By contrast, when we obscure the priestly tradition, we run the risk of becoming legalistic and self-absorbed.

---

10   Thomas B. Dozeman, *Holiness and Ministry: A Biblical Theology of Ordination* (New York: Oxford University Press, 2008).

Zizioulas, attempt to simplify matters by identifying Eucharist with church and church with Eucharist.[2] Regrettably, conceptual miracles like this are not available to us as theologians. There is no conceptual relation between the concepts of Eucharist and church; those who think there is are simply muddled. Yet the effort to chart an intimate relation between Eucharist and church has been a central feature of work in ecclesiology since at least the seminal work of Nicholas Afanasiev. It is surely not too much to say that great hopes have been pinned on the development of a eucharistic ecclesiology. Exploring what those hopes involve will provide the platform for the identification of an alternative ecclesiological venture for Methodism. I will sketch what such a development might look like in what follows.

Eucharistic Ecclesiology

Let me begin by getting a handle of the contours of a vision of the church that makes the Eucharist constitutive of the very being of the church. Everything hinges initially on how we set the table conceptually and theologically. Interestingly, there is a persistent misrepresentation of Afanasiev in the literature. The title of his great work is significant: *The Church of the Holy Spirit*.[3] The bedrock of his thinking began not with the Eucharist but with the Holy Spirit. Moreover, to make him the father of eucharistic ecclesiology runs the additional risk of reductionism. He was vitally interested in breaking down the bifurcations between laity and clergy, between priest and bishop, between local church and institutional church. We might equally refer to his ecclesiology as a pentecostal ecclesiology, given the crucial role that the work of the Holy Spirit plays in its foundations and in its dynamic superstructure. The move to redeploy his work in the interests of a eucharistic ecclesiology is really an effort at domestication, a way to accommodate his more radical proposals to the longstanding convictions of the standard ecclesial manuals in Roman Catholicism and Orthodoxy.

The core elements in eucharistic ecclesiology as they have emerged after the pioneering work of Afanasiev are relatively easy to identify and chart. My aim here is to paint a picture rather than provide an exegetical and historically documented summary of the literature.[4] I shall work at two levels.

---

2   See John Zizioulas, "The Ecclesiological Presuppositions of the Holy Eucharist," 4. Available at http://www.resourcesforchristiantheology.org/?p=99.

3   Nicholas Afanasiev, *The Church of the Holy Spirit*, ed. Michael Plekon, trans. Vitaly Permiakov (Notre Dame: University of Notre Dame Press, 2007).

4   The exception to this is the attention I give to the Ravenna Document below.

At one level, perhaps the highest level theologically, we can think of Eucharist as communion. In turn we can construe communion as participation in the inner fellowship of the Trinity. So our vision of life together in communion essentially involves communion in the Son with the Father through the Spirit. We participate in a primal fellowship with each other that is constituted by the fellowship of the Persons of the Holy Trinity; we are joined in fellowship together because we share in the fellowship of the Trinity. This fellowship is, of course, a fellowship of grace. It is initiated by the Triune Agency of God out of the fecundity of divine love and grace; it is also sustained by divine love and grace. The very life of the Trinity is manifested to us in the wondrous divine economy, which, without counting our trespasses and sins, visits us in salvation and draws us inwardly by the Holy Spirit to the Son who shares with us the very life of the Father.

Methodists can take to this vision of Eucharist as communion like the proverbial duck takes to water. A hallmark of Methodist life across the centuries is its warm fellowship shared in prayer meetings, worship, retreats, hymn-singing, testimonies, Bible studies, conferences, and even committee meetings. It is also visible in quiet conversations around the hearth fire, in the shared suffering and war stories of itinerant preachers, in the joyous encounter with conversion narratives, and in the delight of immediate spiritual friendships across radically different cultural, social, and ethnic borders. Equally, it can be seen in the relaxed sense of recognition when a total stranger is suddenly recognized as a believer; when one experiences that strong inner knowing that whatever may divide us we belong not just to a common cause but to a common Lord. Theologically this sense of fellowship surfaces prominently in Wesley's vision of a catholic spirit. In this there is a native distancing and rejection of sectarianism, bigotry, and exclusivism. The default position calls for a personal hermeneutic of generosity that reaches to identify and celebrate the work of God in persons and communities that do not share the full vision of Christian faith and practice that one inhabits.

To be sure, this sense of fellowship can readily degenerate into mere sociability and niceness; it can collapse into camaraderie and clubbability; it can even descend into a passion for chicken dinners and dessert. Higher up in the social circles of the church this commitment to fellowship can be rechanneled into a passionate and even polemical commitment to this or that caucus or interest group. Outsiders within the church become demonized or dehumanized; favored insiders become saints and heroes; distrust and division multiply. However, we can readily recognize these phenomena for what they are, that is, degenerate photocopies of a much deeper reality. It is communion in God that is the original source and fountainhead. I propose that it is this deeper fellowship and communion that has held my own tribe of Methodists together through the tumultuous challenges of the last half-century. Or at least, we can hope that this is by far the most salient explanation for our precarious unity.

Theologians who revel in the doctrine of the Trinity will be relatively happy with this opening foray into the deep narrative and content of the Christian tradition. They should be on their guard, though, against being carried away by romantic idealization. Hence we need to come down to earth both conceptually and empirically. At this point we move to a second level of investigation. The Eucharist is first and foremost a practice of the church. For Methodists it is one of the two dominical sacraments that are celebrated generally on the first Sunday of every month. The exact form has changed across the years, most notably in the shift from the classical liturgy of the Book of Common Prayer to the ecumenically informed and updated version that now includes the epiclesis, the wonderful invocation of the Spirit toward the end that prepares for the final climax of the service.

Here the connection between Eucharist and church is to be found in the notion of the church as a gathering of the people of God around the Lord's Table on a regular basis. The connection can be pressed to a deeper level. We naturally demarcate a church from, say, a fellowship group of students at a university, precisely by the regular practice of baptism and Eucharist. It is the absence of these that leads us to treat a weekly Bible study of students as a fellowship group rather than a local church.

This distinction shows up nicely in the relevant Articles of Religion in *The Book of Discipline* where a church is identified precisely as a congregation of local Christians where the Word of God is preached and the sacraments aptly celebrated. It also comes to the surface in debates about the historic origins of Methodism as a church. It was when John Wesley moved to ordain elders to administer the sacraments that the fat fell into the fire. Wesley had crossed a line and nothing he said by way of sophisticated casuistry could undo what he had done. He was creating a new church. His followers in North America saw exactly what was happening and acted accordingly by developing the fuller practices, offices, and materials that were essential to finalizing the pathway that Wesley had initiated. Nineteenth-century theologians in both Britain and North America followed this up by a rigorous articulation and defense of their identity as church. The failure of nerve and accompanying doctrinal amnesia that developed in the middle of the twentieth century concealed these crucial components of Methodist history. Treating this unhappy interlude as an occasion to bind up the wounds of the recent past, we should recover our nerve and come back to the main road from the distractions of this detour. Working at this second level we can now grasp afresh that there is an intimate connection between Eucharist and ecclesiology, for one way to identify a church, as opposed to a fellowship group or an order within a church, is precisely the practice of Eucharist.[5]

If we move from theological description to material eucharistic practice within Methodism, then we are faced with all sorts of challenges. Due to the disastrous theological experiments in pluralism in the twentieth century, the situation on the ground can legitimately be described as farcical. Given the long history in Western Christianity in which the epiclesis was omitted, one can tolerate the omission of the epiclesis as a hangover from past tradition. Other developments should be treated with the intellectual derision they deserve. I have been in services where the Eucharist was turned into a party political broadcast for the latest brand of liberation theology just imported from Latin America. In other cases, I have been in services where the passion for pseudo-spiritual spontaneity made it impossible to distinguish between a Eucharist and a love feast. I leave it to the imagination to fill in the possible positions between these two extremes.

Happily, the preceding jeremiad is not the whole story. The work in liturgical renewal across the church in the last generation has borne fruit in the vineyard of Methodism. We now have splendid formal liturgies that have serious content. There is no longer any excuse for the incompetence of egocentric clergy who want to make it up as they go along or who turn to all sorts of silly artistic make-believe in the name of creative innovation. Moreover, we have begun to think through the longstanding but by no means initial practice of Methodism that welcomes all believers to the Lord's Table. Furthermore, our ecumenical encounters are forcing us to revisit the wonderful hymns of Charles Wesley on the Eucharist to find a response to the challenges posed by more metaphysically robust accounts of the presence of Christ in the bread and wine. Most of all, it is patently clear that whatever the confusion of the last generation, there is a native sense that eucharistic practice really does matter not just as a formal matter but in our hearts and in our bones. Eucharist is not just one more means of grace; properly conducted it feeds and nourishes us in ways that cannot be propositionally enunciated in full but that can be known instinctively and intuitively in the depths of

---

5   I am not here committing to a closed conception of "church" where we can readily rattle off the necessary and sufficient conditions of its usage; our usage is in fact essentially contested and context-dependent.

the soul. This is surely one reason why the revolt against the thin liberalism that captured our corporate imagination for a perilous period has struck such a chord among many clergy and laity. The native sensibility of ordinary believers and of competent clergy has come back to life and recovered its voice; the voice of the faithful has been heard in the land again.

The Ravenna Accord

It is precisely at this point that the deepest challenge of recent work in eucharistic ecclesiology has to be joined. I have taken for granted that the Eucharist as practiced within Methodism is legitimate, valid, authentic, and dominical. I have joined a top-down analysis to a bottom-up analysis that has ignored the third level of ministerial order and ecclesial continuity. For a felicitous point of entry into the domain of ecclesial communion, conciliarity, and authority we turn to the Ravenna Document.[6] This fine exhibition of ecumenical dialogue and agreement represents the considered exposition of Roman Catholic and Orthodox teaching on the relation between Eucharist and ecclesiology. I focus carefully only on the salient features relevant to my purposes here.

Ravenna begins with the mystery of ecclesial *koinonia* as rooted in the life of the Trinity. It moves almost immediately to "the role of apostolic succession as the guarantee of the *koinonia* of the whole Church and of its continuity with the Apostles in every time and place" (ibid., no. 2). The challenge it seeks to meet on this score is how to work out the ecclesiological and canonical consequences that flow from the sacramental nature of the Church.

> Since the Eucharist, in the light of the Trinitarian mystery, constitutes the criterion of ecclesial life as a whole, how do institutional structures visibly reflect the mystery of this *koinonia*? Since the one and holy Church is realised both in each local Church celebrating the Eucharist and at the same time in the *koinonia* of all the Churches, how does the life of the Churches manifest this sacramental structure? (ibid., no. 3)

---

6   Joint International Commission for the Theological Dialogue between the Roman Catholic Church and the Orthodox Church, *Ravenna Document*, in the Pontifical Council for Promoting Christian Unity, http://www.vatican.va/roman_curia/pontifical_councils/chrstuni/ch_orthodox_docs/rc_pc_chrstuni_doc_20071013_documento-ravenna_en.html. Henceforth I shall sometimes refer to this document simply as "Ravenna."

Once we make the Eucharist the criterion of ecclesial life, we can see that the stakes have gone up a tad. We now want to know what the criteria for the criterion are. The answer is already partially given in the longstanding and resounding claim of "apostolic succession as the guarantee of the *koinonia* of the whole Church and of its continuity with the Apostles in every time and place." A valid and authentic Eucharist will only be one that is physically related to apostolic succession.

However, Ravenna rightly and understandably presses ahead to insist that mere apostolic succession is not enough. There is more to the church than a bishop presiding or authorizing a valid Eucharist in a local congregation. The church spreads out across space and time; to secure communion at this level local bishops must share life together in a robust and meaningful fashion. While communion begins with baptism and confirmation of local Christians, the bishops of the church have a unique role in proclaiming the Church's faith and clarifying the norms of Christian conduct. To achieve this end and other ends, bishops must come together in communion. Councils provide the principal means of exercising this communion. From here it is plain sailing all the way to a vision of a universal communion mediated in and through the local bishop.

> The Church exists in many and different places, which manifests its catholicity. Being "catholic", it is a living organism, the Body of Christ. Each local Church, when in communion with the other local Churches, is a manifestation of the one and indivisible Church of God. To be "catholic" therefore means to be in communion with the one Church of all times and of all places. That is why the breaking of Eucharistic communion means the wounding of one of the essential characteristics of the Church, its catholicity. (ibid., no. 11)

The next step takes us to the exercise of authority. At this point Ravenna neatly combines epistemic authority and executive authority. It is common teaching "that the people of God, having received 'the anointing which comes from the Holy One' [1 John. 2:20, 27], in communion with their pastors, cannot err in matters of faith [John 16:13]" (ibid., no. 7). However, the general conscience of the church must be identified and articulated. The authority of Christ in the conscience of the faithful belongs within the fuller articulation of that conscience instantiated in Christ himself. It is to Christ and his Word that ultimate authority belongs. He in turn has historically transmitted that authority to his apostles and then through them by the practice of the laying on of hands to their successors in the apostolic episcopate. This does not at all mean that bishops are untethered in the warrants for their teaching. To the contrary, the church is founded upon the Word of God and bishops like everyone else are accountable to that Word. That Word in turn is constituted by Scripture.

> Scripture is the revealed Word of God, as the Church, through the Holy Spirit present and active within it, has discerned it in the living Tradition received from the Apostles. At the heart of this Tradition is the Eucharist (cfr. 1 Cor 10:16-17; 11: 23-26). The authority of Scripture derives from the fact that it is the Word of God which, read in the Church and by the Church, transmits the Gospel of salvation. Through Scripture, Christ addresses the assembled community and the heart of each believer. The Church, through the Holy Spirit present within it, authentically interprets Scripture, responding to the needs of times and places. The constant custom of the Councils to enthrone the Gospels in the midst of the assembly both attests the presence of Christ in his Word, which is the necessary point of reference for all their discussions and decisions, and at the same time affirms the authority of the Church to interpret this Word of God. (ibid., no. 15).

At this juncture we circle back to apostolic succession. It is not enough to have criteria or canons of truth; someone must exercise executive authority and declare what is essential to salvation for the church as a whole.

> In his divine Economy, God wills that his Church should have a structure oriented towards salvation. To this essential structure belong the faith professed and the sacraments celebrated in the apostolic succession. Authority in the ecclesial communion is linked to this essential structure: its exercise is regulated by the canons and statutes of the Church. Some of these regulations may be differently applied according to the needs of ecclesial communion in different times and places, provided that the essential structure of the Church is always respected. Thus, just as communion in the sacraments presupposes communion in the same faith (cfr. Bari Document, nn. 29–33), so too, in order for there to be full ecclesial communion, there must be, between our Churches, reciprocal recognition of canonical legislations in their legitimate diversities. (ibid., no. 16).

The rest of the Ravenna Document spells out how conciliarity and authority function at the local, regional, and universal level. Communion begins with the eucharistic celebration around the local bishop before it reaches outward to communion in its region with other bishops canonically ordained and operating together in synods, where they alone have deliberative voice. Through the same episcopal agents local churches reach out not just to the totality of all local churches across the world but to all the faithful since the beginning and into the future. It is at this level that disputes that naturally arise at the local and regional level are finally resolved. "It is because of this communion that all the Churches, through canons, regulate everything relating to the Eucharist and the sacraments, the ministry and ordination, and the handing on (*paradosis*) and teaching (*didaskalia*) of the faith" (ibid., no. 34).

The Ravenna Document is a model of diplomatic ecumenical conversation. Following the standard model of convergence it works through the common teaching of the Roman Catholic and Orthodox communions as focused on the relation between Eucharist and ecclesiology. Not surprisingly it leaves unresolved the debate about the identity of Ecumenical Councils, the nature of primacy, and the status of the Bishop of Rome; and, in the only footnote in the document, it openly exhibits the deep difference on exactly where the one, holy, catholic, and apostolic church of which the Nicene Creed speaks is to be located. However, there is no equivocation on the criterion for identifying a valid and authentic Eucharist. There is no valid Eucharist without apostolic succession, even as apostolic succession is nested in a complex network of epistemic and executive phenomena. It is apostolic par excellence that is the guarantee of the *koinonia* of the whole church and of its continuity with the apostles in every time and place.

Methodism and Apostolic Succession

There is no point in beating around the bush at this point. If apostolic succession is a necessary condition of a valid Eucharist, then Methodist theology cannot pursue the contours of a eucharistic ecclesiology in Methodism. There is no apostolic succession in the required sense. Wesley himself clearly rejected apostolic succession, and the ecclesial traditions he spawned have never canonically rescinded that conviction. There are at least three options open to us at this point.

First, we can do what we can to make manifest the associated elements that Methodism shares at least formally with Ravenna. We can exhibit our ineradicable commitment to conciliarity; we can display our shared vision of the authority of Christ and of divine revelation mediated in Scripture; we can proclaim our readiness to exercise executive authority with a clear and constructive conscience; we can bear witness to our openness to, if not practice of, the threefold order of deacon, presbyter, and bishop; we can trumpet our sense of the importance of baptism in

Christian initiation; we can confess our love for proper order in the life of the church; we can insist on our rejection of institutionalism as a fall from some kind of illusory, pristine purity; we can bear testimony to the significant fruits of our apostolic labors across the world in evangelism, education, service to the poor, social justice, and the like; and we can repent of our flirtation with liberal and radical forms of Christianity and embrace the great tradition of the catholic heritage as a whole. Some might even press the case for an apostolic succession through the episcopacy of presbyters that stretches back to Wesley and through him to the patristic era. This is certainly no mean catalogue of ecclesial assets. However, there is one thing they lack, namely, apostolic succession, and without this we are doomed to failure if eucharistic practice related to apostolic succession is the desideratum.

This suggests a second alternative. Why not seek out a suitable ecclesial partner and take the apostolic succession into our system? The obvious candidate on the table to date has been various plans to work through our Anglican forbears. Alternatively, we could go straight to Rome or Constantinople.[7] Failing that, we could disband the whole Methodist ecclesial world and join Rome or Constantinople. Failing that, we can quietly quit our membership in the Methodist churches and join Rome or Constantinople as individuals. Some, including very good friends, have taken the last option across the years. Beyond the giddy and silly idea of dying and rising again, say, as an order in a whole new configuration of ecumenical Christianity, the second option has absolutely no realistic prospect of success. So by elimination, the only realistic corporate option is the first one, that is, going home to or uniting with the Anglican Church. This has been tried in England and failed. There are two other weighty reasons for thinking it is even more likely to fail in the future, which can be stated by way of rhetorical questions. Who wants to join a church whose orders are canonically rejected by Rome? Who wants to join a church that is currently riddled with brutal internal divisions and schism?

It is time we looked to a third way forward beyond displaying our formal agreements with Ravenna and our search for a suitable partner who can mediate apostolic succession. We need to question the Ravenna requirements for a eucharistic ecclesiology, and, beyond that, we need to

---

7   The reference to Constantinople stands for the various autocephalous branches of the Orthodox tradition. We might add the Coptic tradition, but this is not likely to be a serious option.

go deeper still and rethink our theological reorientation in ecclesiology. The project I have in mind can only be sketched in what follows; it will require the work of a new generation of creative theologians to flesh it out in both substance and detail.

Note as we proceed that the Ravenna conditions include not just apostolic succession but apostolic succession as nested in a network of wider claims and practices related to conciliatory and authority. Apostolic succession always stands in intimate relation to other desiderata as far as authentic ecclesial identity is concerned. Moreover, once we get beyond the diplomatic applause, it is clear that Ravenna does not begin to solve the thorny issues represented by the identity of Ecumenical Councils, the nature of primacy, the status of the bishop of Rome, and the deep difference on where exactly to locate the one, holy, catholic, and apostolic church.

These are enormously significant and neuralgic challenges. Worse still, it only hints at the epistemological differences lodged in and around the canonical teaching in Roman Catholicism on papal infallibility. Orthodoxy fudges on epistemological issues; Rome does not; either way once epistemological issues are made constitutive of ecclesial identity the problems multiply. Of course, this was not the intention of the Ravenna conversations, so I am not faulting the document on that score. Let me make my initial point negatively and then positively. Negatively, the distance between Roman Catholicism and Orthodoxy is far deeper than an optimistic reading might suggest. Hence the shared vision of eucharistic ecclesiology is at best a very modest achievement. Positively, the best hope for the future in the wake of Ravenna is that Roman Catholicism and Orthodoxy find some way in the providence of God to unite as one church; Methodists can then revisit at that point our ecumenical options. Maybe at that point creative versions of our second option will disband and join the new church that emerges on the unification of Roman Catholicism and Orthodoxy.

The immediate follow-up to the forgoing cuts much deeper and must be stated with total candor. The whole idea of apostolic succession has been falsified by historical investigation into the life of the churches the apostles left behind and by appropriate research on the developments of "the historic episcopate" in, for example, Alexandria. While Wesley had limited access to the best available evidence, he was right to reject the standard Anglican claims he inherited. Once this objection is firmly in place, the eucharistic ecclesiology of Ravenna collapses. One necessary condition, indeed its foundational necessary condition, has been undermined. To be sure, I am not expecting any of the standard-bearers of apostolic succession to give this argument a hearing; they have heard all this before countless times, and they can readily provide ingenious epistemological theories to dispose of the historical evidence. However, here I stand and I can do no other.

A Radically Different Way Ahead

We now have to make yet one more critical decision. Should we rescue and repair the whole idea of a eucharistic ecclesiology, or should we look for a radically different theological orientation for thinking through a Methodist ecclesiology? As regards the first question, my answer is simple: the whole idea of eucharistic ecclesiology is so tied to claims about apostolic succession that it is best to treat the option of rescue and repair as a dead end. We can still harvest the insights the theory has engendered, but as a serious option in ecclesiology the game is over, even though its champions will carry on their work with enthusiasm and flair. So the best bet for the future is to develop a radically different theological orientation. How might we proceed? Let me note three desiderata before I get to the substance of my proposal.

The first desideratum is psychological and sociological. If we are even to begin this journey there will have to be a radical recovery of theological nerve within Methodism. On this score the time is ripe for change, despite all the talk of doom and gloom. As noted at the outset, in the wake of the failure of the campaign to "rethink church" in superficial categories and the failure to achieve organic union, we are now in a period of incubation as far as the quest for a new ecclesial identity is concerned. Complementary to this, the future ecumenical focus will concentrate on the relations between Roman Catholicism and Orthodoxy. As Bishop Hilarion has repeatedly noted, Anglicanism will be left behind.[8] Methodism is not even on this radar screen, given the absence of the so-called apostolic succession. In the wider Evangelical world, Christians will either convert to Roman Catholicism or Orthodoxy, morph into another round of Liberal Protestantism, experiment with various forms of Emergent Church, or retreat into Fundamentalism. There is no serious alternative for Methodists but to cease being intimidated by its older and younger alternatives in the Christian tradition and find its own voice.

The second desideratum is to develop a different narrative of the place of Methodism in the history of Christianity as a whole. Rather than simply

---

8   Most recently in a lecture at Villanova University. See http://www.byzcath.org/
      forums/ubbthreads.php/topics/389923/Metropolitan_Hilarion_at_Villa.

work back from Wesley through Anglicanism to the early church and then to the New Testament, we need to go forward and only then go backward. Wesley and Methodism represent the beginning of a third wave of Christian history beyond the Catholic traditions and the Reformation traditions. That third wave moves up through revivalism and the Holiness tradition on into Pentecostalism and its many expressions in World Christianity. We are dealing with a fresh Pentecost in the life of the modern church. We can then go back into church history and reread the early centuries through the eyes and faith of the great Evangelical Awakenings.

It is no accident that Wesley insisted that Methodism was Primitive Christianity rather than simply Biblical Christianity. In fact he rejected the whole idea that you can find a normative ecclesiology in the New Testament as expressed, say, in a doctrine of ministerial orders. Without reading John Henry Newman, he instinctively was committed to a vision of development, looking to the Holy Spirit to lead the church through the vicissitudes of history. So we need to find a better way to tell the story of Methodism, working first forward and then backward.

Reworking the narrative along lines like this is crucial to undermining the sense of inferiority and intimidation that one so often finds among Methodist theologians and scholars. Some stay with the tradition but cannot get over the conviction that it is really marginal and ephemeral. They rightly eschew smugness and arrogance but are at bottom embarrassed and docile when it comes to their identity. Others assimilate to developments within Evangelicalism across the centuries and find it difficult to think outside the primacy given to this tradition so that Methodism simply becomes the expression of a complex movement in modern Protestantism. Others do what they can to hitch Methodist theology to a favored theological hero, say, Barth or Aquinas, or to a favored theological movement, say, liberation theology or process philosophy. Working with the kind of narrative I have identified will not mean we cease to learn from others, nor does it mean that we become triumphalist and sectarian. It does mean we stop apologizing and get on with the work in hand.

The third desideratum is an extended reengagement with the whole history of Methodist systematic and dogmatic theology. This dovetails with the point just enumerated. The last generation of scholars misled by Albert Outler effectively demonized the first major phase of Methodist systematic theology after Richard Watson. Insofar as scholars took seriously the second phase beginning with Borden Parker Bowne, they co-opted him and his offspring for a Liberal Protestant agenda that ignored the deeply orthodox components of his thinking. There is, to be sure, a measure of truth in these narratives but they remain hopelessly reductionist. Beyond the tendentious Barthian narrative of Chiles,[9] we have next to nothing that really works through the history accurately and with flair. Yet this in itself is not enough; we also need sympathetic and critical engagement with the history of systematic theology that really believes that it is important in its own right. It is only by such engagement that we will internalize the theological riches of our tradition and find our own voice for the future. Within this we can begin to find the crucial theological themes in which to lodge a fresh vision of the church for our own day and generation.

An Ecclesiology of the Third Article

My own hunch is that we will find the relevant themes by articulating an account of the church that locates her origins, life, and ministry in the work of the Holy Spirit. I do not intend this appeal to the Holy Spirit as a labor-saving device. There are, in fact, various ways that this option might be played out.

Consider the following quotation from the hand of Hendrik R. Pieterse in which he applauds the important historical work of Russell E. Richey.

> But perhaps Richey's most important word for United Methodists today is that, at their most authentic, Methodists have understood their connectional covenant as a creature of the Spirit. It is this confidence that has emboldened them "to go with the Spirit, to experiment, to try new things, to change." Counterintuitive as it may seem to many of us, releasing ourselves again into the custody of the Spirit who blows we know not where might just hold the deepest clue to a worldwide United Methodist connection worthy of our deepest commitments.[10]

This comment constitutes the conclusion of a sophisticated and careful analysis of United Methodism in the wake of the General Conference of 2012. My aim here is not to provide a comprehensive summary of Pieterse's proposals, much less an extended analysis. What his work makes clear is that there are going to be several ways of thinking through an ecclesiology of the Third Article; how far they are complementary or contradictory can be left open for now.

---

9   Robert E. Chiles, *Theological Transition in American Methodism* (Nashville: Abingdon Press, 1965).

10   Hendrik R. Pieterse, "A Worldwide United Methodist Church: Soundings toward a Connectional Theological Imagination." Available at http://www.methodistreview.org/index.php/mr/article/view/87.

The core of Pieterse's vision can be stated partially in this way. Methodism is rooted in John Wesley's encounter with the poor and marginalized in the eighteenth century. Operating at the periphery rather than the center, he encountered the God of the gospel provided by these unlikely and unexpected bearers of good news. This encounter gave him leverage against the illusions of Christendom and provided impetus for challenging the social, economic, religious, and political status quo. In time this led Wesley and the early Methodists to develop a connectional system of ecclesiastical structure and governance that sought the welfare of the connection as a whole.

Currently, Pieterse goes on to explain that the connection within United Methodism is undergoing great stress, encumbered as it is by Judicial Council decisions, by its bureaucratic systems, by its recourse to business strategies and discourse, and above all by its obsession with a center-oriented rather than periphery-oriented mind-set. What is needed now, he suggests, is to come to terms with the truth made available at the periphery; the golden opportunity for this is made possible not just by the crisis of the last General Conference but by the unique connectional polity that is constitutive of its very identity. United Methodism, he insists, must develop a "connectional theological imagination" in which it listens to the margins. As it works in genuine partnership and radical mutuality with the periphery within its own household, develops more equitable church structures, engages with the most recent scholarship in mission studies and postcolonial theory, challenges global neoliberal capitalism, and the like, United Methodism could well experience the authentic kind of renewal that it so sorely needs.

> In opening ourselves anew to the unexpected, the peripheral, and the novel in our emerging global experience, United Methodism may yet experience the reviving winds of the divine Spirit who after all blows where it chooses. Otherwise, I fear missiologist Walter Hollenweger's wry observation about the churches in Europe may be said of us also: "Many of us prayed for revival. When it came we did not recognize it because it was black or brown."[11]

Buried in this fascinating reading of the work of the Holy Spirit there is a network of tacit assumptions. Connectionalism has replaced the apostolic episcopacy as constitutive of the church; epistemologically the poor are seen as a privileged site of divine revelation or the interpretation of divine revelation; liberation theology is seen as the harbinger of the most important

---

11   Ibid., 18.

insights of recent theological scholarship; the history of Methodist doctrine is handed over to those historians who systematically ignore its canonical doctrinal commitments; postcolonial theory is regarded as especially insightful in making sense of contemporary global developments; more conservative visions of renewal are either ignored or treated as mere covers for the politicization of the church; "logic" is reduced to the logic of center and periphery and thus ignores a century's work in analytic philosophy. What is most pressing and obvious from a theological point of view, however, is the way in which the work of the Holy Spirit is tacked onto all of these complex theoretical moves as an afterthought. There is no serious engagement with the long history of reflection on the work of the Holy Spirit in Scripture and in the various problems thrown up in the history of the church. Nor, despite a passing nod to current mission studies, is there any serious engagement with the actual phenomenology of the work of the Spirit within contemporary World Christianity. One is very tempted to conclude that we have in fact exactly what Pieterse fears, namely, one more effort on the part of North American United Methodists located in one end of the current institutional establishment in Nashville and elsewhere to co-opt the periphery for its own theological and ecclesial interests.

When time has marched past us all, we will need to look back and harvest the very important insights that Pieterse is exploring but which for now must be subject to comprehensive critical evaluation, conceptually, epistemological-ly, historically, and theologically. Happily, Pieterse is much too good a scholar to challenge this observation; he knows only too well that he is offering only the beginnings of a Methodist ecclesiology. Yet the positive takeaway from his work is the clear intuition that a Methodist ecclesiology will indeed make the work of the Holy Spirit pivotal in its deliberations. I stand resolutely with him on this common ground. But where do I want to go? What alternative tele-grams do I want to send? Here are three by way of conclusion.

First, we need to retrieve not just the work of the Spirit but the work of the Spirit within the work of the Tri-personal agency of God. The core that has to touch everything is not the speculative and contested claim that the emerging "empire" of global capitalism "increasingly determines every part of our lives,"[12] but the earth-shattering claim that the Son of the Father through the work of the Spirit has fully identified with our world as it is, even to the point of redemptive death, and now, risen from the dead, gives the gift of the Spirit to his people in the inauguration of his kingdom not of eating and drinking but of righteousness, peace, and joy in the Holy Spirit.

---

12   Ibid., 16.

Second, where the Holy Spirit is, there is the church and all the fullness of grace and truth. This revolutionary insight enabled the early first Christians (Messianic Jews one and all) to identify afresh the work of the Holy Spirit outside their borders and open the door to Gentile believers. It was equally this insight (experienced and articulated in its own inimitable way in Wesley's canonical sermons) that gave Wesley and the early Methodists the courage, confidence, and power to spread scriptural holiness across the world. I suggest, moreover, that something like this insight may also lie behind both the strong connectionalism and the ineradicable ecumenical disposition so characteristic of Methodism across space and time. However, when we read these latter developments, we begin with the axiom: where the Holy Spirit is there is all the fullness of grace and truth.

Third, where the Eucharist is properly and aptly celebrated there is a celebratory and expectant invocation of the Holy Spirit to make the bread and the wine the body and blood of Jesus and to make us the body of Christ given in service to the world. We have our theological work cut out for us to articulate what this means; we readily admit the mystery, but, given our commitment to rationality, we also acknowledge the challenge of being, with our "Father in the Faith," John Wesley, rational enthusiasts. In this way we come back around to chart an exceptionally close causal and liturgical link between Eucharist and ecclesiology.

SEVEN

Soteriology and Eucharist

Sarah Heaner Lancaster

It has been observed that in England the eighteenth-century general revival of religion and sacramental revival went hand in hand.[1] John Wesley is credited with influencing increased attendance for the sacrament in the Church of England at a time when the Eucharist was offered in some parish churches only a few times a year. He himself received the sacrament often, and he urged Methodists to commune not just frequently but constantly. The people evidently responded to this message. There is evidence that hundreds attended Eucharist when it was offered.[2] This observation suggests that the power of the Methodist movement in England at that time may be displayed in the relation between the way Eucharist was understood and the salvation that John Wesley preached. This chapter will examine the connection between Eucharist and John Wesley's soteriology to show the ways that the Eucharist supported the theological themes of the revival so that Methodists not only earnestly sought salvation but also were drawn to participate in Holy Communion.

The Way of Salvation

To talk about Eucharist and soteriology in the Wesleyan tradition requires as a first step some orientation to how soteriology will be understood here. The preferred manner of thinking of Wesley's soteriology has been in recent years to accept the idea of *via salutis* rather than *ordo salutis*, that is, to describe salvation in terms of a "way" rather than an "order." Randy Maddox gives three reasons for this preference: (1) the Reformed *ordo salutis* implies discrete steps through which a Christian passes, whereas *via salutis* allows a more fluid and interconnected understanding of the Christian life; (2) the image of stages also tends toward the idea of forward progress only, of leaving one stage and moving to the next, whereas the image of traveling a way allows not only going forward but also the possibility

---

1   J. Ernest Rattenbury, *The Eucharistic Hymns of John and Charles Wesley* (London: The Epworth Press, 1948), 4–5.

2   Ibid., 5–6.

of going backward; (3) the idea of an order was cultivated in Protestant scholasticism, a manner of doing theology that worked for clarity and definition in an effort to organize ideas, whereas the clarity and definition that Wesley's theology sought was not strictly organizational but was rather an attempt to describe complex pastoral situations.[3] The use of a way rather than an order to think about soteriology may be less tidy, but it has the advantage of reflecting something of the messiness of life.

If soteriology is understood as a way of salvation, then what is salvation? In the sermon that uses the language for the image of the *via salutis* ("The Scripture Way of Salvation"), Wesley describes salvation as "a present thing, a blessing which, through the free mercy of God, ye are now in possession of." This description is set in intentional contrast to thinking of salvation as only "the going to heaven, eternal happiness," or "a blessing which lies on the other side of death." Of course, Wesley never denied (and in fact hoped for) salvation as the going to heaven after death, but he wanted to call attention to the anticipation of that final salvation in this life. We begin to travel the way of salvation now, and we already enjoy some of the benefits of knowing Christ. Salvation, then, in Wesley's understanding is an expansive concept, embracing "the entire work of God, from the first dawning of grace in the soul till it is consummated in glory."[4] It is this expansive concept of salvation that I will have in mind as I examine the link between soteriology and Eucharist. Participating in the Lord's Supper allowed a person to experience the present effects of salvation.

To consider the way of salvation as a present thing is primarily to think of being saved from sin. The corollary to being saved from sin is to be saved for holiness. The way that we travel takes us from a fallen state toward realization of the life that God intended for humans. Both Wesley's theology and Methodist practices focused on this movement. On this journey, the point of origin and also the destination are described in terms of love. As fallen creatures, we suffer from a distorted image of God. We were made to love God above all else and to find our happiness in that loving relationship, but because of the Fall, the human functions badly and so our love is misdirected. Although it should be animated and ordered by love for God, the will has lost focus on its proper object and so it wanders and attaches itself to other objects.[5]

---

3   Randy Maddox, *Responsible Grace: John Wesley's Practical Theology* (Nashville: Abingdon Press, 1994), 157–58.

4   John Wesley, "The Scripture Way of Salvation," in *The Works of John Wesley: Sermons*, vol. 2, ed. Albert C. Outler (Nashville : Abingdon Press, 1984), 156, §I.1

5   Wesley, "The Image of God," *The Works of John Wesley*, vol. 4, ed. Outler, 294–98, §§I.2 and II.3.

For this reason, when Wesley talks about sin he often uses the language of desire. He commonly categorizes sin in three ways: desire of the flesh, desire of the eye, and desire of praise (the pride of life). Each of these has at its root a misdirected love. Desire of the flesh manifests itself in becoming attached to things that bring sensual pleasure. Desire of the eye involves less concrete and more mental or imaginative pursuits, such as the pleasure we gain from entertainment or being fashionable. Desire of praise leads us to seek to be held in high esteem by others.[6] As desires, each of these categories of sin shows that we are drawn to something other than God more than we are to God, whether a material object, an intangible pleasure, or the way we are regarded by those around us. The root of the human problem, then, is that we do not love as we should.

To be saved from sin, then, means to have our love redirected, away from lesser things and toward its proper object—God. Consequently, being saved for holiness is also described in terms of love. Wesley carefully and intentionally describes the perfection that Christians seek in terms of love, loving God and loving neighbor. To be perfect as a Christian is to be holy, and to be holy as a Christian is to reflect God's holiness by loving as God loves. Wesley reasons in *A Plain Account of Christian Perfection* that love fulfills the Law because love encompasses all that is just and pure and virtuous. This love, then, is perfection.[7] If holiness is the destination of the way of salvation, then the way that Christians travel is to become more and more like God in love, loving God above all else, and loving God's creatures (self and neighbor) as God loves them.

To be saved from sin means being saved both from its guilt and from its power. Wesley understood that we are guilty before God both because of original sin and because of our actual sins. Jesus atoned for our guilt by his sacrificial death, and we receive the benefit of that atonement (pardon) in justification. Wesley understood that we are responsible for our sins, but he also recognized that sin has power over us. Because the image of God has been damaged by the Fall, we are drawn away from God and cannot resist the allure of those things we desire. God deals with the power of sin in our sanctification. As we are made more holy in love, sin has less power over us. Justification and sanctification are the two orienting ideas for understanding what God does in saving human beings.

---

6   Wesley, "Original Sin," *The Works of John Wesley*, vol. 2, ed. Outler, 179–82, §II.9–11. I have more fully articulated the place of desire in the way of salvation in Sarah Heaner Lancaster, *The Pursuit of Happiness: Blessing and Fulfillment in Christian Faith* (Eugene, OR: Wipf and Stock, 2011).

7   John Wesley, *A Plain Account of Christian Perfection* (Kansas City, MO: Beacon Hill Press, 1966), 12.

It is well known that John Wesley held to the possibility of entire sanctification, or perfection in love in this life. It is also known that he and his brother Charles had different viewpoints on perfection. John R. Tyson identifies three points on which the brothers disagreed: (1) Charles understood perfection in a way John thought to be "too high"; (2) Charles saw perfection received gradually over the course of a person's life whereas John held out the possibility of an instantaneous blessing; (3) Charles expected the fullest expression of perfection to occur at death while John urged people to expect it before death.[8] These differences matter for a Wesleyan understanding of the connection between Eucharist and soteriology because Charles's hymns had as much (if not more) effect on Methodist understanding of Eucharist as John's sermons and treatises did. So a short discussion of the difference between the brothers is in order.

Both brothers agreed that perfection was the restoration of the image of God. John thought that Charles's view was "too high" because Charles envisioned perfection as the full, absolute restoration of the image, such that no sin remained at all, which in turn prevented any possibility of falling back.[9] Although John, like Charles, understood that sin could be uprooted, he understood the fully restored image to put us back in the situation of Adam and Eve. They loved God fully before the Fall, but they were capable of falling because even in that state, they were vulnerable to temptation. Like them, even in a state of full perfection, we would still be vulnerable to temptation.[10] In addition to the danger of vulnerability, though, perfection also had the possibility of increase. For John a perfected person not only could fall back, she or he could also go forward. For him, there could always be more love, so we could continue to grow even as perfected beings. For this reason, he would not call perfection "absolute."[11]

The question of gradual or instantaneous perfection brought an exchange of letters between the brothers.[12] John and Charles each had practical reasons for placing their emphasis on perfection differently. For Charles, emphasizing gradual perfection guarded against enthusiasm

---

8   John R. Tyson, "The One Thing Needful: Charles Wesley on Sanctification," *Wesleyan Theological Journal* 45, no. 2 (Fall 2010): 177–95.

9   J. W. Cunningham, "The Methodist Doctrine of Christian Perfection: Charles Wesley's Contribution Contextualized," *Wesley and Methodist Studies* 2 (2010): 25–44.

10   Wesley, "The Repentance of Believers," *The Works of John Wesley*, vol. 1, ed. Outler, 346-47, §I.20; "Christian Perfection," *The Works of John Wesley*, vol. 2, ed. Outler, 104, §I.8.

11   Wesley, "Christian Perfection," *The Works of John Wesley*, vol. 2, ed. Outler, 104–05, §I.9.

12   See Tyson, "The One Thing Needful: Charles Wesley on Sanctification," *Wesleyan Theological Journal*.

and premature claims that would need to be recanted later. For John, emphasizing instantaneous perfection placed the promise of holiness constantly before the believer, and constant expectation that God would complete the work of salvation in us actually opens us to receive God's work.[13] Because Charles emphasized gradual perfection, he reasonably saw the fullest expression of holiness to come at the end of one's life, as the culmination of one's journey. Because John emphasized instantaneous perfection, he held that even before death it was possible to enjoy the full love of God that constituted the full restoration of the image of God (albeit still vulnerable to temptation).

Although John thought the expectation of instantaneous perfection was important, he did not deny God's gradual work in us. Even very early in his theological reflection on perfection, Wesley recognized that the movement away from sin and toward holiness involved a maturing in Christ. In his 1741 sermon "Christian Perfection," Wesley acknowledged that although no real Christian, even a babe in Christ, would "commit sin" (what he would later describe as "outward sin" or an "actual, voluntary 'transgression of the law'"), only those who are "strong in the Lord" would be free of sinful thoughts and tempers (or "inward sin").[14] Wesley's later reflections on perfection took up the problem of this inward sin that remained in believers, even if it did not rule over them. By 1767, Wesley was using the three categories of sin described above to talk about the way that sin, as desire, can still cling to the words and actions of maturing Christians.[15] The remaining presence of sin requires continual reliance on God's forgiving grace, as well as continuing to respond to God's graceful empowerment to move forward. As he entered his late period of reflection, Wesley spoke of how our hearts might be "truly, yet not entirely renewed."[16] These words indicate the importance of growing in the Christian life toward the entire renewal that Christ offers.

John Wesley's theology, then, is clear that the salvation that is available to Christians in this life is to have our distorted wills healed so that our love may

---

13 Wesley, "Scripture Way of Salvation," *The Works of John Wesley*, vol. 2, ed. Outler, 168–69, §III.18.

14 Wesley, "Christian Perfection," *The Works of John Wesley*, vol. 2, ed. Outler, 117, §II.21; "The Great Privilege of Those that are Born of God," *The Works of John Wesley*, vol. 1, ed. Outler, 436, §II.2; "On Sin in Believers," in *The Works of John Wesley*, vol. 1, ed. Outler, 320, §II.2. In the 1872 edition of *A Plain Account of Christian Perfection*, the phrase "strong in the Lord" appears as "grown Christians."

15 Wesley, "The Repentance of Believers," *The Works of John Wesley*, vol. 1, ed. Outler, 335–52.

16 Wesley, "On Sin in Believers," *The Works of John Wesley*, vol. 1, ed. Outler, 325–26, §IV.1.

be redirected toward God. Since this healing takes time, he is also clear that we journey toward salvation, both guided and empowered by God. In Sermon 101, "The Duty of Constant Communion," described by Albert Outler as "Wesley's fullest and most explicit statement of his eucharistic doctrine and practice," Wesley makes it just as clear that both the happiness and holiness we seek in salvation are supported by participation in the Eucharist.[17] Wesley considers the Lord's Supper to be both a command and a mercy. God's particular mercy to human beings is for us to be happy in God, which is the end for which we were made. Our happiness in God was lost in the fall, so our journey toward salvation—the healing of the image of God in us—restores us to the happiness for which we were made. God knows, though, that we are unable to achieve this happiness on our own, that we must be helped by grace along the way toward this salvation, so God has provided us with means of obtaining this help. As Wesley says, "One of these is the Lord's Supper, which of his infinite mercy he hath given for this very end: that through this means we may be assisted to attain those blessings which he hath prepared for us; that we may obtain holiness on earth and everlasting glory in heaven."[18]

Eucharist is a means of helping us along the way of salvation so that we may enjoy the blessing of salvation that is available to us in this life precisely because it gives us what we need for the journey: "the forgiveness of our past sins and the present strengthening and refreshing of our souls."[19] Eucharist provides what we need at every point along our journey. As John Wesley wrote in his journal, "The Lord's Supper was ordained by God to be a means of conveying to men either preventing or justifying, or sanctifying grace, according to their several necessities."[20] Eucharist is a means of grace according to our need, so it is clear why we have a duty of constant communion. Eucharist provides for us in whatever state we find ourselves before God, so we ought to make use of it in every state.

Let us turn now to consider how Eucharist serves as a means of grace along the topography of the way of salvation.

Converting Ordinance

Although Wesley says Eucharist is a "means of conveying" prevenient

---

17   Albert C. Outler, introductory comment to Wesley, "The Duty of Constant Communion," *The Works of John Wesley*, vol. 3, ed. Outler, 427–28.

18   Wesley, "The Duty of Constant Communion," *The Works of John Wesley*, vol. 3, ed. Outler, 432, §II.5.

19   Ibid., 429, ¶2.

20   John Wesley, Saturday, June 28, 1740, in *The Works of John Wesley*: Journal and Diaries, vol. 19, ed. W. Reginald Ward and Richard P. Heitzenrater, 159.

grace, it may be more accurate to talk about how prevenient grace draws us to Eucharist rather than its being received in the sacrament itself. A person only starts to travel along the way of salvation when that person has an understanding of a need to be saved. One of the functions of prevenient grace is to give us a conscience that makes us uneasy in our present condition and so moves us to seek the salvation God offers. Grace works this way in every person, unless or until this light is quenched by lack of response.[21] Response to these slight stirrings leads to greater conviction of sin and therefore greater awareness of the need for deliverance. God's grace works preveniently to convict us of sin even without Eucharist, but by making the offer of forgiveness plain (and thus implying the need for forgiveness), Eucharist may goad the conscience to be more aware of our sin. The beginning of the Methodist societies was marked by acknowledgment of sin and desire to flee from the wrath it brings, and this remained the single condition for membership.[22]

If admission to the societies clearly depended on conviction of sin, it was not at first so clear that admission to the Eucharist was to be based solely on this conviction. John Wesley's journal refers to a question of his time as to whether the Lord's Supper was to be considered a converting or a confirming ordinance.[23] It is important to be aware that in this context "converting" did not mean a change from no religion or another religion to being Christian. Rather it meant a change from being a Christian in name only (as most people would already have been baptized) to being what a Christian really should be (having received the Holy Spirit). The question, then, was whether sinners come to the Table to be regenerated or whether only regenerate, godly Christians come to the Table to be confirmed and strengthened in their godliness. In the Church of England in Wesley's time, any baptized person could participate in Eucharist. Some Anglicans, though, stressed the importance of being worthy for taking Communion, and there were many manuals to assist people in preparing for Eucharist properly. Puritans also shared a concern for worthy partaking and examined communicants to determine their fitness to receive.[24] In his

21   Wesley, "On Working Out Our Own Salvation," *The Works of John Wesley*, vol. 3, ed. Outler, 206–07, §II.1 and III.4.
22   John Wesley, "The Nature, Design, and General Rules of the United Societies, in *The Works of John Wesley:* The Methodist Societies, vol. 9, ed. Rupert E. Davies, vol. 9, (Nashville: Abingdon Press, 1984ff), 69–70, ¶1 and 4.
23   Wesley, Friday, June 27, 1740, *The Works of John Wesley:* Journals and Diaries, vol. 19, ed. Ward and Heitzenrater, 158.
24   Lorna Khoo, *Wesleyan Eucharistic Spirituality* (Adelaide, Australia: ATF Press, 2005), 29 31.

early years, John Wesley held to the importance of adequate preparation for communion, and this requirement became a source of conflict in his congregation in Georgia.[25]

The question whether Eucharist was a converting or confirming ordinance had its own history in the colonies because a few had practiced admitting unconverted (unregenerated) Christians to the sacrament instead of restricting the sacrament only to the converted (regenerated). Among those who engaged in this practice was Jonathan Edwards's maternal grandfather, Solomon Stoddard. Stoddard received criticism for this practice, and Edwards published a careful and thorough reflection on the question, comparing Stoddard's position with the criticisms of Solomon Williams. In working through the issue himself, Edwards found he could not embrace his grandfather's view and practice, so he argued for some qualification to be admitted to the Lord's Table.[26] In contrast, Wesley's own continued reflection led him away from the expectation of showing evidence of worthiness in order to receive Communion.

By the time Wesley wrote about the Lord's Supper as a converting ordinance in his journal, he had moved from his earlier position, namely that a person needed to prepare to be worthy to partake, and instead held that "no fitness is required at the time of communicating but a sense of our state, or our utter sinfulness and helplessness; every one who knows he is fit for hell being just fit to come to Christ, in this as well as all other ways of his appointment."[27] The only preparation, then, is the desire to receive the grace that God offers in this meal. In 1740, Wesley held this conviction so strongly that he called the denial that the Lord's Supper was a converting ordinance to be a "gross falsehood."[28] In making this assertion, Wesley appeals to the experience of many who said they had been converted, or even deeply convicted of sin, in taking the Lord's Supper. He refused to accept unworthiness as a legitimate excuse for not receiving Communion.[29]

This understanding of Eucharist as a converting ordinance is reflected in the *Hymns on the Lord's Supper*. The invitation that is given in these hymns

---

25   Ibid., 34.
26   Jonathan Edwards, *An Humble Inquiry into the Rules of the Word of God, concerning the Qualifications Requisite to a Complete Standing and Full Communion in the Visible Christian Church*, in *The Works of President Edwards*, 10 vols. (New York: S. Converse, 1830), 4:291–451.
27   Wesley, Saturday, June 28, 1740, *The Works of John Wesley*: Journals and Diaries, vol. 19, ed. Ward and Heitzenrater, 159.
28   Wesley, Friday, June 27, 1740, *The Works of John Wesley*: Journals and Diaries, vol. 19, ed. Ward and Heitzenrater, 158.
29   Wesley, "The Duty of Constant Communion," *The Works of John Wesley*, vol. 3, ed. Outler, 433–36, §II. 7–13.

to come or draw near makes it clear that sinners may come to the Table: "Come to the Supper come / Sinners there is still room / Every soul may be his guest." One hymn describes the things that lead people into sin: "Come hither all, whose grov'ling taste / Enslaves your souls and lays them waste," "Come hither all, whom tempting wine / bows to your father Belial's shrine." The specific sin that creates the need for forgiveness, though, matters less than one's willingness to approach the Table looking for help from God: "Sinner with awe draw near / And find thy Saviour here." [30]

The Eucharist, then, has a role even at the beginning of the way of salvation. When we are moved by prevenient grace to receive the offer of Christ, the Lord's Supper makes the gift of Christ available. The appropriate preparation and fitness, then, is recognizing need. What makes one worthy of coming to the Table is knowing that one needs to be there. This idea matters not only for individuals who are made welcome to come as they seek salvation, but also for the whole community. By eating the Lord's Supper together, the ones further along the way of salvation are joined in the body of Christ with those who are just beginning. Even at different places along the journey, all recognize their sin and their need for God's grace, as we will see in the next section.

Forgiveness

By opening the Table to sinners rather than restricting it to the godly, Wesley embraced the idea that the grace offered in the Lord's Supper would forgive. The benefit of Christ's atoning work was available through bread and cup. He understood the sacrament as sacrifice, not as a reenactment of Christ's sacrifice, but as conveying the ongoing effect of the original sacrifice made on the cross. The preface to *Hymns on the Lord's Supper* (an extract of Daniel Brevint's treatise) explains that the Lord's Supper is more than a memorial, it is the place where we actually meet Christ ("I haste to this Sacrament for the same purpose that SS Peter and John hasted to His sepulcher—because I hope to find him there"). [31] Because the presence of Christ in the Eucharist is real, the bread and wine convey Christ's blessings, although the way in

---

30   John and Charles Wesley, *Hymns on the Lord's Supper* (Bristol: Farley, 1745), 7 and 29. Hereafter referred to as HLS. Page numbers are to the upper right in the online document, which are different from the pdf number. Accessed in Charles Wesley's Published Verse, Duke Center for Studies in the Wesleyan Tradition. https://divinity.duke.edu/sites/divinity.duke.edu/files/documents/cswt/27_Hymns_on_the_Lord%27s_Supper_%281745%29.pdf.

31   Rattenbury, *Eucharistic Hymns*, 181–82.

which this happens is not explained.

As a means of forgiving grace, Eucharist has a role in our justification (pardon). It is all too easy to think of Wesley's way of salvation as a series of steps or stages, making it function as an order of salvation. This happens whenever justification is presented exclusively as a step before sanctification. Of course, it is important to maintain the idea that we are forgiven before (and not because of) holiness, but to think of forgiveness and holiness as sequential steps obscures more subtle nuances of their relationship. To understand justification in Eucharist, this subtlety must be highlighted.

Because the way of salvation begins with knowledge of sinfulness and desire to be forgiven, the first thing that grace must do when we turn to God is to forgive and assure us of our forgiveness. This act of grace is justification, but "initial justification" is not the whole of justification.[32] We are forgiven for past sin in justification and are thus delivered from its guilt. Initial justification is all that is needed for eternal life with God if we have neither time nor opportunity because of immediate death to participate further in God's saving activity in this life. If we continue to live, though, we are expected to continue to respond to God's work in our lives in order to participate in salvation as a present reality. For those who live beyond the time of their initial justification, Wesley spoke of a "repentance consequent upon" justification.[33] This repentance is necessary because sin remains (as inward sin) even if it does not rule (lead to committing an outward sin). Even if one does not "yield" to it, one is still aware of desire of the flesh, of the eye, and of praise. As long as this inward sin remains, it needs forgiveness of the atoning work of Christ. John Wesley's hope, of course, was that even this inward sin could be overcome in this life, but he admits that if one has no instantaneous deliverance but only gradual change "we must be content, as well as we can, to remain full of sin till death. And if so, we must remain guilty till death, continually deserving punishment."[34] It is this sin and guilt that makes repentance and continual justification still necessary. Even though this guilt deserves punishment, believers do not need to fear condemnation because they are confident in God's forgiving grace.

---

32 Randy Maddox uses language of "initial" and "final" justification taken from George Bull to illumine the way that Wesley came to think about the subtle connection between justification and sanctification. Maddox, *Responsible Grace*, 169.

33 Wesley, "The Scripture Way of Salvation," *The Works of John Wesley*, vol. 2, ed. Outler, 164, §III.4.

34 Wesley, "The Repentance of Believers," *The Works of John Wesley*, vol. 1, ed. Outler, 346–47, §I.20.

During the time between initial justification and perfection, the believer should respond to God's grace with good works, works of mercy, and works of piety.[35] These works keep us growing to be more Christlike as grace sanctifies us. Because present salvation is not finished all at once, we still struggle with the sin that remains. While we are maturing in Christ, the Lord's Supper is a means of forgiveness of the sin that continues to cleave to our words and actions, as well as a source of providing us with strength to resist temptation. Wesley explains:

> The grace of God given herein confirms to us the pardon of our sins by enabling us to leave them. As our bodies are strengthened by bread and wine, so are our souls by these tokens of the body and blood of Christ. This is the food of our souls: this gives strength to perform our duty, and leads us on to perfection.[36]

Constant communion during this time, then, serves two purposes. The Lord's Supper is a means of grace for forgiveness of the sin that remains, and it is a means of grace to strengthen us to work. As long as sin remains in a believer growing toward holiness, her or his life will likely reflect some struggle. The Lord's Supper strengthens us to prevail in that struggle.

With sinners coming to the Table seeking forgiveness for their sins, it is not surprising that a large number of *Hymns on the Lord's Supper* express not only the need but also the gift that may be received in the Eucharist. The first hymn in the collection explicitly makes the connection between the body and blood offered at the Table and the atoning sacrifice on the cross that makes forgiveness possible: "This is my blood which seals the new / Eternal covenant of my grace / My blood so freely shed for you / For you and all the sinful race."[37] This forgiveness could be known again and again, as often as it was needed during the struggle with sin, by participation in Eucharist.

Perfection

The time between initial justification and perfection may be thought of as not only a time of struggle but also a time of healing. Wesley could describe the distortion of the image of God as disease. His sermon on original sin (after he describes the way our desires are misdirected) ends with the

---

35 Wesley, "The Scripture Way of Salvation," *The Works of John Wesley*, vol. 2, ed. Outler, 164, §III.5.
36 Wesley, "The Duty of Constant Communion," *The Works of John Wesley*, vol. 3, ed. Outler, 429.
37 "In That Sad Memorable Night," HLS, 1.

injunction: "Know your disease! Know your cure!"[38] Sinners could approach the Table knowing that not only would they be forgiven throughout their struggle, but the disease of their nature was being healed: "O Taste and see that God is here / To heal your souls, and sin subdue."[39] The injuries that killed Jesus become the source of healing for our sin-sickness: "From thy blest wounds life let us draw / Thine all-atoning blood."[40] Those who come to the Eucharist properly may expect to receive in the bread and cup "salutary meat" and "saving health."[41] They hoped to be fully healed, with sin completely subdued, in perfection.

Despite their disagreement about timing, both John and Charles Wesley shared this goal and knew that for most who came to the Table the goal remained at some distance. One hymn on the Lord's Supper describes waiting for perfection this way: "Long we for thy love have waited / Begging sat by the wayside / Still we are not new-created / Still we are not sanctified / Thou to some in great compassion / Hast in part their sight restored / Show us all thy full salvation / Make the servants as their Lord."[42] Although John thought that the idea of instantaneous perfection was needed to keep the expectation for perfection constantly before us, Charles found a way to keep people reminded constantly of that goal as they sang hymns at the Eucharist.

> O thou Pascal Lamb of God,
> Feed us with thy flesh and blood,
> Life and strength thy death supplies,
> Feast us on thy sacrifice.
>
> Quicken our dead souls again,
> Then our living souls sustain,
> Then in us thy life keep up,
> Then confirm our faith and hope.
>
> Still, O Lord, our strength repair,
> Till renewed in love we are,
> Till thy utmost grace we prove,

---

38   Wesley, "Original Sin," *The Works of John Wesley*, vol. 2, ed. Outler, §III.5.
39   "Come Hither All," HLS, 8.
40   "O Thou, Whom Sinners Love," HLS, 73.
41   "How Dreadful is the Mystery," HLS, 40.
42   HLS, 83.

> *All thy life of perfect love.*[43]

The Eucharist strengthens and enlivens the soul as God continues God's saving work. It is plain that such help is needed for maturing Christians. From Charles's point of view regarding gradual perfection, one needs strength to continue growing to the end of one's life. Even from John's point of view of instantaneous perfection in this life, those who have been entirely perfected would also have need of God's strengthening, sustaining, and confirming help because, as he points out, "In this world we are never free from temptations," so we need the strength that the Lord's Supper provides to resist them.[44] Although John and Charles held somewhat different understandings of perfection, the Eucharist served a common purpose of empowering us to receive the fullness of God's saving work in this life.

Conclusion

Because the Lord's Supper had a role to play at every important landmark along Wesley's way of salvation, it is no wonder that Methodists gathered in such crowds to receive Holy Communion. They understood its relevance for the work that God was doing in them, and they sought its empowerment for their journey. Together, the Eucharist and the instruction the people received through the sermons provided a mutually supporting and compelling vision of how God works in human lives for salvation. Such intersection between theological understanding and liturgical practice provides powerfully effective spiritual formation. Because Methodists understood salvation not merely as something that occurred after death, but also as healing that takes place in this life, the benefits of the Eucharist had immediate relevance. The experience of grace at the Lord's Table was a powerful affirmation of God's saving work. Eucharist was a truly joyful occasion of celebrating that work. Those who seek to revitalize the Methodist tradition in a new time would do well to contemplate the power of this connection, which has proved its effectiveness.

---

43   HLS, 35.
44   Wesley, "The Duty of Constant Communion," *The Works of John Wesley*, ed. Outler, 429, ¶2.

EIGHT

Eschatology and Eucharist

Brent D. Peterson

A Failed Imagination

For too many Christians, the Lord's Supper has failed to offer both the eschatological hope and thanksgiving, which is the very visceral ethos of the celebration. An impaired eschatological imagination has exacerbated a "Christian" culture of individualism, judgmentalism, fear, anger, and violence of all kinds. This culture infects Christians with a gnostic triumphalism that can, ironically, be coupled with a strain of neo-Constantinian ambition for being politically successful, powerful, and influential, and at the same time yielding the destruction and rape of the earth while ignoring the "least of these." The primary concern is not condemnation of Christians but a pastoral invitation into the robust eschatological imagination of the eucharistic divine-human event, because at the root of the Gospels is the revelation of and encounter with Jesus Christ and the apocalyptic irruption of the kingdom of God, proclaiming and embodying an audacious hope.

There is good news, not in spite of the present circumstances but precisely because of present circumstances. The hope of Scripture is that God's kingdom is here in part, but *will* come on earth in fullness as it is in heaven, not unlike the rushing of a mighty wind. The hope of being captured by such an imagination invites Christians into a type of doxological living that more faithfully opens them to being used as God's vessels to bring about the present and future irruption of the kingdom of God, the redemption of the world. The Eucharist is both a proclamation of such a promise and a participation in the coming of the kingdom. Such an eschatological imagination encountered and embodied in the Eucharist releases Christians from fear and frees them to be joyfully broken and spilled out with an imagination of eucharistic, doxological martyrdom for the world.

With an ecumenical Wesleyan lens, this chapter will first briefly survey some of the roots and beginnings of the eschatological aroma from the Christian Scriptures to Jewish and Christian liturgies. Second, this chapter will consider how Christ's presence at the Table is an eschatological healing memory, emphasizing not past nostalgia but a memory of presence that is never fully exhausted. Moreover, such a memory does not fixate on Calvary but instead on a present encounter of the Last Supper that both illumines and inaugurates the kingdom of God aimed at a cosmic theosis, the renewal of all things into the Triune Godhead. Third, the chapter details this theotic encounter that both renews the church as the body of Christ and sends the church out in hope with a doxological ethic as the martyr-church so that the church can become who it is and is becoming. The eschatological event at the Table is a further irruption and participation of the coming kingdom. In order to explore the eschatological imagination of the coming kingdom in the Lord's Supper, this chapter explores the works of Geoffrey Wainwright, E. Byron Anderson, John and Charles Wesley, John D. Zizioulas, Alexander Schmemann, Bruce Morrill, Louis-Marie Chauvet, and Craig Hovey.

Eschatological Roots

Jewish Passover

Many Jewish prayers of blessing (*berakah*) and thanksgiving (*tōdah*) affirmed a confident hope in the redemption that was to come. J. Heinemann distinguishes three main topics in Jewish prayers: creation, revelation (the giving of the Law), and redemption.[1] These prayers saw a collapse of the past and the future and offered hope in an uncertain present. Jasper and Cuming note that this is especially seen in the prayers for Passover and specifically the four cups.[2]

New Testament

The New Testament also offers broad proclamations of hope including the present and future coming of the kingdom (see 1 Cor 15:20-28 and Phil 2:9-11). Both the Gospels of Matthew and Luke record Jesus' own eschatological proclamation in the Last Supper narrative.

> He said to them, "I have eagerly desired to eat this Passover with you before I suffer; for I tell you, I will not eat it until it is fulfilled in the kingdom of God." Then he took a cup, and after giving thanks he said, "Take this and divide it

---

1   Joseph Heinemann, *Prayer in the Talmud* (Berlin: Walter de Gruyter, 1977), 77–97.
2   R. C. D. Jasper and G. J. Cuming, *Prayers of the Eucharist: Early and Reformed* (Collegeville, MN: Liturgical Press, 1980), 9.

among yourselves; for I tell you that from now on I will not drink of the fruit of the vine until the kingdom of God comes" (Luke 22:15-18, NRSV).

In the hope of past, present, and future deliverance of the Passover, Jesus affirms that he is the meal's fulfillment. Joel Green notes that the celebration is not simply about Jesus' death and hence fulfillment of the Passover sacrifice, but about the hope of the full realization of the kingdom and God's redemption of the world. Like the Passover, Jesus' table fellowship in Luke was "in anticipation of the completion of God's purpose and spoke of the coming eschatological banquet in which his [Jesus'] own meal practices would be the norm."[3] In Paul's liturgical instructions for the church in Corinth regarding the Lord's Supper this eating and drinking in remembrance was a proclamation to be done until Christ returns (1 Cor 11:26).[4]

Didache

The Didache is largely believed to be a first-century document used broadly among the young Christian church. The Didache petitions, with hope, God's gathering and uniting the scattered church to become one. "As this broken bread was scattered over the mountains, and when brought together became one, so let your Church be brought together from the ends of the earth into your kingdom; for yours are the glory and the power through Jesus Christ forevermore."[5] This prayer notes the significance of the eucharistic emblems of bread and wine that synergistically were made by God from many grains of wheat and bushels of grapes crushed and pressed by human hands to form the loaf and wine. The eschatological hope celebrates the scriptural teachings from the Apostle Paul that there is just one Lord, one faith, and one baptism (Eph 4:4-6).

The Liturgy of Saints Addai and Mari

This fifth-century anaphora was composed in Syriac after the Council of Ephesus. This liturgy celebrates the hope of the kingdom while also invoking God's continual peace and redemption of more and more of creation. "And grant us your tranquility and your peace for all days of this age (repeat) *People:* Amen. That all the inhabitants of the earth may know you, that you alone are the true God and Father, and you sent our Lord Jesus Christ, your

---

3 Joel B. Green, *The Gospel of Luke*, New International Commentary on the New Testament (Grand Rapids: Eerdmans, 1997), 761.
4 It is noteworthy that the verb *érchomai* in this verse is in the subjunctive.
5 Cited in Jasper and Cuming, *Prayers of the Eucharist*, 23.

beloved Son . . .'"[6] Not only is the prayer for God to offer peace in the present
to inhabitants of all the earth, this prayer also seeks God's sanctification
of the offering, which may serve as a hope for the future resurrection.

> May your Holy Spirit, Lord, come and rest on this offering of your servants,
> and bless and sanctify it, that it may be to us, Lord, for remission of debts,
> forgiveness of sins, and the great hope of resurrection from the dead, and new
> life in the kingdom of heaven, with all who have been pleasing in your sight."[7]

This prayer appears to serve as a rough *proto*-epiclesis asking the Spirit
to help sanctify this offering to serve for the church's healing offering the
great hope of the resurrection from the dead.

Liturgy of St. James

The *Liturgy of St. James* is thought to be a combination of the *Liturgy of St.
Basil* and an old Jerusalem rite. It was widely used around Jerusalem until
the twelfth century. The eschatological prayer in this rite seeks not only the
unity of the church but peace in all the world.

> Remember, Lord, all men for good; on all have mercy, Master; reconcile us all,
> bring peace to the multitudes of your people, disperse the scandals, abolish
> wars, end the divisions of the churches, speedily put down the uprisings of
> the heresies, cast down the insolence of the heathen, exalt the horn of the
> Christians, grant us your peace and your love, God our savior, the hope of all
> the ends of the earth.[8]

This prayer seeks peace in all the earth. It is the peace of Jesus Christ that is
petitioned to reign in all conflict and hostility.

The Liturgy of St. John Chrysostom

The *Liturgy of St. John Chrysostom* supplanted the *Liturgy of St. Basil* as
the principal and normal rite of the Orthodox Church by 1000 CE. In this
anaphora, the epiclesis seeks the "changing" of the blood so those who partake may encounter the fullness of the kingdom:

> And that which is in this cup and precious blood of your Christ, changing it
> by your Holy Spirit, Amen; so that they may become to those who partake

---

6   Ibid., 43.
7   Ibid.
8   Ibid., 95.

for vigilance of soul, for fellowship with the Holy Spirit, for the fullness of the kingdom [of heaven], for boldness toward you, not for judgment or condemnation.[9]

The emphasis of the "change" of the blood, similar to the notion of transubstantiation in the Roman Catholic tradition, is not solely focused on the wine itself, but how the wine can foster and assist in the church more properly becoming again the body of Christ, an eschatological becoming. This small sampling of eucharistic liturgies throughout the early centuries includes an eschatological dimension that has often not been properly remembered by the church at present, but invites the church again to do so.

The Eucharistic Encounter

Cosmic Eschatological Healing: Geoffrey Wainwright

Geoffrey Wainwright's *Eucharist and Eschatology* is the standard work when considering Wesleyan eschatology as embodied in eucharistic practice as well as its ecumenical roots and implications.[10] In this work Wainwright focuses on three primary images of the Eucharist: the messianic feast, the advent of Christ, and the first fruits of the kingdom.

Wainwright suggests that eschatology is the primary lens of theology. Eschatology encompasses the "already–not yet" tension that forms the church's mission as a messenger of the kingdom and the church's unity as the body of Christ.[11] Certainly the Eucharist provides a sense of the "alreadyness" and participation in the heavenly feast, but it calls out for a fuller and richer consummation.[12] Wainwright critiques a version of Christian eschatology that too frequently reduces salvation to an individualized and psychologized anthropology, failing to envision a cosmic eschatology, the creation of a new heaven and a new earth.

In light of this cosmic redemption in the Wesleyan tradition, salvation as ongoing healing is grounded in an eschatological imagination. The continual healing of sanctifying grace occurring in the Eucharist is an eschatological event and an act of becoming. E. Byron Anderson, drawing upon Wainwright, suggests that "What is 'already' is provisional; it is until. There is more to come. In this sense what is 'already'

---

9   Ibid., 133.
10   Geoffrey Wainwright, *Eucharist and Eschatology* (New York: Oxford University Press, 1981).
11   Ibid., 124–26.
12   Ibid., 128–30.

is 'not yet.'"[13] Yet Anderson presses deeper as to the nature of the "not yet," the teleological creation of humanity by God. Speaking directly of Wesley, Anderson writes,

> The experience of salvation in the present life prepares the individual for the life of the kingdom and represents a present realization of that life. The present experience of sanctification, of happiness and holiness, provides an entrance into what remains future, the believer not only living and walking toward eternity but also living the life of eternity, the life of love which characterizes the Kingdom of God.[14]

This further sanctifying healing must never be seen as achievement or personal success, but must be grounded in the continual growth of love for God and neighbor participating in the kingdom's further coming.

In light of the already and not-yet, Wainwright is convinced this must frame the discourse regarding Christ's presence at the Lord's Supper. For Wainwright, too much space has been spent on the ontology of Christ's presence while failing to pay adequate attention to the eschatological dimension of presence at the Eucharist.[15] Wainwright draws upon several *anaphoras* along with other liturgies of the church that offer an eschatological vision of Christ's coming.[16] Wainwright understands *anamnesis* at the Table to be a second epiclesis, a "throwing forward" of Christ's final advent into the present.[17] In other words, Christ's presence in the Eucharist offers a vision of the fullness of Christ's presence to be celebrated at the coming messianic feast.

At the Lord's Supper what is remembered/encountered eucharistically is not the past event of Calvary but Christ present. An improper focus hampers and misses the eschatological tenor of each eucharistic celebration. Ernest Rattenbury suggests that the nuanced memorialist position for the Wesleys is not being present to the past event of Calvary, but to Christ.[18] The Eucharist focuses not primarily on Calvary, 30 CE, but on a present encounter with

---

13   E. Byron Anderson, *Worship and Christian Identity: Practicing Ourselves* (Collegeville, MN: The Liturgical Press, 2003), 173.

14   Ibid., 177. In this final phrase Anderson is citing Henry H. Knight III, *The Presence of God in the Christian Life: John Wesley and the Means of Grace* (Metuchen, NJ: Scarecrow Press, 1992), 71.

15   Wainwright, *Eucharist and Eschatology*, 107–8.

16   Ibid., 60–73.

17   Ibid., 80–84.

18   John Ernest Rattenbury, John Wesley, Charles Wesley, and Timothy J. Crouch, *The Eucharistic Hymns of John and Charles Wesley: To Which Is Appended Wesley's Preface Extracted from Brevint's Christian Sacrament and Sacrifice Together with Hymns on the Lord's Supper*, American ed. (Cleveland: OSL Publications, 1990), 16–17.

the risen Christ whose body remains doxologically broken and mutilated. Focusing solely on the past event may offer only memorial options of what has already occurred. The dangerous reduction is that one can mentally consider Calvary, yet be closed off to the new event of Christ's dynamic healing presence. Xavier Léon-Dufour concurs that the emphasis is not on the death but on the presence of Jesus at the Table. The command of liturgical anamnesis is "that the disciples must 'do this,' not 'in memory of my death' but 'in memory of me.'"[19] This remembrance does not sentimentally long for the past. This is not a disembodied commemoration of Calvary or a human pledge to "keep the story alive." Simple nostalgia for first-century events would not be transforming and, for the Wesleys, would not be sacramental.

Eschatological Memory: John D. Zizioulas

Metropolitan John D. Zizioulas also considers eschatology as the central vision and schema for the Eucharist. Zizioulas pushes against the reduction of eucharistic remembrance to a psychological nostalgia of the past. As the Eucharist is an eschatological memory of Christ, Zizioulas notes how the encounter (remembrance) with Christ is personal. Zizioulas also highlights how the church's remembrance at the Table is not simply oriented to who Christ was, but "in the Eucharist, however, the church remembers the risen one who is to come."[20] Moreover, drawing upon an Irenaean Christology of recapitulation, he affirms Christ's coming as an ontological healing for the whole of creation. "In Jesus Christ we see the future of creation, for in him God's will to share his life with creation is revealed and realized" (ibid.). In this way Christ serves as an eschatological firstfruits for all of creation. Hence, every eucharistic celebration is a further coming and healing of creation. Zizioulas further notes that as "creation ultimately will receive her being from Jesus Christ, who comes to us from the *eschaton* (as *ho eschatos*), our very being is eschatological" (ibid.). Creation is not simply that which it *has been,* but what it *will be.* It is the future that continues to call and redeem creation.

Therefore, Zizioulas emphasizes that the eucharistic liturgy is an *icon* of the kingdom. This is to claim that the eucharistic liturgy "bears the image of the eschatological Kingdom of God through participation in it" (ibid.). The church is not simply acted upon, but in the dynamic

---

19   Xavier Léon-Dufour, *Sharing the Eucharistic Bread: The Witness of the New Testament,* trans. Matthew J. O'Connell (New York: Paulist Press, 1987), 67.
20   John D. Zizioulas, *The Eucharistic Communion and the World,* ed. Luke Ben Tallon (New York: T&T Clark, 2011), x.

transforming event of the eucharistic liturgy, the church encounters and offers itself to God with Christ by the Spirit as a participation in receiving and becoming who the church is and will be.

Even within this emphasis of participation, some might be nervous that such an eschatological emphasis of the church may fall prey to an un-witting gnosticism where the past and present, *being in the world*, become irrelevant and profane. Zizioulas allays those fears by emphasizing the significance of the epiclesis in the eucharistic prayer. Christ's person can-not be divorced from his *"work* in space and time, the taste of the *eschaton* given in the Eucharist cannot be isolated from either the fruits of *creation* (the bread and the wine) or the *history* [sic] the people of God" (ibid., xi). This eschatological becoming of the church and the rest of creation while coming from the future, invades the very darkness, powers, and princi-palities of this age. Moreover, Zizioulas notes that this does not lead to a type of triumphalism of the church because it is only by the Spirit that the gift of resurrected life continues to irrupt in the world.

> Far from leading to triumphalism, the Eucharist *intensifies* the Church's strug-gle with evil and death present in the world . . . the Church cannot oppose death by fleeing space and time, materiality and history; for in the Eucharist, the life of the world to come meets the Church in space and time, indicating that it must be transformed, not abandoned" (ibid.).

The eschatological encounter at the Eucharist participates viscerally in the very redemption of the world. Zizioulas also emphasizes how the Spirit offers charisms to the church to participate in the world's redemption.

One important example Zizioulas offers is the importance for Chris-tians to love enemies. "This love is not simply a matter of *ethics*—of a different *action*. Rather, it is a matter of *eschatology*, knowing others not as they have been (past sins, etc.), but as they may be in the *eschaton* (a member and neighbor in the Kingdom)" (ibid., xiii). Loving an enemy is precisely the posture for how one will participate in faithfulness in the martyr-church that will be explored below. Zizioulas strongly re-sists any type of moralism that reduces the eucharistic imagination to a bigoted list of do's and do not's. This is about the redemption of all the creation come what may.

Eschatological Memory of Christ's Last Supper: Alexander Schmemann and Bruce Morrill

Alexander Schmemann suggests that the emphasis of this eschatolog-ical memory of Christ is not simply Golgotha, but all of Christ's life. The memorial acclamation proclaims: Christ has died, but also Christ is risen; Christ will come again.

> The very essence of faith, therefore, consists in believers' memory of Christ, a knowledge of Christ that entails remembrance of all aspects of his life, death, and resurrection, and glorification. Rather than being mere knowledge about Christ, such remembrance is a participation in life everlasting; it is the gift of new life in Christ.[21]

This memory participates in the very source of new life in Christ. This memory not only remembers what Christ has done, but who Christ is and what Christ will do. David Power also notes an eschatological horizon into the Roman Rite of Mass a new prayer of the people in the Anamnesis and Acclamation, "We proclaim your Death, O Lord, and profess your Resurrection until you come again" and "When we eat this Bread and drink this Cup, we proclaim your Death, O Lord, until you come again."[22] This is prayer of expectation of Christ's return in glory where all things will be reconciled to him. [23]

Bruce Morrill also suggests that such a memory of encounter describes precisely why "liturgy is eschatological. It is a moment in our fragmentary experience that reveals the fullness of history that Christ will achieve in the *eschaton*."[24] This memory transforms the present as it symbolically (participates into that to which it points) offers a vision of the consummation, which also brings the coming kingdom closer.

If being present to Christ and not Calvary defines the eucharistic celebration, in what context is Christ present? Alexander Schmemann, in his book *The Eucharist*, asserts that what the church encounters through remembering in the Eucharist is not Golgotha but the eschatological encounter of the Last Supper. Schmemann concludes that the church's commemoration is not being present to a past event but ascending to God's kingdom that is coming.

---

21   Bruce T. Morrill, *Anamnesis as Dangerous Memory: Political and Liturgical Theology in Dialogue* (Collegeville, MN: Pueblo Book, 2000), 143.

22   Eucharistic Rite I, No 91, acclamations 1 and 2, in *A Commentary on the Order of the Mass of 'The Roman Missal,"* ed. Edward Foley (Collegeville, MN: Pueblo, 2011), 241.

23   David Power, "Theology in Latin Text and Rite," in *A Commentary on the Order of the Mass of 'The Roman Missal,"* ed. Edward Foley (Collegeville, MN: Pueblo, 2011), 266.

24   Morrill, *Anamnesis as Dangerous Memory*, 144.

> The remembrance is the confession of the knowledge of this mystery, its reality, and likewise faith in it as the salvation of the world and man. Like the entire Eucharist, the remembrance is not a repetition. It is the manifestation, gift and experience, in this world, and therefore again and again, of the Eucharist offered by Christ once and for all, and our ascension to it.[25]

This event is the surprising, yet contiguous irruption of the kingdom of God. In the Eucharist, the church experiences the gift and consummation of the kingdom first celebrated on the night in which Jesus was betrayed. "The entire endless joy of this commemoration is precisely that it remembers the last supper not as a 'means' but as a manifestation, and even more than a manifestation, as the presence and gift of the very goal: the kingdom for which God created the world" (ibid., 203). Schmemann asserts that Christ prays for this kingdom in John 17. For Schmemann this kingdom is the manifestation of " I in them, and thou in me, that they may be made perfect in one . . . that the love wherewith thou hast loved me may be in them, and I in them" (John 17:23, 26, KJV). This immersion of creation into the Godhead is a way to think about theosis. Theosis is a fitting imagination of the telos of the kingdom, which the Last Supper, not Golgotha, manifests. Schmemann clarifies how the eschatological inbreaking of the kingdom occurs at the Last Supper: "We call the last supper an ultimate event because, being the manifestation of the goal, it is the manifestation of the end" (ibid., 204). The end of the kingdom is communion in God with one another. This appears to be in full agreement with Wesley's *ordo salutis*, where sanctification renews persons into the image of God so they can better love God and others. Therefore, because we continue to remember, we continue on the way toward perfection. This Wesleyan understanding of Christian perfection (sanctification) should be linked to the notion of theosis. The kingdom of God's end is that all of creation will be caught up in God, and God will be all in all (1 Cor 15:20-28).

The Last Supper as the Climax of Theosis

If the eucharistic encounter is more about the Last Supper than Golgotha, so too the Last Supper is a kind of climax of Jesus' ministry. Schmemann declares, "With the last supper Christ's earthly ministry was completed" (ibid.). Immediately one may inquire about the cross and Resurrection.

---

25   Alexander Schmemann, *The Eucharist*, trans. Paul Kachur (Crestwood, NY: St. Vladimir's Press, 1987; Reprint 2003), 224.

Schmemann anticipates this question. "Everything that Christ accomplished after the last supper, and that the eucharistic prayer commemorates after it, is revealed in this prayer [John 17] and in the faith and experience of the Church as a consequence of this manifestation of the kingdom, as its first, decisive and saving *victory* in the world and over the world" (ibid.). Christ's death and resurrection are a consequence of this offering of love at the Last Supper and the manifestation of the kingdom and not a constitution of it. In other words, while Christ's death and resurrection are central to Christ's narrative, they speak into the kingdom that is Christ's entire life and ministry inaugurated by the Spirit. Christ's death and resurrection must be read in light of his entire ministry and posture of oblation (thank-offering) to the Father. Moreover, in looking for a climax to Christ's narrative, Schmemann argues it is in the Last Supper and not Calvary "that we find the consummation of the full, complete self-sacrifice of this love" (ibid., 205). Schmemann suggests that the Last Supper manifests the fullness of the kingdom. Schmemann clarifies that such a claim does not eschew the cross, but sees it in light of the whole and not an isolated event. However, in light of the relational healing of sanctification toward theosis, the Lord's Supper embodies the important climax of the kingdom of God. Within this emphasis of Last Supper, it is important to see this meal as the culmination rather than an isolated, punctiliar, abstract moment from Jesus's ministry. In other words, Jesus' teaching, healings, and other meals are also occasions that participated in the inauguration of the kingdom of God that Christ embodied.

With the Last Supper as the pinnacle of the kingdom, Schmemann concludes that Christ had few options moving from the Last Supper. "After the last supper Christ also had *nowhere to go* than to this encounter, to the deadly duel with sin and death. . . . Christ *condemned* himself to the cross with the last supper, with the manifestation in it of the kingdom of love" (ibid., 206). Christ's oblationary sacrifice led to conflict. Schmemann declares that as a citizen of this kingdom who lives "in the world, does not the cross—betrayal, crucifixion, suffering and death—become *unavoidable*" (ibid., 205). Perhaps the unavoidability of the cross only makes sense to the church in light of the hope of the Resurrection. Thus what Christ does, becomes an invitation of the church to join him in a doxological oblationary sacrifice captured by an eschatological imagination of theosis through an ethical embrace of martyrdom.

The Eschatological Constitution and Ethical Vocation of the Church

The healing memory of the Eucharist is also the memory of the constitution of the church. This eschatological encounter is not only an individualistic healing memory but an ecclesial healing memory. Forgetting God also exacerbates an individual's propensity to forget others. When someone forgets God, so too the need to love, care, and be present to others is forgotten. An individualized memory leaves open the possibility of idolatry by manipulating the memory to a self-enclosing nightmare of forgetfulness: such nightmares only dream of me trying to secure my own future by turning all around me into objects that provide for my present and future "happiness" or "wholeness." In attempting to secure my own existence and identity, I forget God, and thus myself and others. Such a nightmare never offers hope, it only offers insecurity and spreads the disease of selfishness. This healing of memory is not of isolated persons, but in Christ it is the healing memory of the body of Christ. Schmemann describes how this eschatological encounter of the Last Supper at the Table reimagines the beginning of the church.

This encounter offers "Eucharistic knowledge in the last supper of the ultimate manifestation of the kingdom of God, and thus of the beginning of the Church, her beginning as the new life, as the sacrament of the kingdom" (ibid., 201). At the Table the church encounters "the ultimate manifestation of the kingdom of God." This encounter with the Last Supper also remembers the church's beginning as the sacrament of that kingdom. Schmemann suggests that in the Last Supper, Christ does not institute the right or authority to transform bread and wine; "he instituted the Church" (ibid.). In the eucharistic event, this union in God unites the church for ministry. In this event, the church momentarily encounters the consummation of the kingdom as a present communion of the Last Supper. This empowers the church to doxologically (in praise) live into God's transformation of the world, into the present yet coming kingdom.

Morrill, in his book *Anamnesis as Dangerous Memory*, similarly asserts that this encounter continually shapes the church toward the eschatological vision of what the church will be.[26] This eschatological encounter heals through the gift of God's memory that makes possible the church's dangerous memory of God, calling for the church to live into its eschatological conversion.[27] As with psalms of lament, asking God to remember is not hoping to ease divine senility; rather, it implores God to heal again as God has done before. God's gift of remembering (active and present healing) offers the church a dangerous memory. Morrill calls this memory dangerous as a political posture where conflict may come to those who take this memory seriously and live it out.

---

26   Morrill, *Anamnesis as Dangerous Memory*, 106–7.
27   Ibid., 141–44.

"The threat of serious conflict (danger) looms in concrete situations where the praxis of faith begins to have tangible impact in a particular political situation."[28] The invitation to imitate Christ by participating in Christ is dangerous. The *imitatio Christi* is "'dangerous' both in the conversion it requires of its parishioners, away from a privatized view of salvation, and in the threat it poses to the conventional (evolutionary) wisdom of society."[29]

Morrill and Schmemann affirm that this active commemoration—the gift of the healing memory of God—is itself a healing that renews the church and empowers it to love and care for the world as God moves the world toward full redemption. Through memory the church participates in this transformation, because memory is not simply a passive cognitive reflection. "In the liturgy we have been commanded to celebrate, we do not *repeat* and we do not *represent*—we *ascend* into the mystery of salvation and new life."[30] The encounter of this healing eucharistic memory moves the church to doxological living. To anamnestically remember and partake in Communion celebrates an encounter with Christ in the eschatological Last Supper. In this sacrament of remembrance, we experience Christ not primarily individually or personally, but ecclesially.[31]

Morrill emphasizes the soteriological foundation of this eschatological, anamnestic healing of memory, which politically constitutes the church in God. This healing memory is soteriological because this constitution guides, empowers, and demands the political nature and, thus, ethical ministry of the church in the world. The church's ministry participates in and continues the ministry of the Incarnation. The church participates with and in Christ: "For this reason memory is of irreducible importance to the theory and practice of Christian faith. What Christians glean from the narrative remembrance of Jesus is the pattern of his life, a pattern of prayer and action, of . . . mysticism and politics."[32]

Morrill agrees with Dahl concerning the deep connection between worship (mysticism) and ethics (politics). Memory in the New Testament emphasizes not only the past but something of the present or future. Further, memory is "not a mere recalling or recollection of its object but, rather entails a far greater degree of subjective involvement."[33] This subjective involvement moves

---

28 Ibid., 42.
29 Ibid., 140.
30 Schmemann, *The Eucharist*, 221.
31 I have in mind John D. Zizioulas, in *Being as Communion: Studies in Personhood and the Church* (Crestwood, NY: St. Vladimir's Press, 1985). Zizioulas claims that through the ecclesial encounter individuals can fully be persons. See especially 15–19, 49–61.
32 Morrill, *Anamnesis as Dangerous Memory*, 146.
33 Ibid., 146–47.

those remembering to action. Therefore, "the manner of remembering entails bringing the object of one's memory into linguistic expression. Such expressive activity has an impact upon those who perform it or participate in it."[34] Morrill maintains that "the Christian exercise of memory is for the purpose of transforming believers' perspective and praxis."[35] The presence of Christ can be discussed only as the church recognizes the healing eucharistic memory as an eschatological encounter of the Last Supper that renews the church and sends it out to participate in the ongoing ministry of the Incarnation of Christ.

With the celebration of the present unity fashioned at the Table, the eschatological tension reminds the church of the *dis-unity* that marks the present fractured Table. Therefore, the Table celebrates both *what is* and *what will be*, which simultaneously illumines *what is currently not*. Eschatology moves soteriology beyond my personal morality into how God is calling and empowering the church into ministry in the world. Wainwright claims that meals eaten with an eschatological vision powerfully shape the ecclesial ethic and vision of the kingdom. This eschatological eating moves beyond material consumption to spiritual "indigestion." A proper eating causes the church to no longer accept the status quo of oppression and alienation before them as all that can be hoped for. This eating seeks to transform and renew these gathered persons to be the body of Christ in and for the world as a participation in creation's redemption.[36]

Ironically, Wainwright claims that because the memory of the eschatological future has been forgotten, the memory of Christ and resulting ecclesial vocation has also been misplaced. The eucharistic *anamnesis* (remembrance) not only seeks Christ's presence but acts as a continual judgment upon the church's ethical character. This ethical character works in anticipation of the gathering of the world at the coming great heavenly feast.[37] In a chapter on ethics in *Doxology*, Wainwright contin-ues to press for the ethical consequences and presuppositions of liturgy. He suggests that worship is either insincere or ineffective if the church is not shaped to live out its worship in the world. The church lives in light of the kingdom that is both present but also coming.[38]

---

34   Ibid., 147.
35   Ibid., 147.
36   Wainwright, *Eucharist and Eschatology*, 144–46.
37   Ibid., 80–84, 89–91.
38   See Geoffrey Wainwright, *Doxology: The Praise of God in Worship, Doctrine, and Life* (New York: Oxford University Press, 1980), 399–431.

Eschatological Hope

It must be envisioned, however, that this vocational invitation from the Table is grounded in the hope of what will be. Because the Eucharist offers eschatological healing, John and Charles Wesley could affirm that it is a pledge of the future and final healing that is to come. From the Wesley brothers' collection of eucharistic hymns titled *Hymns of the Lord's Supper*, this pledge is affirmed at the Table.

> *Sure pledge of ecstasies unknown*
> *Shall this divine communion be,*
> *The ray shall rise into a sun,*
> *The drop shall swell into a sea.*[39]

The Lord's Supper provides a real and present taste of the coming future hope and glory. The Wesleys affirmed that the Lord's Supper serves both as a "pledge and assurance that God will, as it were, keep *his* side of the covenantal agreement."[40] In God's promise, the church is commanded in doxology to continue its participation in the further coming of the kingdom. Therefore, the church is sent out in mission in the world in hope that what God commands, God is promising to accomplish. Yet what the church seeks to accomplish is faithfulness to Christ that names the body of Christ as the martyr-church.

Doxological Oblation into the Martyr-Church

At the Eucharist the church receives the oblationary offering of Christ, by offering itself as a sacrificial oblation (thank-offering) with Christ's offering by the Spirit to the Father. This joint oblation begins at the Table but continues as the church is exhaled by the Spirit to continue to be the broken body and spilled blood of Christ for the present and future coming kingdom. Louis-Marie Chauvet further illumines why ethics must be shaped by eschatology. God sends the church to embody its return gift by caring for the world as its continual becoming the body of Christ participating in God's further restoration. "To become historically and eschatologically the body of him whom they are offering sacramentally, the members of the assembly are committed to live out their own oblation of themselves in self-giving to others as Christ did, a self-giving called agape between

---

39 *Hymns on the Lord's Supper* (Bristol: Farley, 1745), no. 101, st. 4, 87. See also no. 53, st. 2, 44; and no. 95, st. 3, 83.
40 Ole Borgen, *John Wesley on the Sacraments* (Grand Rapids: Zondervan, 1985), 80.

brothers and sisters."[41] Craig Hovey names this doxological oblation in the world as communion into the martyr-church. As the church is the body and blood of Christ, broken and spilled out for the world, the invitation to martyrdom is never couched in fear of securing a future or a strategy to achieve anything. "It is true that there is no reason for disciples to die, in that they accomplish anything by their deaths. But this is not sufficient to keep them from becoming martyrs, since . . . martyrs do not die for 'reasons.'"[42] Being open to martyrdom is a witness to being in solidarity with Christ as both the undoing and absorbing of violence in the world, the kingdom of God.

> Breaking and dividing does not mean waste and poverty; distribution does not mean depletion; consumption does not mean exhaustion. The loss of bread, like the loss of life, names a free expenditure in the face of the promise for restoration. The church gives away its bread as it gives away its body—in the hope of the resurrection by which its common life is renewed with replenished resources and in which its suffering members are preserved in its witness to the world through the same miracle.[43]

This openness to martyrdom does not seek or desire death or proclaim the death of a martyr as a good, but it remains receptive to being blown by the Spirit, come what may. This posture of being broken and spilled out is always done in doxological joy because of the hope of the Resurrection. A church opened up to the possibility of martyrdom is not throwing away its future, but fully embracing it, an open-armed reception. Life is received and embodied through brokenness. Too often idolatrous ecclesiologies are guided by an ethic of self-preservation. An eschatological imagination of the Eucharist in the Wesleyan tradition proclaims that doxological living means being willing to be broken open for the world and released from the fear of death. An eschatological imagination of the Eucharist in the Wesleyan tradition means being freed from holding any person or empire as an enemy but participating in the world's redemption.

Hovey continues to speak of the frailty of the church that becomes the broken body:

---

41   Louis-Marie Chauvet, *Symbol and Sacrament: A Sacramental Reinterpretation of Christian Existence,* trans. Patrick Madigan and Madeleine Beaumont (Collegeville, MN: The Liturgical Press, 1995), 277.

42   Craig Hovey, *To Share in the Body: A Theology of Martyrdom for Today's Church* (Grand Rapids: Brazos, 2008), 93.

43   Ibid., 94–95.

"We break this bread to share in the body of Christ". . . with these words the church also confesses its belief that broken bread does not lead to no-bread, that its martyred members are not silent members, that its frailty is met with the promise of resurrection. It does not exchange weakness for power or stop sharing bread in an attempt to shore up for itself the remnants of its remaining strength. Instead it gives of itself all the more freely to the extent that its memory of the Father's faithfulness to the Son is enacted in the very constitution of its existence.[44]

Just like Christ, the martyrs, though killed, live through the church's present ministry and testimony. The eschatological resurrection hope moves the church in joy to keep being broken and spilled out in love for the world as a further participation in theosis. The body of Christ, the church, is to be broken and spilled out for the world as the continual doxological *latreia* of its sacrificial oblation offered at the Table.

The "So What" of an Eschatological Imagination of Doxological Martyrdom

Such an imagination seeks to transform persons from selfish-materialistic individuals to become the body of Christ gathered at the Table in hope and healing and then to be sent out to become the broken body and spilled blood of Christ. This is the ongoing sanctification of the church.

Archbishop Oscar Romero serves as a powerful witness of one whose oblationary doxological sacrifice ended in his own life being taken. His very testimony serves as a confirmation of the resurrected theotic hope into which the church is invited to live. In a phone interview two weeks prior to his murder, Archbishop Oscar Romero proclaimed,

As a shepherd, I am obliged by divine mandate to give my life for those I love—for all Salvadorans, even for those who may be going to kill me. If the threats are carried out, from this moment I offer my blood to God for the redemption and for the resurrection of El Salvador. . . . Martyrdom is a grace of God that I do not believe I deserve. But if God accepts the sacrifice of my life, let my blood be a seed of freedom and the sign that hope will soon be a reality. Let my death, if it is accepted by God, be for my people's liberation and as a witness of hope in the future.[45]

---

44   Ibid., 95.
45   Archbishop Oscar Romero, from Bryan P. Stone, *Evangelism after Christendom: The Theology and Practice of Christian* (Grand Rapids: Brazos, 2007), 302, quoted in James R. Brockman, *Romero: A Life*, rev. ed. (Maryknoll, NY: Orbis, 1989), 248.

PART II

Eucharist and Ministry

NINE

Eucharist and Worship

Robin Knowles Wallace

The 166 Eucharistic *Hymns on the Lord's Supper* (HLS) by John and Charles Wesley in 1745, with nine printings during their lifetime,[1] give us, through the medium of congregational song, the breadth and depth of human life lived in God's presence.[2] This essay will focus on the closing hymns in the section now called "After the Sacrament," numbers 158–66 in HLS,[3] to consider why

---

1   John & Charles Wesley. *Hymns on the Lord's Supper* (Bristol: Farley, 1745). (Duke online edition available at http://divinity.duke.edu/initiatives/cswt/john-wesley). This is the version from which the texts are quoted throughout this paper. Additional editions include:
    2nd Bristol: Farley, 1747
    3rd London: Cock, 1751
    4th London: sold at the Foundery, 1757
    5th Bristol: Pine, 1762
    6th Bristol: Pine, 1771
    7th London: Hawes, 1776
    8th London: Hawes, 1779
    9th London: Paramore, 1786

2   The foundations for this essay may be seen in Carlton R. Young's vast work in congregational song including editing the Methodist and United Methodist hymnals of 1964 and 1989; *Music of the Heart: John and Charles Wesley on Music and Musicians: An Anthology* (Carol Stream, IL: Hope, 1995); and his work with Global Praise through the General Board of Global Ministries. Don E. Saliers's work includes *Worship as Theology: Foretaste of Glory Divine* (Nashville: Abingdon Press, 1994) and *Worship Come to Its Senses* (Nashville: Abingdon Press, 1996). Other Wesleyan scholars whose work confirms these foundations are Geoffrey Wainwright, *Doxology: The Praise of God in Worship, Doctrine, and Life: A Systematic Theology* (New York: Oxford University Press, 1980); and Susan J. White, "Charles Wesley and Contemporary Theology," in *Charles Wesley: Life, Literature and Legacy*, ed. Kenneth G. C. Newport and Ted A. Campbell (Werrington, Peterborough, U.K.: Epworth, 2007), 515–31, and the teaching life of Kendall McCabe.

3   Comparison of Brevint's textual organization and the Wesleys' hymnic organization:
    Section 1 The Importance of Well Understanding the Nature of this Sacrament
    Section 2 Concerning the Sacrament, as it is a Memorial of the Sufferings and Death of Christ
    Section 3 Concerning the Sacrament as it is a Sign of Present Graces
    Section 4 Concerning the Sacrament, as it is a Means of Grace
    Section 5 Concerning the Sacrament, as it is a Pledge of Future Glory

eucharistic worship is essential to Christian theology and living as it acknowledges human brokenness and, through Christ's redeeming work, celebrates
and gives thanks for God's astonishing gifts of salvation and grace.

Hymns on the Lord's Supper first appeared with John Wesley's abridgment
of Church of England clergyman Daniel Brevint's *The Christian Sacrament
and Sacrifice* (1673). Wesley's use of Brevint's work was organized into eight
sections, which became five sections of hymns. The nine hymns in the sixth
section may have been an appendix, added during the late stages of publication.[4] They were not grouped into a section, "After the Sacrament," until
the second edition of the collection in 1747. Of the nine hymns, four[5] were
previously published in *Hymns and Sacred Poems* (HSP) in 1739, with one of
these based on a text by George Herbert and, some believe, adapted by John
Wesley.[6] The final text (no. 166) of twenty-two stanzas is described by Daniel Stevick as "clearly not a hymn to be sung, but a final reflection, challenge
and prayer to be read and considered by the Church."[7] While none of these
texts can be definitively said to be authored by Charles Wesley,[8] for over

---

Section 6 Concerning the Sacrament, as it is a Sacrifice. And First, of the Com-
    memorative Sacrifice.
Section 7 Concerning the Sacrifice of Ourselves
Section 8 Concerning the Sacrifice of our Goods
Section 1 As it is a Memorial of the Sufferings and Death of Christ, 1–27
Section 2 As it is a Sign and a Means of Grace, 28–92
Section 3 The Sacrament a Pledge of Heaven, 93–115
Section 4 The Holy Eucharist as it implies a Sacrifice, 116–27
Section 5 Concerning the Sacrifice of our Persons, 128–57
Added in the 1747 edition: Section 6 After the Sacrament, 158–66

4   Frank Baker, "Approaching a Variorum Edition of Hymns on the Lord's Sup-
     per" in *Proceedings of The Charles Wesley Society*, vol. 2 (1995): 10–11.
5   No. 160 "Welcome delicious sacred cheer" appeared first in *HSP* (1739), 126–28;
     no. 161 "Lord, and God of heavenly powers" appeared first in *HSP* (1739), 128;
     no. 163 "Glory be to God on high" appeared first in HSP (1739), 128–29; and no.
     164, "Sons of God, triumphant rise" appeared first in *HSP* (1739), 190–92.
6   Editorial Introduction for *HLS* (1745) online. See also Daniel B. Stevick, *The Al-
     tar's Fire: Charles Wesley's Hymns on the Lord's Supper, 1745 Introduction and Expo-
     sition* (Werrington, Peterborough, U.K.: Epworth Press, 2004), 245.
7   Stevick, *The Altar's Fire*, 219.
8   According to the "First Line Index of all Verse by John or Charles Wesley in
     Editions They Published during Their Lifetime" (http://divinity.duke.edu/
     initiatives-centers/cswt/research-resources/wesley-studies-resources) eight of
     the texts are questionably by Charles, the three brought over from *HSP* and the
     four new to this collection. It is interesting to note that the question of authorship
     does not appear in all discussions on these texts; notably J. Ernest Rattenbury, *The
     Eucharistic Hymns of John and Charles Wesley* (London: Epworth Press, 1948), 128.
     Stevick follows the understanding that John adapted George Herbert's text for
     160 HLS but says nothing about the other eight hymns in this section, 214–222;
     Stevick's appendix on "Authorship in Question," 245–49, studies three other

their first forty years in print, they formed for Methodists a summing up of thanksgiving and praise for salvation from the brokenness of human life into the joys of relationship with God.

Charles's diary for Easter Day, April 14, 1745, suggests the first public use of this collection, and his entry for the following Tuesday stated, "We kept the octave, communicating every day; and the Lord never sent us away without a blessing."[9] These final hymns suggest the experiential reasons for "constant communion"[10] during weekly worship, reminding followers of the Wesleys of the joys of communion that can be experienced during every worship service. As Stevick notes, "these hymns that follow the sacrament express only gratitude, joy and praise."[11] We will introduce the texts individually, discuss the themes that emerge collectively, and then discuss the importance of Eucharist for worship.

The Hymns

Hymn 158

> [1] *All praise to God above*
> *In whom we have believed!*
> *The tokens of whose dying love*
> *We have ev'n now received,*
> *Have with his flesh been fed,*
> *And drank his precious blood:*
> *His precious blood is drink indeed,*
> *His flesh immortal food.*
>
> [2] *O what a taste is this*
> *Which now in Christ we know,*
> *An earnest of our glorious bliss,*

---

texts and suggests this is a field for future study. S. T. Kimbrough Jr. includes two of the nine texts in *The Lyrical Theology of Charles Wesley: A Reader* (Eugene, OR: Cascade Books/Wipf and Stock, 2011), 217–18, 236–38, and mentions two others on 57, without raising questions of authorship.

9   Rattenbury, *The Eucharistic Hymns of John and Charles Wesley*, 12.

10   John Wesley, "The Duty of Constant Communion," in *The Works of John Wesley: Sermons*, vol. 4, ed. Albert Outler (Nashville: Abingdon Press, 1986). On Luke 22:19.

11   Stevick, *The Altar's Fire*, 214.

Our heaven begun below!
When he the table spreads,
How royal is the cheer!
With rapture we lift up our heads,
And own that God is here.

[3] He bids us taste his grace,
The joys of angels prove,
The stammerers' tongues are loosed to praise
Our dear Redeemer's love.
Salvation to our God
That sits upon the throne;
Salvation be alike bestowed
On his triumphant Son!

[4] The Lamb for sinners slain,
Who died to die no more,
Let all the ransomed sons of men
With all his hosts adore:
Let earth and heaven be joined
His glories to display,
And hymn the Saviour of mankind
In one eternal day.

This hymn of praise begins with proclamation of our belief in God and Christ in response to receiving Communion and it testifies to the work of Communion in bringing us salvation and joy. It is one of the five original texts that appear in this section, but research does not uncover its reprinting in its full form in any hymnals beyond HLS, at least in the United States.[12] What does occur in eight instances, related to the Methodist Episcopal Church, South, and the CME Church in America, is a selection of stanzas 2 and 4, "O what a taste is this," divided into four stanzas and placed under the heading "The Lord's Supper."

---

12 Hymnary.org was used for research on appearances of texts in hymnals in the United States, accessed February 27–March 2, 2013. This research site is supported by Christian Classics Ethereal Library, Calvin Institute of Christian Worship, Calvin College, The Hymn Society in the United States and Canada, and the National Endowment for the Humanities.

Hymn 159

> *[1] All glory and praise to Jesus our Lord!*
> *His ransoming grace we gladly record,*
> *His bloody oblation, and death on the tree,*
> *Hath purchased salvation and heaven for me.*

> *[2] The Saviour hath died for me and for you,*
> *The blood is applied, the record is true;*
> *The Spirit bears witness, and speaks in the blood,*
> *And gives us the fitness for living with God.*

This hymn, the second original to HLS, gives praise for grace and records Christ's gift of salvation for us. It states the personal belief that Christ died for each of us (specifically, *me* and *you*) and that the Spirit bears witness and gives us fitness "for living with God." It bears brief but clear testimony to the bloody work of Jesus in ransoming us through grace.

A text by Charles Wesley that begins the same but diverges in the second line—"All glory and praise to Jesus our Lord! So plenteous in grace and so true to his word"—appears in twenty-nine hymnals in the United States through the 1800s, paired with the gospel refrain "Hallelujah, thine the glory." The Communion text does not appear to have been reprinted in the States.[13]

Hymn 160

> *[1] Welcome delicious sacred cheer,*
> *Welcome my God, my Saviour dear!*
> *O with me, in me, live and dwell;*
> *Thine, earthly joy surpasses quite,*
> *The depths of thy supreme delight*
> *Not angel-tongues can fully tell.*

> *[2] What streams of sweetness from the bowl*
> *Surprise and deluge all my soul,*
> *Sweetness which is, and makes divine,*
> *Surely from God's right hand they flow,*
> *From thence derived to earth below,*
> *To cheer us with immortal wine.*

---

13   According to hymnary.org.

[3] Soon as I taste the heavenly bread,
What manna o'er my soul is shed,
Manna that angels never [k]new!
Victorious sweetness fills my heart,
Such as my God delights t' impart,
Mighty to save, and sin subdue.

[4] I had forgot my heavenly birth,
My soul degen'rate clave to earth,
In sense and sin's base pleasures drowned,
When God assumed humanity,
And spilt his sacred blood for me,
To wash, and lift me from the ground.

[5] Soon as his love has raised me up,
He mingles blessings in a cup,
And sweetly meets my ravished taste;
Joyous I now throw off my load,
I cast my sins and care on God,
And wine becomes a wing at last.

[6] Upborne on this, I mount, I fly;
Regaining swift my native sky,
I wipe my streaming eyes, and see
Him, whom I seek, for whom I sue,
My God, my Saviour there I view,
And live with him who died for me.

"Welcome, delicious sacred cheer" first appeared in HSP (126–28). It is closely based on George Herbert's "The Banquet" from his collection *The Temple* (Cambridge: Buck & Daniel, 1633; 175–77, no. 153). The variation builds on Herbert's images of Communion cup, bread, and flight. Herbert's meter of 73.7.73.7 is changed to 88.8.88.8 often simply by adding adjectives: *delicious, earthly, supreme, angel, immortal, heavenly* (twice), *base, sacred, ravished, native,* and *streaming.* John Wesley retains Herbert's rhyme scheme of AABCCB and three-quarters of Herbert's original rhyming words, and condenses Herbert's nine stanzas into six. This is a sensual poem and hymn, particularly in its opening three stanzas, about the sweetness of the wine and the blessed nature of the bread, which Wesley twice names *manna.* The joys of the wine and bread are symbolic of God's deep love for humanity, including our heavenly birth and God's taking on flesh, the cleansing of our sin and fallenness, the freedom granted by forgiveness, and the lifting up of our spirits to see and live with God/Christ. This hymn does not appear in hymnals in the United States.

Hymn 161

"Therefore with Angels and Archangels . . ."

[1] Lord, and God of heavenly powers,
Theirs—yet Oh! Benignly ours;
Glorious King, let earth proclaim,
Worms attempt to chant thy name.

[2] Thee to laud in songs divine,
Angels and archangels join;
We with them our voices raise,
Echoing thy eternal praise.

[3] Holy, holy, holy Lord,
Live by heaven and earth adored!
Full of thee they ever cry
Glory be to God most high!

This text appeared first in HSP (no. 128). It is drawn from the Preface to Holy Communion in the Book of Common Prayer, still used in Communion prayers today introducing the Sanctus:

Therefore with Angels and Archangels, and with all the company of heaven, we laud and magnify thy glorious Name; evermore praising thee, and saying, Holy, holy, holy, Lord God of Hosts: Heaven and earth are full of thy Glory. Glory be to thee, O Lord Most High.

The first two stanzas of the hymn weave together God's praise by angels/archangels and we/our/earth/worms. The third stanza begins with the threefold *holy, holy, holy,* and *heaven* and *earth* join in, and then the stanza ends with *glory.*

It appeared in full in eleven hymnals in the United States in the 1800s, primarily in various editions of *A Collection of Hymns for Use in Public, Social and Domestic Worship; Hymnbook of the Methodist Protestant Church;* and *Songs of Zion: or, The Christian's New Hymnbook, for the Use of Methodists.*

Hymn 162

> [1] *Hosanna in the highest*
> *To our exalted Saviour,*
> > *Who left behind*
> > *For all mankind*
> *These tokens of his favour:*
> *His bleeding love and mercy,*
> *His all-redeeming Passion,*
> > *Who here displays*
> > *And gives the grace*
> *Which brings us our salvation.*
>
> [2] *Louder than gathered waters,*
> *Or bursting peals of thunder,*
> *We lift our voice*
> *And speak our joys,*
> *And shout our loving wonder!*
> *Shout all our elder brethren,*
> *While we record the story*
> *Of him that came,*
> *And suffered shame*
> *To carry us to glory.*
>
> [3] *Angels in fixed amazement*
> *Around our altars hover,*
> *With eager gaze*
> *Adore the grace*
> *Of our eternal lover:*
> *Himself and all his fulness*
> *Who gives to the believer;*
> *And by this bread*
> *Whoe'er are fed*
> *Shall live with God forever!*

The placement of this third of the original texts between the Preface and the Gloria in Excelsis from the Book of Common Prayer's service of Holy Communion may suggest the communion liturgy as its source as well, as "Hosanna in the highest" appears there following the Preface. The first stanza praises Christ for his grace and favor in leaving this meal for us. The second stanza begins with the gathered waters of Genesis 1 and the thunder of Revelation[14] over which our voices join those of previous Christians (*elder brethren*) in telling the story of Jesus. The third stanza joins our praise with descended angels in praise of "our eternal lover" who through communion gives us life forever.

This hymn appears in *Hymns Ancient and Modern* (related to the Church of England), revised 1924, at no. 724, as the final hymn in the section on Communion. In the revised 1950 *Hymns Ancient and Modern*, it appears at no. 421 in the section on Holy Communion with an alternative beginning for the tune by Sir S. H. Nicholson for stanzas 2 and 3 which helps the natural word accent fall appropriately on the first syllable, on *louder* and *angels*, as opposed to hosanna in stanza 1, with its accent on the second syllable. It does not seem to have appeared in hymnals in the United States.

Hymn 163

> "*Glory be to God on High, and on Earth Peace . . .*"
>
> [1] *Glory be to God on high,*
> *God whose glory fills the sky;*
> *Peace on earth to man forgiven,*
> *Man the well-belov'd of heaven!*
>
> [2] *Sovereign Father, heavenly King,*
> *Thee we now presume to sing,*
> *Glad thine attributes confess,*
> *Glorious all and numberless.*
>
> [3] *Hail by all thy works adored,*
> *Hail the everlasting Lord!*
> *Thee with thankful hearts we prove,*
> *Lord of power, and God of love.*
>
> [4] *Christ our Lord and God we own,*
> *Christ the Father's only Son:*
> *Lamb of God for sinners slain,*
> *Saviour of offending man.*
>
> [5] *Bow thine ear, in mercy bow,*

---

14   Revelation 4:5; 6:1; 8:5; 11:19; 14:2; and 16:8.

Hear, the world's atonement thou:
Jesu, in thy name we pray,
Take, O take our sins away.

[6] Powerful advocate with God,
Justify us by thy blood!
Bow thine ear, in mercy bow,
Hear, the world's atonement thou!

[7] Hear, for thou, O Christ, alone,
With thy glorious Sire art One,
One the Holy Ghost with thee,
One supreme eternal Three!

"Glory be to God on high" no. 163, found first in HSP (128–29), was based on the Gloria in the liturgy of the Book of Common Prayer. The first three stanzas of the hymn refer to the opening of the Gloria:

Glory be to God on high,
   and on earth peace, good will towards men.

We praise thee, we bless thee,
   we worship thee,
   we glorify thee,
   we give thanks to thee for thy great glory,
   O Lord God, heavenly King, God the Father Almighty.

Stanza 4 of the hymn picks up the Gloria lines about Jesus, with stanzas 5 and 6 speaking of Christ's work of atonement, taking our sin away:

O Lord, the only-begotten Son, Jesus Christ;
O Lord God, Lamb of God, Son of the Father,
   that takest away the sins of the world,
   have mercy upon us.

Thou that takest away the sins of the world,
   receive our prayer.
Thou that sittest at the right hand of God the Father,
   have mercy upon us.

Stanza 7 of the hymn, like the closing of the Gloria, sings of the Trinity and its unity:

> *For thou only art holy;*
> *thou only art the Lord;*
> *thou only, O Christ,*
>   *with the Holy Ghost,*
>   *art most high in the glory of God the Father. Amen.*

Notice the repetition of lines 5ab at lines 6cd. As we will see, in later versions of this text accommodations are made so that that repetition does not occur. The only changes made in this hymn text between 1739 (HSP) and 1745 (HLS) are the subtraction of exclamation marks; while the setting at no. 163 in HLS has five in its seven stanzas, the earlier version has twice as many.[15] These exclamation marks are matched in exuberance by the language of the text in describing both the Trinity and God's work on our behalf. The first three stanzas relate to God our creator; the adjectives and names used include: *glory* (twice), *glorious* (twice), *sovereign Father, heavenly King, numberless thy attributes, everlasting Lord, Lord of power, God of love.* The next three stanzas sing of Jesus, and in these stanzas there are more names for Jesus than in any of the other eight hymns of this section: *Christ our Lord and God, Lamb of God, Christ the Father's only Son, Savior of offending man, Jesu, powerful advocate with God,* and *the world's atonement* (twice).

Human beings are, beginning in stanza 4, sinners and offensive, in need of having our sins removed, and justified by Christ's blood. Jesu is listening to our cry to bow his ear in mercy and to take our sins away, as stanzas 5 and 6 plead for forgiveness, bookended with the lines "Bow thine ear, in mercy bow, / Hear, the world's atonement thou." The condition of humanity is that for which we now sing glory to God: *man forgiven, man the well-belov'd of heaven.* We presume to sing, glad to confess God's attributes, we hail God who is adored by all God's works, with thankful hearts we prove that God is a God of power and love. The final doxological stanza is Trinitarian: *Christ is one with his glorious Sire and one with the Holy Ghost, one supreme eternal Three.*

In a survey of 108 appearances, beginning with the opening lines of this text, from hymnals primarily published in the United States between 1790 and 1917,[16] forty-one occurrences use the first stanza of Wesley's hymn followed generally by three other stanzas of praise by Unitarian John Taylor

---

15   HSP, additional exclamation marks in lines 2:1, 4:2, 4:4, 5:2 and 7:4.
16   Found at hymnary.org.

(1750–1826) that were printed first in *Selection of Hymns for Social Worship* (London: Norwich, 1795). Nine appearances add an anonymous stanza in the midst of Taylor's stanzas and six appearances diverge at the third line, creating a general psalm-like hymn of praise. That leaves fifty-two appearances using only Wesley's text, with eleven using all seven stanzas as is and seventeen combining stanzas 5 and 6 most often to say:

> *Jesu, in thy name we pray,*
> *Take, O take our sins away*
> *Bow thine ear, in mercy bow,*
> *Hear, the world's atonement thou.*

Nine appearances omit stanza 6 altogether, and the rest have a combination of stanzas. Except for one instance—*Hymn and Tune Book of the Methodist Episcopal Church, South,* 1902, where it appears under the category "The Lord's Supper"—the text appears under categories of worship such as adoration, praise, worship, thanksgiving, or introduction to worship. It should be noted that this is the first hymn in this section to be widely used, in its various forms, by various denominations—not only Methodists, but United Christian Friends, Lutherans, Universalists, Church of Christ, Baptists, Wesleyan Methodists, and Christian Scientists.

Hymn 164

> *[1] Sons of God, triumphant rise,*
> *Shout th' accomplished sacrifice,*
> *Shout your sins in Christ forgiven,*
> *Sons of God, and heirs of heaven!*

> *[2] Ye that round our altars throng,*
> *List'ning angels join the song;*
> *Sing with us, ye heavenly powers,*
> *Pardon, grace, and glory ours!*

> *[3] Love's mysterious work is done;*
> *Greet we now th' atoning Son,*
> *Healed and quickened by his blood,*
> *Joined to Christ, and one with God.*

[4] *Christ, of all our hopes, the seal,*
Peace divine in Christ we feel,
Pardon to our souls applied,
Dead for all, for me he died.

[5] *Sin shall tyrannize no more,*
Purged its guilt, dissolved its power,
Jesus makes our hearts his throne,
There he lives, and reigns alone.

[6] *Grace our every thought controls,*
Heaven is opened in our souls,
Everlasting life is won,
Glory is on earth begun.

[7] *Christ in us; in him we see*
Fulness of the deity,
Beam of the eternal beam;
Life divine we taste in him.

[8] *Him by faith we taste below,*
Mightier joys ordained to know,
When his utmost grace we prove,
Rise to heaven by perfect love.

This hymn first appeared in HSP as "Hymn After the Sacrament." Like no. 162 above, "Hosanna in the highest," it quickly repeats the imperative to *shout*. Stanza 3's "Love's mysterious work is done" is echoed as "Love's redeeming work is done" in the familiar Wesley hymn for Easter, "Christ the Lord is risen today,"[17] also appearing in HSP. The following line—"Greet we now th' atoning Son"—was originally *th' accepted*; the phrase was changed to *th' atoning* in the fourth edition of HSP in 1743, and in HLS.

This hymn, in versions of three (st. 1, 3, and 8) and four (st. 1, 2, 3, and 8) stanzas, appeared in hymnals in the United States from 1845 to 1902. Like "Glory be to God on high" above, it only appears once under the heading "The Lord's Supper"; more often it appears under "Mediation of Christ" or other headings. Stanzas 1 and 8 do include mention of *sacrifice* and *taste* but

---

17   HSP, 1739, no. 209.

[7] *O what a flame of sacred love*
  Was kindled by the altar's fire!
They lived on earth like those above,
  Glad rivals of the heavenly choir.

[8] *Strong in the strength herewith received,*
  And mindful of the crucified;
His confessors for him they lived,
  For him his faithful martyrs died.

[9] *Their souls from chains of flesh released,*
  By torture from their bodies driven
With violent faith the kingdom seized,
  And fought and forced their way to heaven.

[10] *Where is the pure primeval flame,*
  Which in their faithful bosom glowed?
Where are the followers of the Lamb,
  The dying witnesses for God?

[11] *Why is the faithful seed decreased,*
  The life of God extinct and dead?
The daily sacrifice is ceased,
  And charity to heaven is fled.

[12] *Sad mutual causes of decay,*
  Slackness and vice together move,
Grown cold we cast the means away,
  And quenched our latest spark of love.

[13] *The sacred signs thou didst ordain,*
  Our pleasant things are all laid waste;
To men of lips and hearts profane,
  To dogs and swine, and heathen cast.

[14] *Thine holy ordinance contemned* [sic],
  Hath let the flood of evil in,
And those who by thy name are named,
  The sinners unbaptized out-sin.

[15] *But canst thou not thy work revive*
　　Once more in our degenerate years?
O wouldst thou with thy rebels strive,
　　And melt them into gracious tears!

[16] *O wouldst thou to thy church return!*
　　For which the faithful remnant sighs,
For which the drooping nations mourn,
　　Restore the daily sacrifice.

[17] *Return, and with thy servants sit,*
　　Lord of the sacramental feast,
And satiate us with heavenly meat,
　　And make the world thy happy guest.

[18] *Now let the spouse, reclined on thee,*
　　Come up out of the wilderness,
From every spot, and wrinkle free,
　　And washed, and perfected in grace.

[19] *Thou hear'st the pleading Spirit's groan,*
　　Thou know'st the groaning Spirit's will:
Come in thy gracious kingdom down,
　　And all thy ransomed servants seal.

[20] *Come quickly, Lord, the Spirit cries,*
　　The number of thy saints complete,
Come quickly, Lord, the bride replies,
　　And make us all for glory meet.

[21] *Erect thy tabernacle here,*
　　The New Jerusalem send down,
Thyself amidst thy saints appear,
　　And seat us on thy dazzling throne.

[22] *Begin the great millennial day,*
　　Now, Saviour, with a shout descend,
Thy standard in the heavens display,
　　And bring thy joy which ne'er shall end!

Simply, in the third stanza, second line, was changed to *simple* in the 1771 sixth edition and following editions. The entire text appears in S. T. Kimbrough Jr.'s *The Lyrical Theology of Charles Wesley: A Reader,*[20] under the heading "Eucharist/Holy Communion/Lord's Supper" and the subheading "The Community of Faith," at 115 entitled "Constant Communion." It has never appeared in hymnals in the United States, Methodist or otherwise. We will return to the message of this text after lifting up a few common themes from all these texts.

Common Themes

These "After the Sacrament" hymns deal with the human condition without God by describing humanity as: hungry and thirsty (no. 158); cast down to earth, groveling on the ground, laden with sins and care, in tears (no. 160, stanzas 4–6); worms attempting to "chant thy name" (no. 161, st. 1:4); in need of salvation and grace (no. 162); offensive sinners (no. 163); in need of healing and pardon, tyrannized by sin (its guilt and its power) (no. 164); and chained by flesh, decaying, slack, grown cold (no. 166).

Christ's redeeming work is praised: he gives immortal food, spreads the table, gives salvation (no. 158); ransoms with grace, purchases salvation, bears witness, and makes us fit to live with God (no. 159); assumed humanity, raised us up by love, bears our burdens, gives us wings (no. 160); gives grace which brings salvation, came and suffered shame to carry us to glory, our eternal Lover (no. 162). Jesus is the Lord of Power, God of Love, Lamb of God, Saviour, World's Atonement, powerful advocate (no. 163); Eternal Beam, Life Divine, makes us heirs of heaven, seals our hopes (no. 164); our meeting place (165); our lamb-like Lord and wise Master (no. 166).

God through Christ changes our human life, so that we are fit to live with God (no. 159); earthly joy is surpassed, as we experience depths of delight and streams of sweetness and are overwhelmed with wine and manna. Though we had forgotten our heavenly birth—we are now raised up with blessing and sweetness, joyous, fly, regain our native sky, and see God face to face (no. 160). We praise loudly, lift our voices, speak our joys, and shout our loving wonder (no. 162); and we recognize thankfully that we are well-beloved (no. 163). We become triumphant, rising, shouting, singing, greeting, joined to Christ and God, hopeful, freed from guilt and power of sin, filled with grace, a place of heaven and glory, and light (no. 164). In sweet accord and perfect harmony (no. 165), we are transported to Eden

---

20   S. T. Kimbrough Jr., *The Lyrical Theology of Charles Wesley: A Reader* (Eugene, OR: Cascade Books/Wipf and Stock, 2011), 236–38.

in eating with Christ, rivals of the heavenly choir, Christ's happy guest, washed and perfected in grace, free from every spot and wrinkle, fit for glory, and have joy which never ends (no. 166).

Frequency of Communion

> For I received from the Lord what I also handed on to you, that the Lord Jesus on the night when he was betrayed took a loaf of bread, and when he had given thanks, he broke it and said, "This is my body that is for you. Do this in remembrance of me." In the same way he took the cup also, after supper, saying, "This cup is the new covenant in my blood. Do this, as often as you drink it, in remembrance of me." For as often as you eat this bread and drink the cup, you proclaim the Lord's death until he comes. 1 Corinthians 11:23-26 (NRSV)

These words of institution suggest frequent Communion, with their phrase "Do, this, as often as you drink it, in remembrance of me." So the church at times in its history has stressed weekly, and sometimes even daily, Communion. For certain branches of the church, the Eastern Orthodox for example, if Communion is not celebrated, the church has not worshiped. The early Reformers tried to move the church from yearly reception of Communion to weekly, but only succeeded in quarterly reception. For English-speakers, Cranmer's success with morning and evening prayer in the Book of Common Prayer meant that Communion was no longer the "normal" Sunday service.[21]

Yet, John Wesley writing to "Our Brethren in America" from Bristol on September 10, 1784, said, "I also advise the elders to administer the Supper of the Lord on every Lord's Day."[22] But this did not become the practice, as Methodist liturgical historian Paul S. Sanders reminds us:

> Certainly the Lord's Supper was not central to Methodist worship. The Love Feast may at first have been as important; it was more frequently held, and in a revivalistic atmosphere the fervent testimonies of awakened believers may have caused it to seem more vital. Still, the Eucharist would have been celebrated at every quarterly visitation by the presiding elder riding his rounds; the people may have exerted more effort to be present at those quarterly meetings than it would occur to modern Methodists to suspect.[23]

---

21   James F. White, *Introduction to Christian Worship* (Nashville: Abingdon Press, 2001), 142–43.

22   John Wesley, Letter to "Our Brethren in America," September 10, 1784, *Letters of the Rev. John Wesley, A.M.*, vol. 7, ed. John Telford (London: Epworth Press, 1931), 239.

23   Paul S. Sanders, "The Sacraments in Early American Methodism," *Church History* 26, no. 4 (December 1957), 369.

Writing in 1976, J. Robert Nelson suggested that Methodist eucharistic usage had moved from constant Communion (referring to Wesley's sermon, "The Duty of Constant Communion") to benign neglect to sacramental recovery.[24] Thirty-seven years later, The United Methodist Church still varies in its celebrations of Communion from quarterly (following Reformation and circuit-rider rhythms) to monthly (generally first Sundays) to more frequent.

Let us return to the final hymn of the collection, "Happy the saints of former days" (no. 166). J. Ernest Rattenbury suggests that part of the interest in this text derives from "the use Anglo-Catholics made of its emphasis of the Daily Sacrifice in the controversies of 1870. There are several instances of Wesley's valuation of the Daily Sacrifice in these hymns."[25]

Stanzas 1 and 2 of the hymn speak of the early church receiving every joyful day the tokens of Jesus' dying [expiring] love: their frequent remembrance of his sacrifice, breaking the bread from house to house, and drinking the spirit transmitted in the sacred cup. The following stanzas remind us that with this frequent communion Jesus' constant presence was felt, leading forward into eternity, and strengthening Christians through the hardships of this earthly life.

Stanza 10 asks the questions "Where is that passion nowadays?" "Where are the works?" "Where are the dying witnesses?" Beginning in stanza 11 the answer comes: "because the daily sacrifice is ceased," we've grown cold, and while God has set these things out we have profaned and wasted the gifts we were given. Stanza 14 says, "we have turned away from your holy ordinance," and Christians are "out-sinning the unbaptized." The hymn turns again in stanza 15 to address God, asking for revival of God's work, melting the hardness of us "rebels of God," pleading for God's return to the church and restoration of the daily sacrifice.

The daily sacrifice, the heavenly meal, where the Lord sits with the servants, is then what can make the world God's happy guest. Here will then be the return from the wilderness, the washing and perfecting in grace. Here the Spirit will plead and groan with us, to call God's kingdom into being, and indeed the text picks up energy here: come quickly, come quickly, complete the number of your saints, seal your ransomed servants, erect your dwelling place [tabernacle], appear among us, bring in "the great millennial day" of your glory and joy.

---

24 J. Robert Nelson, "Methodist Eucharistic Usage: From Constant Communion to Benign Neglect to Sacramental Recovery," *Journal of Ecumenical Studies* 13 (Spring 1976): 278–84.

25 Rattenbury, *The Eucharistic Hymns of John and Charles Wesley*, H-54, n. 2 in American Edition, ed. Timothy J. Crouch (Cleveland: OSL Publications, 1990).

So the text moves from the simple practice of the early church in its daily sacrifice/Communion through the neglect of the sacrifice/Communion and then pleading through the Spirit for communion to return, that things spoken about the great future promised might come to pass with joy. These were the hopes of the Wesleys, that God's Spirit through more frequent reception of Communion would move the church to greater witness in the world. These are the hopes of many in the United Methodist movement, teaching and leading in United Methodist seminaries and churches—that through participation in the sacrament, the holy act of Communion with God and neighbor, the United Methodist Church might glimpse again the joy and delight of God's great mercy and grace and show the world a clearer picture of the happiness to be found by living lives full of God's grace and love.

It may be, of course, too simple to say that the world and the church will regain its passion for God and holy fellowship by communing daily or weekly, but the gifts of joy and relationship with the Triune God and one another which have traditionally benefited Christians gathering at table should not be underestimated or ignored. May we indeed be like those early followers and those vital Wesleyans communing often and witnessing to the grace and goodness of God.

TEN

Eucharist and Preaching[1]

Richard Eslinger

"It is very meet, right, and our bounden duty . . . "[2]

The single most critical point of clarification at the outset is to understand that the Preface—that liturgical material bookended by the conclusion of the Dialogue and the beginning of the Sanctus—is not a preface. This initial portion of the Prayer over the Gifts by the presiding minister is not a preface *to* the Prayer but the opening sequence *of* the Prayer. In fact, prior to the insertion of the Sanctus within the Eucharistic Prayer—a development first in the East and later in the West—the preface can be discerned as that opening material following the Sursum Corda embodying the dynamics of thanksgiving. In this respect, the Preface may have its origins in the opening portion of the tripartite Jewish after-meals prayer, the *berakah*. The initial section of the *berakah* focused on a joyful thanksgiving to God for the gifts of creation and for covenant.[3] Once the Sanctus was located within the seam between the first and second sections of the anaphora, the Roman rite began to speak of this opening section in Latin as *praefactio*, which "does not mean a preliminary, but a proclamation."[4]

Lamentably, the title was misunderstood and the canon itself (only in the West) was increasingly thought to consist of the Post-Sanctus. Once this notion of *"praefactio"* as "preface" gained currency, it was reinforced in the West by such practices as differing stances for each, the assembly standing for the Preface and kneeling for the Post-Sanctus. The Continental reformers of the sixteenth century simply deleted the Preface entirely, typically beginning the Prayer with the Words of Institution. Among American Methodists, the standard practice was for the minister,

---

1   Much of this chapter is taken from chap. 3 in *Preaching and the Holy Mystery* (San Antonio: Order of Saint Luke, 2016) and used with permission.

2   The Methodist Church Commission on Worship, *The Book of Worship for Church and Home*: With Orders of Worship, Services for the Administration of the Sacraments and Other Aids to Worship According to the Usage of the Methodist Church (Nashville: The Methodist Publishing House, 1965), 19.

3   See Louis Bouyer, *Eucharist* (Notre Dame, IN: University of Notre Dame Press, 1989), 78–90.

4   W. Jardine Grisbrooke, "Preface," A Dictionary of Liturgy and Worship, ed. J. G. Davies (New York: Macmillan Company, 1972), 322.

"facing the Lord's Table" to say two sentences for a preface, the first responding to the last line of the Dialogue ("It is meet, right, and our bounden duty . . . ") and the second introducing the Sanctus ("Therefore with angels and archangels . . .").[5]

Following the reforms of the Second Vatican Council of the Roman Catholic Church, the first three core Eucharistic Prayers of the Mass were provided with numerous Proper Preface options (numbering into the dozens) which related to various seasons, festivals, and occasions. Eucharistic Prayer IV, based upon an Eastern pattern, provided only an invariable preface. The further revisions of the New Roman Missal of 2011 provided for over eighty prefaces, again specified for various days and festivals within the temporal and sanctoral calendars as well as other pastoral and liturgical occasions. Many begin with an opening phrase that essentially repeats and intensifies the last line of the Dialogue. The Tridentine Latin Mass expressed this intensification and repetition simply:

> *Response:*   *Dignum et justum est.*
> *("It is meet and just")*
>
> *Priest:*   *Vere dignum et justum est,*
> *("It is truly meet and just,*
>
> *Aequum et salutare,*
> *right and profitable . . .")*

Now, in the New Missal of 2011, many of the prefaces open with the following:

> *It is truly right and just, our duty and our salvation, always and everywhere to give you thanks, Lord, holy Father, almighty and eternal God, through Christ our Lord.*[6]

---

5   The Methodist Church, *The Book of Worship*, 1964, 19. This last in the series of Communion Ritual services in the tradition of the Anglican Book of Common Prayer for American Methodists did contain four "Proper Prefaces for Certain Days" (ibid., 23). In my own experience in both rural and urban Methodist churches prior to the reforms of the liturgy, these Proper Prefaces were rarely employed in place of the two-sentence Preface in the text of the Ritual..

6   Catholic Doors Ministry, "Preface IV of Lent," http://www.catholicdoors.com/prayers/english5/p03393.htm.

Most of the Western traditions that inherited the variable preface of the Eucharistic Prayer, including the Anglican, Lutheran, Presbyterian, and Methodist communions, also paralleled the Roman Catholic reforms after the Second Vatican Council. For example, the Episcopal Church provided for an increased number of Proper Prefaces in the Book of Common Prayer revision of 1979. The Episcopal Church also continues to offer occasional supplemental liturgical resources, and the 1998 publication *Enriching Our Worship* provides three additional Eucharistic Prayers, each containing distinctive prefaces.[7]

Lutheran revisions of the Eucharistic Prayer have followed along similar trajectories. The *Lutheran Book of Worship*, 1978, provided two settings of the Sunday Service of Holy Communion. In both liturgies, the Sursum Corda is followed by the opening line of the Preface with an accompanying rubric, "The preface appropriate to the day or season is sung or said."[8] In *Evangelical Lutheran Worship*, 2006, ten musical settings of Holy Communion are provided with Setting Two providing distinctive full texts of the Great Thanksgiving for "Advent—Epiphany of Our Lord" and "Ash Wednesday—Day of Pentecost."[9]

Along with other denominations during the 1970s and 1980s, The United Methodist Church issued provisional liturgical texts for the Sunday Service as well as the Service of Holy Baptism and those for weddings and funerals. In 1980, the General Conference of the United Methodist Church approved versions of these services for approved alternate use in local congregations (the Ritual of the 1965 *Book of Worship* remaining for the time in place along with that of the former Evangelical United Brethren Church). The final version of "Word and Table," along with the other services, was approved at the 1988 General Conference and then published in *The United Methodist Hymnal* and *The United Methodist Book of Worship*. Throughout the series of revisions during the "test run" of the Sunday Service, the overall shape of the Sunday liturgy was fully in harmony with that of the broad ecumenical reforms begun by the Second Vatican Council. However, when the Eucharistic Prayer was examined, it was evident immediately that the United Methodist text had diverged from that of

---

7   Episcopal Church, Standing Liturgical Commission, *Enriching Our Worship 1: Supplemental Liturgical Materials* (New York: The Church Pension Fund, 1998), 50–71.

8   Inter-Lutheran Commission on Worship, *Lutheran Book of Worship,* (Minneapolis: Augsburg Fortress, 1978), 68, 88.

9   Evangelical Lutheran Church in America, *Evangelical Lutheran Worship* (Minneapolis: Augsburg Fortress, 2006), 132–33.

the Roman Catholic, Lutheran, Episcopal, and even the prior Methodist pattern. The Western practice of employing a Proper Preface for the various days, festivals, and occasions had been abandoned in favor of a through-composed prayer specific to each liturgical event. The Preface was no longer the proper; rather, the entire Eucharistic Prayer became the proper. This shift in liturgical organization of the anaphora did not affect the opening and closing phrases of the United Methodist Preface. All of these Great Thanksgiving propers began with a version of the familiar repetitive and intensifying statement following the last line of the Dialogue:

> It is right, and a good and joyful thing, always and everywhere to give thanks to you, Father Almighty, creator of heaven and earth.[10]

The final statement of the Preface also follows ancient tradition as well as the contemporary ecumenical practice in providing a smooth segue to the Sanctus:

> And so, with your people on earth and all the company of heaven we praise your name and join their unending hymn:[11]

However, between the opening and closing lines of the new United Methodist Preface, the terse rhetoric of the other Western prefaces was loosened and the Preface became more of a narrative of the paradigmatic events of covenant history, chiefly focused on those related to God's covenant people Israel. In this format, the narrative aspects of the Post-Sanctus focused more on the Incarnation of Jesus Christ and the Spirit's work in the church. Again, these narratives emphasized distinctive occasions and festivals both in the Preface and the Post-Sanctus. Numerous Eucharistic Prayers in their entirety therefore were needed to provide for the different "proper" occasions within the liturgical year and among various pastoral occasions.[12]

---

10 "Service of Word and Table I," *The United Methodist Book of Worship* (Nashville: The United Methodist Publishing House, 1992), 36.

11 Ibid. .

12 A United Methodist "sacramentary," *At the Lord's Table*, was published during the trial use season for these "Supplemental Worship Resources." Since its publication in 1982, however, a new sacramentary for the United Methodist Eucharistic Prayer propers has not been forthcoming. Also see: Timothy Crouch and the Order of Saint Luke, *Offices and Services (Proposed) After the Usage of the Order of Saint Luke* (Hackettstown, NJ: Order of Saint Luke, 1984), 12–24.

These liturgical retrievals and reforms related to the expansion in proper preface texts included the development of a significant corpus related to days, festivals, and occasions. Also evident has been an unambiguous emphasis on a rhetoric of thanksgiving within these prefaces ecumenically. That venerable resource, *The Catholic Encyclopedia*, noted that two qualities distinguished the earliest extant prefaces in the Latin Church, their "shortness and changeableness."[13] We may also add a third quality, that of the sequential logic of the texts. The opening and closing lines of most any preface serve as predictable bookends, leading from the Dialogue and leading to the Sanctus. Sandwiched within these frames, the variable material focuses on the occasion, day, or festival. A sequential logic obtains within most every Proper Preface.

Qualities of the Proper Preface and "Proper Preaching"

Continuing a homiletical mystagogy, we will explore these three enduring qualities of the Preface of the Eucharistic Prayer with regard to their implications for proclamation. Again, we are assuming an interplay between the qualities of the liturgical acts of the eucharistic rites and the dynamics of the sermon. The three qualities, resident within most every preface after the reforms of the liturgy, include the succinct nature of the rite, its "changeableness," and its reliable pattern of sequential logic. Each has important implications for the sermon.

Compact, Succinct Content

There are traditions, chiefly Roman Catholic and Anglican, in which the liturgical homily is typically marked by a brevity or "shortness." This emphasis on the "brief homily" is on one hand the outcome of teaching as to what the homily should not be. Such "definition by negation" is grounded, for these traditions, in a theological understanding of the gathered faithful at the Eucharist. *Fulfilled in Your Hearing* sets up one parameter for the liturgical homily this way: "The liturgical gathering is not primarily an educational assembly."[14] Moreover, the assembly gathered for Eucharist on the Lord's Day is not a

---

13 A. Fortescue, "Preface," in The Roman Catholic Encyclopedia (New York: Robert Appleton Company, 1911), http://www.newadvent.org/cathen/12384a.htm.

14 Catholic Church, National Conference of Catholic Bishops, Bishop's Committee on Priestly Life and Ministry, *Fulfilled in Your Hearing* (Washington, DC: Office of Pub. Services, United States Catholic Conference, 1982), 18.

group of non-baptized inquirers; neither is it a political party or a caucus for some ideological cause. The baptized who assemble for worship at the Holy Meal are Christ's body and have come to receive deeper faith, to be fed with the Bread of Life, and to be strengthened for their mission in the world. Preaching on other occasions—that is, at times and contexts other than that of the Sunday Eucharistic Feast—and preaching to other communities—such as the catechumens who are seeking faith in Christ and Holy Baptism—may well be more educational, evangelistic, or prophetic. *Fulfilled in Your Hearing* states the case directly: "A homily presupposes faith". William Willimon speaks of this distinctive quality of the liturgical homily as "baptismal preaching." It is "not so much a matter of being didactic, of explaining something, as it is of testifying to something, struggling to describe an event that has already happened to the congregation, bringing into view the significance of our baptism with words."[15] Boundaried by such concrete and distinctive purpose, it becomes increasingly clear what the homily at Eucharist is not to be. A liturgical homily's brevity, then, is a function of its context, its purpose, and its rhetorical and methodological parameters. Discerning what the homily *is not* brings clarity regarding its brevity. Becoming aware of what the homily *is* then leads to a brighter vision of its depth.

We have alluded to a rhetorical dimension to the insistence on a "brief" homily in some liturgical traditions. The critique here leading to an insistence on the brevity of the homily is applicable across the span of preaching styles and ecclesial traditions. "We tend towards overkill in our use of words and towards neglect in our use of silence," insists James Wallace.[16]

However, the issue of linguistic overkill is not solely a quantitative matter. Rather, there are certain kinds of words that provide the listeners with "empty calories," spoken entities that bloat the sermon while actually lowering the ability of its language to communicate. David Buttrick has explored these empty-calorie words extensively and in depth.[17]

For example, Buttrick finds that fond pulpit words such as "very," "truly," "really," and "indeed" add little to oral speech and serve to "make language thick and less accessible to consciousness."[18] Moreover, Buttrick argues that adjectives serve mostly to obscure and weaken our speech, in spite of their overdone usage in Romantic literature. Verbs, on the other hand, are the grammar of vivid

15   William H. Willimon, *Peculiar Speech: Preaching to the Baptized* (Grand Rapids: Eerdmans, 1992), 5.

16   James A. Wallace, *Preaching to the Hungers of the Heart: The Homily on the Feasts and Within the Rites* (Collegeville, MN: Liturgical Press, 2002), 92.

17   See David Buttrick, Homiletic: Moves and Structures (Philadelphia: Fortress, 1987), 187–221.

18   Ibid., 212.

and concrete communication. "Excitement in preaching is usually created by verb color and precision."[19]

A graphic depiction of the rhetorical alternatives may be conceived as follows, with the "color and precision," verb-heavy side providing the terse, compact preface-like prose.

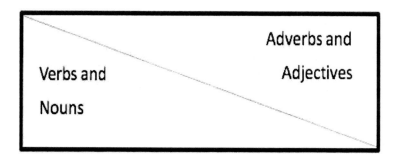

Once again, the issue is not simply that of the quantity of words employed while developing a single thought in the sermon; the congregation's retention of the language in the first place depends upon more qualitative issues such as the presence or blessed absence of "empty-calorie" words and an overabundance of adjectives.

Of course, there are other preaching traditions in which the performance of the liturgical homily is not highly valued in contrast to temporally more extended sermons. To be sure, an African American Baptist or Pentecostal congregation would probably be shocked if their preacher delivered a homily-sized sermon on a Sunday morning. This is not to say that African American sermons should be stereotyped as all lacking "preface-like prose." Rather, Cleophus LaRue notes, there are a number of factors that make for longer moves within the black sermon. These include:

> The black sermon as performed word usually runs longer than the traditional mainline sermon.
>
> The black preacher often engages in prolonged and precise detailing of some text, image, metaphor, or slice of life centered around one thought.
>
> The listening congregation expects and has grown accustomed to following an elongated story plot without losing sight of the defining thought that occasioned the move.[20]

---

19   Ibid., 217..
20   Cleophus J. LaRue, *The Heart of Black Preaching* (Louisville: Westminster John Knox, 2000), 71.

Even given the more extensive time frame of many sermons in the African American church, there remain widely held protocols as to the rhetorical boundaries of the preacher. For example, LaRue raises a cautionary note regarding the practice of inserting a closing reference to Jesus in a sermon on an Old Testament text where "Jesus appears as an afterthought tacked on to the end."[21] Moreover, the length and rhetorical amplitude of sermons expands beyond those of the liturgical homily in many contexts apart from ethnic minority or majority considerations. One significant factor, of course, is that the schism between Word and sacrament in many North American churches has resulted in the sermon becoming "a kind of homiletical ocean liner preceded by a few liturgical tugboats."[22] Given the dominance of the non-eucharistic model of the Sunday Service, the sermon in such a liturgical context tends to expand to fill the void left from noncelebration of the Holy Meal.

A Changeable Focus

As was noted, most prefaces within Western Eucharistic Prayers are "proper," that is, they change in focus and theme from liturgical season to season and from occasion to occasion. A proper preface retains the opening that repeats and intensifies the last line of the Dialogue and closes with a rather standard introduction to the Sanctus. However, the material sandwiched between the opening and closing lines is "proper" to an occasion, day, or season and is therefore noted not only by its essential brevity, but also by its changeableness, its variability. For example, in the Church of England's *Common Worship*, the Proper Preface for Trinity Sunday is as follows:

> *And now we give you thanks because you have revealed the glory of your eternal fellowship of love with your Son and with the Holy Spirit, three persons equal in majesty, undivided in splendor, yet one God, ever to be worshipped and adored.*[23]

Within this brief Proper Preface, we note qualities that obtain for most prefaces as well as elements that are distinctive to the occasion (in this case,

---

21   Ibid., 110.

22   Charles L. Rice, *The Embodied Word: Preaching as Art and Liturgy* (Minneapolis: Fortress Press, 1991), 31.

23   Church of England, Archbishop's Council, "Preface for Trinity Sunday 1," *Common Worship: Services and Prayers for the Church of England* (London: Church House Publishing, 2000), 509.

Trinity Sunday). With reference to the enduring qualities, it is particularly evident in this Preface that it along with the entirety of the Eucharistic Prayer is addressed to the First Person of the Trinity. The reference to "your Son and the Holy Spirit" is a carefully worded phrase retaining this address to the Father.

Another enduring quality of any preface conforming to the Western church tradition is that it is offered by the presiding minister at the Table in concert with the entire people.[24] Certain prayers at the Offertory within the Western tradition are shaped to express the first-person petitions of the presider/priest. (Hence, the "*Suscipe, sancte Pater . . .*" of the Tridentine Mass of the Roman Catholic Church.) However, the Preface within a Eucharistic Prayer, though offered by the presider, is offered on behalf of the whole assembly and the Prayer is consistently in the plural "we." On the other hand, the variable foci of the proper preface are immediately evident. A Eucharistic Prayer beginning with this proper, expressing the mystery of the Holy Trinity, will not be offered, say, on the First Sunday of Advent or on All Saints. There is no question as to the particular day or occasion to which this prayer is "proper." One interesting note, though, is the way in which the church has seen the applicability of one proper to another occasion. So, for example, in the resource published by the Anglican Church of Canada for the propers of the liturgical year, the prefaces for most of those commemorated as saints are specified as that "*Preface of an Apostle,*" "*Preface of a Martyr,*" or, simply, "*Preface of a Saint.*" However, when the occasion is that of The Birth of Saint John the Baptist (June 24), the "*Preface of Advent*" becomes the Proper Preface of the Eucharistic Prayer.[25] In United Methodist eucharistic praying, one text suffices for "All Saints and Memorial Occasions." If a biblical saint was to be recalled and celebrated, for example, a different preface is not available to provide focus to that occasion. Rather, a version of the ancient diptychs is located within the Post-Sanctus and the saint would be memorialized there.[26] This feature

---

24 The United Methodist statement on Holy Communion witnesses to the "in con-cert" roles of presiding minister and congregation by affirming that "an elder or authorized pastor leads the congregation in praying the Great Thanksgiving, in which the whole assembly takes an active role." (See Gaye Carlton Felton, *This Holy Mystery: A United Methodist Understanding of Holy Communion* [Nashville: Discipleship Resources, 2004], 26.)

25 Stephen Reynolds, compiler, "The Birth of Saint John the Baptist," *For All the Saints: Prayers and Readings for Saints Days,* rev. ed. (Toronto: ABC Publishing, 2007), 205.

26 "The Great Thanksgiving for All Saints and Memorial Occasions," *The United Methodist Book of Worship,* 74–75.

of some Eucharistic Prayers in the early church was the location where brief intercessions were made or specific saints were recalled and celebrated. The practice continues in some Western rites.

Homiletical Implications

Considering this core quality of changeability within the preface of the Eucharistic Prayer, the homiletical implications immediately focus on practices where a lack of that trait degrades the hearing of the Word. These practices range from matters of sermon delivery to issues related to the deployment of illustrative material and to questions related to sermon method itself. Each element constitutes a situation where a certain changeability is needed by the listeners but is not provided by the preacher. Some of these "stasis-issues" (characterized by a chronic lack of dynamics or mobility) are as follows:

A. Regarding the preacher's inflection within a sermon, I will predictably encounter one or two students in my introduction to preaching class whose vocal inflection in other contexts is normal and appropriate to their subject. Then, when they rise to preach during the sermon lab, their pulpit speech becomes "preachery" as, for instance, it drops vocal tone by a musical third or fourth at the end of most sentences. The effect is dulling and detracting. It is not that someone in particular has advocated for this unnatural inflective habit in preaching. Rather, there seems to be an abiding consensus among some colleagues that pious and religious speech should sound this way. It then becomes habitual until some caring mentor or homiletics professor takes the preacher aside and calls attention to this vocal pattern. (The habit also infects the offering of public and liturgical prayer, again usually susceptible to intervention and analysis.)

A related issue dealing with sermon delivery relates to the preacher's entire persona accompanying her or his sermons. Once again, a stasis obtains, though in this case it deals with the emotive "preacher" voice that is presented from the pulpit. Persons who otherwise exhibit various affective moods and expressions in other contexts, turn on a pulpit persona that is stereotyped and unchanging. Thus, I have experienced charming and expressive persons who, when coming to preach, adopt a consistently stern facial expression and deep, solemn voice. In other instances, I have experienced pulpit personae of chirpy merriment and, at the other end of the spectrum, ordinarily nice folks who morph into the Hulk when preaching. All of these pulpit "voices"— the solemn, happy, angry, and so on—share several characteristics. First, they are stereotyped, perhaps derived by imitation from some pulpit personality. Second, they are static and predictable in their deployment. Third, these personae will override the particular affective quality of the biblical text and specific sermon content.[27] The liturgical preface changes with context and occasion. The delivery of the sermon—its inflection along with the voice of the preacher— similarly will be "proper" to its text, context, and occasion.

B.   A series of issues related to some sort of homiletical stasis afflict the material in the sermon intended to bring concretion to its conceptual material. Generically labeled "illustrations," these materials actually include brief illustrative narratives, one or more examples, and, finally, the depiction of imagery.[28] A number of problems cluster within the deployment of the conventional sermon illustration—that anecdote intended to reinforce or make vivid the "point" in the message. One changeability issue emerges when the preacher offers the same illustrative subject on a recurring basis. Whatever else may change— the liturgical season, the biblical texts, the events of church and world—one note of deadening consistency obtains, the congregation will hear yet again about the preacher's pet topic. So one congregation will not be able to hear any sermon without the knowledge ahead of time that a golf story will illustrate something or other (or weaving, sailing, or collecting Belgian lace, and so forth).[29] The chronic playing of the same illustrative

---

27   In one preaching lab, a student came to the pulpit to read her lesson and preach. Immediately, she put on her pulpit persona of the Hulk. She growled out her scripture (1 Corinthians 13!) and raged on in the sermon about the greatest of these being love!

28   See Buttrick, *Homiletic*, 137–70. Also see my *Web of Preaching: New Options in Homiletical Method* (Nashville: Abingdon, 2002), 246–85.

29   Only the lace-collecting preacher is an invention in my experience. For myself, I have a deep passion for aviation and am a certified flight instructor in gliders. Since the realm of soaring obviously has applications within every sermon I am

category that has become beloved by the preacher will no longer serve to illustrate anything but that preacher. Consequently, the ethos of the preacher will suffer from such self-illustration.

With preachers having at their disposal such a broad and diverse suite of concretion strategies—story illustration, examples, and imagery—the sermon suffers a rhetorical diminishment if only one type of concretion is deployed again and again. Once again, the preface's changeability is an encouragement to seek the "proper" strategy for bringing lived experience to the sermon. However, some preachers will serve their listeners only an unvaried diet of illustrative material. So, in sermon after sermon, some congregations will hear only story illustrations when the preacher turns to specific application. Other assemblies may only hear lists of examples as the reiterative concretion scheme. A few preachers, perhaps those with vigorous and undisciplined intuitive personality preferences, will boggle the congregation with a myriad of imagery whatever the occasion. The foundational issue here is that the strategy for bringing a move to concretion within the sermon is weighted with theological as well as rhetorical import. Particularly if the story illustrations all derive from one cultural context or historical era, the subtext of these stories will be that the gospel is best lived out within that idealized narrative world. Moreover, a subtle bias is conveyed that the individual and communal life of the hearers is best lived out by way of orderly narrative.[30] The matter of gender bias also infects the choice of illustrations by some male preachers. Not only are illustrations the chief diet served to these congregations in order to provide concrete

---

shaping, I will not mention gliders or flying in any of them!

30   Several commentators have recently noted that postmillennial generational cohorts tend to depict themselves in mostly nonnarrative ways. Thomas Long analyzes the claims of Galen Strawson that two quite distinct ways to be human are now evident: those persons who are "Diachronic," finding a narrative experience of life as both normal and normative, and the "Episodic" ones for whom no narrative self-interpretation is needed or even possible. "As an Episodic," Long reflects, "Strawson lives in a series of present tense moments . . . [He] has no narrative, wants no narrative, and needs no narrative." Thomas G. Long, *Preaching from Memory to Hope* (Louisville: Westminster John Knox, 2009), 12. See Galen Strawson, "Against Narrativity," Ratio (new series) 18, no. 4 (Dec. 2004): 428–52.

experiences, the characters in the stories are likely to be males who display agency and heroic virtues. By contrast, those same illustrations will depict women as passive or dependent upon the male heroes. Once again, the proper preface embodies changeability, so a caution to men in the pulpit is not only to vary their concretion strategies within the sermon, but sometimes to shift the gender focus of illustrations when they are deployed.

A companion transgression often accompanies an undue dependence on story illustrations within the sermon. The congregation is served almost exclusively storied types of illustrative material, but those stories will be almost entirely about the preacher and his or her family. In such cases, it is not a by-product of the rhetorical strategy that the sermonic stories serve to illustrate the preacher rather than the conceptual issue at hand. To the contrary, it seems to be the intended purpose of the first-person tales that they illustrate the preacher. (Otherwise, what is the rationale for such predominance of these personal references from the pulpit?) With an excessive dependence on such first-person narratives, the preacher may unwittingly convey several profound distortions of Christian faith. First, there is an unsubtle message conveyed that the Christian life is most fully lived by the ordained rather than by the laity, the whole people of God. So the message is clear in these over-done first-person narratives: "Want to be a complete Christian? Become ordained and serve as pastor and preacher." Second, the second-class status of the laity is reified in the insistence that they must access the means of grace and the virtues of the faith in ways mediated by and translated through the experiences of their preacher. If the subject at hand is God's call to persons to be about faithful discipleship, then the congregation will hear the story of the preacher's call to ministry. Or, if the message is dealing with perseverance in a season of adversity, the congregation will hear the story of the preacher and the preacher's spouse when they were struggling with a very ill child. And if, on All Saints Day or Sunday, the sermon focuses on the lives of some recent saints, the preacher will relate the stories of a beloved grandmother or grandfather. It all stays in the family. After a steady dose of these first-person illustrations, most any congregation is very ready for changeability to redeem this predictable habit. If used at all, first-person story illustrations should "go communal" with ease and rapidity. Otherwise, the illustrations should be congruent with the conceptual content of the particular homiletical move. Thus, if the conceptual focus is ecclesial—a matter of the Body of Christ—then any individualistic illustration is a wayward tactic and a first-person individualistic story doubles the transgression.

Sequential Logic

The Preface, throughout its "default" or proper variations, maintains a sequencing that links it in place between the Dialogue and the Sanctus. As we have noted, most any preface opens with a statement intensifying the last line of the Dialogue. Thus, in United Methodist euchological practice, the concluding line of the Dialogue ("It is right to give our thanks and praise") is followed in the Preface's opening phrase by an intensified restatement of the *"dignum et justum est"* ("It is right, and a good and joyful thing . . ."). At the aft end of the Preface, a statement transitions from the particular focus and thematic content of the Prayer to an introduction of the Sanctus, also serving to cue the assembly to their entrance into the Eucharistic Prayer. This statement in the 1662 Book of Common Prayer expresses the rhetorical and liturgical genius of the writer of the first prayer books, Archbishop Cranmer:

> *Therefore with angels and archangels, and with all the company of heaven, we laud and magnify thy glorious Name; evermore praising thee, and saying:*[31]
>
> *(Here follows the Sanctus.)*

Between the dependable opening and closing lines of the Preface, the specific thematic and imagistic material embodying the action of making Eucharist is developed.

---

31   The Church of England, Book of Common Prayer, http://www.churchofengland. org/prayer-worship/worship/book-of-common-prayer/the-lord's-supper-or-holy-communion.aspx.

Homiletical Implications

The resonance between this dynamic of the Preface and that of the sermon centers in their held-in-common grounding in a plotted logic. Reflecting on the homiletical plot from this distinctive narrative perspective, Eugene Lowry notes that plot "deals with some kind of *sequential ordering*."[32] Lowry continues by depicting "sequential ordering" as a narrative plot that "typically includes an opening conflict, escalation or complication, a watershed experience (generally involving a reversal) and a denouement (that is, the working out of the resolution)."[33] Other homileticians would concur with Lowry concerning the essential quality of sequential ordering, but would look elsewhere than the dynamics of narrative for the sermon's plot. David Buttrick, for example, insists that the sermon must embody some sort of sequential ordering. "Underlying the movement of a plot is some sort of 'logic' by which parts are assembled and travel."[34] (Buttrick here could be depicting the sequential ordering of the Eucharistic Preface!) In some cases, especially when preaching *in* the mode of immediacy[35] and preaching *from* a biblical narrative, the sermonic plot will trace the Scripture's narrative scenic progression. However, Buttrick also extends the notion of plot to include the "logic" of most any pericope; an ordered sequence will still shape the homiletical plot. That plot—whether derived from a biblical narrative or, for example, the Pauline epistolary logic—always tries "to bring out some structure of meaning within a field of consciousness."[36] By way of contrast, the old "point"-based preaching assembled a series of propositional statements that contained no underlying sequential ordering. For example, a quick internet search spotted the following sermon points for the Parable of the Good Samaritan:

> A neighbor is one in need whom we can help.
> The incongruity of divorcing neighborliness from religion.
> The cost of compassion.[37]

As with the majority of such sermon-building points, there is no necessary sequential ordering of the thematic. A preacher could just as easily begin

---

32 Eugene L. Lowry, *Doing Time in the Pulpit: The Relationship between Narrative and Preaching* (Nashville: Abingdon Press, 1985), 23.
33 Ibid.
34 Buttrick, *Homiletic*, 291.
35 See the discussion of Buttrick's mode of immediacy at p. 57 in *Homiletic*.
36 Buttrick, *Homiletic*, 297.
37 See Higher Praise, "The Parables of Jesus: The Good Samaritan (Luke 10:25-37)," http://www.higherpraise.com/outlines/pa/pa_20.htm.

with the third point about compassion, shift to the first related to the concept of neighborliness, and conclude with this elusive point about the incongruous divorcing of helping neighbors from religion. The points of this sermon—in whatever order they are arranged—invite the congregation to ignore the point of view of the one who has been robbed and beaten. In fact, the distance from the parable's world is stunning, especially when the congregation is invited to considerations of the incongruity of divorcing neighborliness from religion. On the other hand, the scandal of being unable to prevent compassionate help from a despised enemy is bypassed as well.[38] Put simply, the parable's narrative plot is irrelevant to the points of this sermon. Any sequential logic is simply ignored.

Proper Preface and "Proper Preaching": The Lectionary

The Preface has as its companion "propers" several other variable-to-the-occasion elements within the Sunday service. These have included such liturgical components as the Introit (the opening fragment of a hymn or psalm within the Latin Mass and elsewhere),[39] the Collect (the opening prayer of the day), and the reading from Scripture (also specific to the day and occasion). The latter proper readings for the day, of course, have a direct and immediate relationship to the ministry of proclamation; the lectionary is a compilation of lections for every Sunday and festival within the church year. Within ecclesial traditions in which a lectionary is mandated or commended as determining the scriptures for the liturgical occasion—thus becoming one of the propers of that day—the preacher is provided with the texts from which or through which the sermon is to proceed.[40] Since the various Western Church ecclesial communities vary widely on the use of a formal lectionary, and therefore to what extent if any the sermon should be based on such propers, it is essential that we turn to consider the origins and development of this proper and the contemporary issues regarding its use. Simply put, the question we now address has a two-fold structure: How did we come to have this three-year lectionary (whether the Roman Catholic Lectionary or the Revised Common

---

38   See Bernard Brandon Scott, *Hear Then the Parable: A Commentary on the Parables of Jesus* (Minneapolis: Augsburg Fortress Press, 1989).

39   In the Latin Mass prior to the Second Vatican Council, a rubric directs: "The priest now makes the sign of the cross, and, standing at the Epistle Corner, begins the Introit, which will be found in the Mass proper to the day." Thompson Bard, *Liturgies of the Western Church* (Philadelphia: Fortress Press, 1980), 59.

40   Roman Catholic Church, *Fulfilled in Your Hearing*, emphasizes that "The homily is not so much *on* the Scriptures as *from* and *through* them," 20.

Lectionary) and what are the compelling issues at stake in use or disuse? An investigation regarding the origins of this lectionary seems warranted.

In synagogue worship of the postexilic period, the Jewish practices regarding the selection of scriptures varied according to three systems. These included, Marion Hatchett notes, "(1) the synagogue ruler's discretion; (2) 'in-course' readings (*lectio continua*); or (3) a fixed lectionary."[41] Within the New Testament, evidence is abundant that all three of these systems remained in use in early Christian worship. Lessons from the Hebrew Scriptures (though in fact the Greek Scriptures of the Septuagint) were derived by way of one of the same practices in usage in postexilic Judaism. A reading or singing of a psalm may have followed the first lesson and further readings were selected from early Christian writings. Hatchett now makes a striking conclusion with regard to these early Christian writings: "Those lections which found regular place in liturgical usage eventually became the New Testament Canon."[42] Here, a remarkable reversal is asserted to that more conventional assumption as to the relationship between the canon and ordered liturgical practice of scripture usage. Conventional "wisdom" is that after the canon was closed, the post-New Testament church began its alignment of particular lessons to specific occasions resulting eventually in some lectionary scheme or other. Hatchett turns this prevalent viewpoint on its head, proposing instead that the New Testament churches were already in the business of selecting liturgical occasions for particular texts from the early Christian writings. The canon, from this point of view, is derivative in part from the ordering of these writings within the communities constituting early Christianity.

The ordering of the New Testament writings according to occasions and days, however, did not end with the close of the canon. Once again, an interplay seems to have obtained between text and liturgical occasion. So it is no surprise, for example, that as Saint Augustine chose lections for various occasions within the church year, the texts were those that were actually generative of those liturgical days. We are not surprised, then, to find Augustine preaching on texts that gave birth to the liturgical event in the first place. So, the Christmas narrative in Luke 2 was his reading for, of all things, Christmas Day, while Matthew 28 was the Gospel lesson for the Easter Vigil and Acts 2 was the Epistle lesson for Pentecost. The interaction between text and occasion is dynamic. On one hand, the lection

---

41   Marion Hatchett, *Sanctifying Life, Time, and Space: An Introduction to Liturgical Theology* (New York: Seabury Press, 1976), 22.
42   Ibid., 45.

points the church to the day and focus of its observance. On the other hand, the text then becomes the obvious lesson for the occasion. Given this interplay between text and liturgical context, the outcome is the emergence of the church year itself as well as the arrangement of biblical texts that will become a fully developed lectionary. In the course of this complex development, the New Testament texts first generated the occasions within the Paschal cycle of the year (what we would later term the Lent-Easter cycle). For example, the lections for the Great Fifty Days—the Season of Easter—were among the earliest to be fixed, including the church's decision to focus on readings from the Acts of the Apostles during this Season.[43] The last of the Sundays to be given a specific lection were those following Pentecost, the long series of Sundays now included in Ordinary Time.

The first complete lectionaries date from the seventh century,[44] although those of the eighth century are more prevalent and determinative for the future. Various regions followed their own distinctive arrangements—for example, the Gallican eighth-century Lectionary of Luxeuil. By contrast, the lectionary of the Roman Rite during this same era was distinctive in two respects—the lections "were shorter than those typical of other rites" and there existed "a particular dearth of Old Testament readings."[45] The latter distinctive characteristic was to have grave consequences for the Western Church until the reforms of the Second Vatican Council (1963–1965). Once the Old Testament lesson was largely deleted from the readings for Sundays and festivals, the psalm that functioned as a response to that reading was also lost. With the triumph of the Roman Rite in the West by the eleventh century (excepting a few local rites of particular distinctiveness), the Western church would limp through the next nine hundred years with a lectionary composed on most occasions of an Epistle lesson and a Gospel. Moreover, the lectionary of the Roman Rite, adopted with minor variations after the Reformation by Lutheran and Anglican communions, provided only for a one-year sequence of these lections.[46] Not only was the church deprived of the Old Testament in its Sunday worship, the churches retaining this lectionary suffered an inadequate diet of New Testament readings as well. The sea change came in 1963 with the first decree approved by the Second Vatican Council, "The Constitution on the Sacred Liturgy." Here, a principle

---

43   See Peter G. Cobb, "The Liturgy of the Word in the Early Church," in *The Study of Liturgy*, ed. Cheslyn Jones, Geoffrey Wainwright, and Edward Yarnold (Oxford: Oxford University Press, 1979), 185.

44   D. M. Hope, "Liturgical Books," in *The Study of Liturgy*, 66.

45   Hatchett, *Sanctifying Life, Time, and Space*, 72–73.

46   See Luther Reed, *"The Lutheran Liturgy,"* (Minneapolis: Fortress Press, 1947), 450–575.

was announced that from a later perspective was a reform badly needed by most every tradition within Western Christianity: "The Scriptures are to be opened more lavishly to the people."[47] The Roman Catholic Lectionary for Mass (RCL) that resulted from this reforming action of the Council was first promulgated in 1969. It was organized around a three-year sequence and the Gospel lessons for each year focused on one of the Synoptic Gospels. Hence, Year A belonged mostly to the Gospel of Matthew, Year B to Mark, and Year C to Luke. The Gospel of John was featured in the seasons of Lent and Easter during every year, and in Year B—St. Mark being the shortest Gospel—the Bread of Life Discourse of John 6 was intercalated into the Markan sequence during Ordinary Time. The First Lesson for each season, Sunday, or other occasion was derived from the Old Testament except during the Season of Easter when, in accordance with ancient practice, readings from the Acts of the Apostles became the First Lesson. In addition, a Psalter selection responded to the First Lesson and an Epistle reading completed the offerings. The First Lessons were selected with regard to some connective logic to the Gospel Lesson, whether by way of thematic congruence, a promise and fulfillment motif, or typological connection.

During the next decade, various Protestant denominations along with the Episcopal Church adopted the RCL, though in every instance, modifications were made either by way of shortening or lengthening the verses in a given lection or, in a number of cases especially related to the selections from the Acts of the Apostles, replacing texts from the RCL with others. (The latter dynamic, it was discovered, involved the replacement of the community-building pericopes of Acts in the RCL with other texts embodying kerygmatic proclamations of the New Testament church.) However, by the latter years of the 1970s, it was becoming clear that the initial motivations for an ecumenical consensus with regard to the readings within a new three-year lectionary were being threatened by denominational and Protestant-Catholic centrifugal forces. Two denominations—the three Lutheran synods about to merge into the Evangelical Lutheran Church of America (ELCA) along with the Episcopal Church—published official resources that already canonized their own variants of the lectionary. Other denominations were at least potentially heading in the same direction. Therefore, The Consultation on Common Texts (CCT) convened a conference on calendar and lectionary in late March of 1978 and thirteen denominations participated in the discussions.

---

47   Roman Catholic Church, "Constitutional on the Sacred Liturgy," *The Documents of Vatican II*, ed. Walter M. Abbott (New York: American Press, 1966).

Given the evidence of a potential squandering of the gift of unity promised in the advent of the three-year lectionary, the CCT established the North American Committee on Calendar and Lectionary (NACCL) with a charge to attempt a Common Lectionary. A Common Lectionary was achieved by NACCL and several years later some further revisions produced the Revised Common Lectionary, which has persisted as the alternative to the Roman Catholic Lectionary.[48]

The two primary purposes of a lectionary, as noted in *Fulfilled in Your Hearing*, are to establish appropriate Scripture lessons for the various days, festivals, and seasons of the liturgical year and "to provide for a comprehensive reading of the Scriptures."[49] The former purpose—establishing lessons appropriate for various occasions in the year of grace—needs to be nuanced with regard to the dynamics of the New Testament canon and the emergence of the two Christological cycles of Incarnation and the Paschal Mystery (Advent/Christmas and Lent/Easter). In a number of instances, by the fourth century, various "historic-feasts" were being established that have their origin in specific narratives within the New Testament. So, for example, the Christian festival of Pentecost is entirely dependent upon Saint Luke's rendition of the Pentecost story in Acts 2. The same may be said with regard to the fourth-century creations of Christmas in the West and Palm Sunday in the East. None of these festivals would have emerged in the early church except for the generative force of specific biblical narratives. Thus, in these and other cases, a lectionary does not as much *establish* appropriate lessons as it does *recall* for the church the Scriptures that gave birth to the liturgical occasions in the first place. By way of drilling into these relationships between an ordered sequence of Scripture lections and the church year, one other purpose gains a central importance while a second fades to the margins of our considerations. The core purpose of the lectionary—whether the Roman Catholic or Revised Common Lectionary—is to shape a service of the Word such that the hearing and proclamation of these lessons forms a people such that they come to the Eucharist with faith, expectancy, and joy. Put simply, both versions of the three-year lectionary are eucharistic projects with a sacramental lens governing the selection of texts and occasions. Here, we encounter once more the interplay between proclamation

---

48   A detailed history of the development of the reforms in calendar and lectionary within the North American churches is available in Hoyt L. Hickman, Don E. Saliers, Laurence Hull Stuckey, and James F. White, *The New Handbook of the Christian Year* (Nashville: Abingdon Press, 1992), 28–33. Also see the Consultation on Common Texts, http://www.commontexts.org/.

49   Roman Catholic Church, *Fulfilled in Your Hearing*, 20.

and Eucharist. The proper preface for the liturgy is grounded in the same biblical texts that will become the lessons through which the sermon is given birth. Given the rich sources for proper prefaces to the Great Thanksgiving, and even entire "proper" Eucharistic Prayers, during Ordinary Time the careful preacher in many traditions will find a mode of eucharistic praying that resonates effectively with the lessons and the sermon.

There is one rationale for the use of the lectionary that is voiced from time to time, especially by church judicatories and publishing houses. "The lectionary," these voices chime, "is a fine preaching plan for the Christian Year." The obvious subtext of this persuasive argument is that a preacher may come up with any number of "preaching plans," but the abundance of lectionary-based preaching resources is a compelling rationale for using this particular plan. The problem here is not with the abundance of homiletical and liturgical resources based on the lectionary; rather, it is with the implication that the preacher and her or his choice of a preaching plan is the governing principle. Thus, we hear preachers announce that their sermon series for Easter, for example, will be based in the chapters of a new book on spiritual formation. (Such a series, of course, might be a gem of a project for an adult education class.) The issue here is not the relative merit of this or that author's book on spiritual formation. Rather, it is that of the source of our authority as those called to preach the gospel. Must control over the choice of scripture, themes, and topics for our preaching always remain with ourselves? Or, to the contrary, is the authority more grounded in the nature and work of Christ's church through the power of the Holy Spirit? Stanley Hauerwas is perhaps the most provocative spokesperson for the latter, ecclesial location of the preacher's authority as he argues:

> For preaching to be a practice intrinsic to the worship of God requires that the preacher, as well as the congregation, stand under the authority of the Word. That is why preaching should rightly follow a lectionary. To preach from the lectionary makes clear that preaching is the work of the church and not some arbitrary decision by the minister to find a text to fit a peculiar theme that currently fits the preacher's subjectivity. Rather, the exercise of the ministry of proclamation requires the minister to make clear that the Word preached is as painful to him/her as it is to the congregation. Such an acknowledgement makes clear that preaching is not just another speech but rather the way this people here, including the preacher, is formed into the Word of God.[50]

---

50   Stanley Hauerwas, *Sanctify Them in the Truth: Holiness Exemplified* (Nashville: Abingdon Press, 1998), 237.

The Ordo of the eucharistic liturgy—the sequence of liturgical words and actions we are tracing in this homiletical mystagogy—is the work of the church and not an arbitrary decision of any minister at the Table. So, too, the proclamation of the ordered lessons of the Word is a gift and task to the one called to preach. The Proper Preface offers the variable themes, imagery, and narratives of the church year, various pastoral occasions, and local and global issues to qualify eucharistic praying and to locate the assembly in some context or other. "Proper preaching" is grounded in the lections of the church year in order that vital enduring relationships obtain between the Service of the Word and the Service of the Table. Also, "proper preaching" safeguards the preacher from returning to favorite texts, themes, and issues in place of "the whole counsel of God" (Acts 20:27, NKJV). The qualities of the Proper Preface—compact, succinct content; a changeable focus; and an inherent sequential logic—all inform the shape of the liturgical homily. These qualities, then, will also be embodied in "proper preaching."

ELEVEN

Eucharist and Evangelism

Elaine A. Heath

In thinking constructively and critically about the relationship between evangelism and the Eucharist, I would like to begin with *why*. I am by vocation a theologian and an evangelist. I cannot, nor would I wish to, remove my theoretical work from its foundation in holy praxis. Whatever I postulate about the meaning of the Eucharist with regard to the practice of evangelism, it needs to make sense and ring true in the ministry context in which I serve, among the friends and amid the struggles we face together in life. It cannot simply be a theory or a tradition, and it cannot be based on a white, middle-class, exclusively masculine, or American experience.

My daily context outside of academia is among women, men, and children who have survived childhood sexual abuse, domestic violence, torture, war, rape as a weapon of war, theft of land, destruction of home, religious and political persecution, government-backed death squads, and genocide. In addition to serving as professor of evangelism at Southern Methodist University, I founded and helped to lead a missional, new monastic community of refugees, asylees, and middle-class Americans in Dallas, Texas.

Whatever I think, say, or practice with regard to the Eucharist, if it is not dignifying, life-giving, and healing to survivors of the worst that overlords can offer, something is wrong. If my theory and practice of Holy Communion does not include, empower, and liberate persons who are already marginalized outside of the church, something is amiss. The leveraging of ecclesiastical power with the Eucharist as the fulcrum is much more than inherited tradition. There are deep political and ethical ramifications to our praxis. Let us consider those.

I am not nearly so worried that my evangelistic, liturgical theology will be seen as eccentric by the guardians of liturgical orthodoxy, as I am mindful that theology can and does either challenge or perpetuate systemic exploitation, manipulation, and violence against the least of these. All too often in our Christian history the latter has been true.

How we enact the Eucharist is central to our theology of everything else. Who is present at the Table? Who serves and who is served? What is a liberating theology of evangelism and the Eucharist? How might eucharistic theology become central in a liberating, Spirit-breathed, Wesleyan vision for the church? These are the questions at hand, and for me they are much more than academic reflection. So as I ponder, pray, and write my way through this essay I do so with the faces of real people before me, friends who came to the United States as refugees from the Democratic Republic of Congo, Rwanda, Eritrea, Burundi, Iraq, and Bhutan. In them I encounter the One who is broken and poured out. They are sons and daughters of God in whose faces I see the face of God. I write this for them.

In the pages ahead I propose among other things that committed Christian laity are more than capable of learning to preside at Table with integrity and that the restriction of the serving of sacraments to a powerful hierarchy of ordained clergy is not only incompatible with the gospel of Jesus and with missional ecclesiology and praxis, but is complicit with ecclesiological and political systems that create hierarchies of power that inevitably neglect, render invisible, muffle, oppress, exploit, and in general do violence against women, children, and every kind of "other."[1] I make my argument drawing from Wesleyan Pentecostal pneumatology,[2] kenotic

---

1   Let me state that although I continue to follow the requirements of my tradition, Methodism, in this essay I raise serious questions about our practice because I believe our tradition is dynamic, not dead, and at times can and does change. Within The UMC we have only had the ordained order of deacon without sacramental authority for less than twenty years. Creating that order was a change in our tradition. In 2008, the General Conference changed the rules about deacons and sacraments, allowing that in very specific circumstances a bishop may grant a deacon sacramental authority. This, too, was a change.

2   While on the one hand Pentecostalism is a global phenomenon indigenized and expressed through multiple theological traditions, in North America it emerged directly from Methodism, initially through the work of John Fletcher, followed by Phoebe Palmer, whose fully developed articulation of sanctification increasingly used the nomenclature of "baptism of the Spirit," especially in her seminal work *The Promise of the Father*. The final emergence of Pentecostalism from Methodism took place with Methodist preacher Charles Parham's and erstwhile disciple William Seymour's evangelistic ministries, leading to the advent of the Azusa Street revival. See Donald Dayton, "Methodism and Pentecostalism," *The Oxford Handbook of Methodist Studies*, ed. William J. Abraham and James E. Kirby (Oxford: Oxford University Press, 2009), 181–87; and Allan Anderson, *An Introduction to Pentecostalism* (Cambridge: Cambridge University Press, 2004), 23–35. With regard to my appropriation of Pentecostal pneumatology, I came into The United Methodist Church from Pentecostalism, and I value and retain a pneumatological orientation, particularly in ecclesiology and theological anthropology. Like many Pentecostal Christians from the Global South, I experience Pentecostalism primarily as God-breathed liberation from sinful divisions between genders, races, ethnic groups, classes, and other categories of human beings, and the full equipping of the church to partner with God in the *missio Dei*.

ecclesiology, a therapeutic and feminist reading of Scripture and tradition, the language of the Service of Word and Table I in the *United Methodist Hymnal*, and some of Charles Wesley's hymns, among other sources. In short, I believe that the opening of both sides of the eucharistic Table to laity is a missional imperative, not only because laity can and should be empowered to serve, but because the very notion of using the sacraments as a means of exclusion and empire building is rooted not in the gospel but in a fallen world.

Pneumatological Considerations

Let us begin with the Holy Spirit, a truly Wesleyan concern. We cannot escape the fact that the Spirit is the giver of gifts and the caller of persons into ministry. The Spirit gives to whom the Spirit will, irrespective of race, class, gender, economic status, or other identifiers that we have used in the church to segregate and exclude people. Saint Paul reminds us that the Holy Spirit is the one who baptizes us and distributes gifts according to divine, not human wisdom. "We were all baptized by one Spirit into one body, whether Jew or Greek, or slave or free, and we all were given one Spirit to drink".[3] The giving of gifts described in 1 Corinthians 12–14 and elsewhere is not related to being ordained or laity. Indeed, we cannot escape the fact that Jesus and every one of the apostles were laity. What are we to do with the fact that Jesus, the one who initiated the Eucharist, was a carpenter? Surely his vocation as "a working man" matters in this discussion. He "was teaching them like someone with authority, and not like their legal experts" (Matt 7:29,) because of the call of the Father and gifts of the Holy Spirit and for no other reason. He is our exemplar.

So we must begin our reflections with the indwelling presence of the Holy Spirit as our authority and inspiration for ministry that leads people to Christ. As Jesus taught his disciples in preparation for his death, God the Holy Spirit "will glorify me, because he will take what is mine and proclaim it to you. Everything that the Father has is mine. That's why I said that the Spirit takes what is mine and will proclaim it to you" (John 16:14-15). The Holy Spirit in the believer is the source of authority that is mediated through the means of grace. When we pronounce the epiclesis upon the bread and wine, we are invoking the authority of the Holy Spirit. The real question with which we must grapple here is whether or not the person presiding at Table is filled with the Holy Spirit, and thus has authority in God's eyes, to mediate real grace to those who partake.

---

3   1 Cor 12:13, CEB. The following verses are also CEB.

As already stated, Spirit baptism is not reserved to the ordained. It is a promise and Jesus' hope for every Christian.

There is also the example of Jesus' own life that utterly redefines authority, lordship, and power. In the great Kenotic Hymn of Philippians 2:5-11, Saint Paul writes:

> Adopt the attitude that was in Christ Jesus:
>
> Though he was in the form of God,
>
> he did not consider being equal with God something to exploit.
>
> But he emptied himself
>
> by taking the form of a slave
>
> and by becoming like human beings.
>
> When he found himself in the form of a human,
>
> he humbled himself by becoming obedient to the point of death,
>
> even death on a cross.
>
> Therefore, God highly honored him
>
> and gave him a name above all names,
>
> so that at the name of Jesus everyone in heaven, on earth, and under the earth might bow
>
> and every tongue confess that Jesus Christ is Lord, to the glory of God the Father.

Christ the Kenotic Icon of the Unseen God

In the Kenotic Hymn we find a clear, unambiguous theology of kenotic leadership and a strong text supporting kenotic ecclesiology,[4] for we are enjoined in the prelude to the hymn to let ourselves take on this same orientation, corporately, that is manifest in Jesus. This is the premier text of the epistles with which the church must contend in our day. Jesus is the icon—the exact image—of the unseen God, St. Paul writes elsewhere (Col 1:15). He is our exemplar of what the *imago Dei* means. To believe in

---

4   *Kenotic* refers to the self-emptying of Christ in v. 7, in which Christ freely and lovingly laid aside hierarchical power in order to become a servant and to find solidarity with all who are of low station and who suffer injustice.

and follow the God of Jesus, the Father of the Holy Trinity, revealed to us in Christ by the Spirit, is to live, think, and serve kenotically. This is an orientation of divine, evangelistic, missional wisdom that intentionally and repeatedly lays aside our hierarchies of power and privilege in order to find solidarity with the least of these. This is God's way of salvation.

Kenosis and the Missional Wisdom of God

People ask me sometimes why I use the term "missional wisdom" to describe evangelism. They want to know what it means and where it came from. It is a term grounded in kenotic ecclesiology.

The word *missio* simply means "sent out." Missional ecclesiology is the fundamental Christian identity of the church being God's sent-out people. This identity is both communal and individual. We are, in the words of Henri Nouwen, "taken, blessed, broken and given."[5] A missional life is always a eucharistic life. To take the bread and drink the cup is to say to God, "Here am I, Lord, send me."[6]

There are many definitions of wisdom, but one of the best understandings I have received is that wisdom is knowledge gained through suffering. I learned this from Wendy Miller, my dear friend and gifted teacher of spiritual direction. The wisest people I've ever known are those who have suffered and whose ministry is with those who suffer.

So being people of missional wisdom means we are God's people, gathered, forgiven, healed, blessed, and distributed to participate in God's mission of healing and redeeming the cosmos. To be people of missional wisdom is to go fully informed and listening to the knowledge gained through suffering, the knowledge that we receive from others who suffer, among whom we are sent, and the knowledge we ourselves bear as wounded healers.[7]

In this era of postcolonialism and neocolonialism, the first voices of suffering we must deeply hear are those who have been harmed by

---

5   Henri J. M. Nouwen develops this fourfold meditation in his beautiful little book *Life of the Beloved: Spiritual Living in a Secular World* (New York: Crossroads, 2002).

6   Isa 6:8. This text grounds one of the most widely used sending-forth hymns in *The United Methodist Hymnal*, "Here I Am, Lord," which is found in the section of the hymnal focusing on ecclesiology. Dan Schutte, "Here I Am, Lord," *The United Methodist Hymnal* (Nashville: The United Methodist Publishing House, 1989), hymn 593.

7   Becoming a wounded healer is not automatic. It requires intentionality, a contemplative orientation, sometimes therapeutic and focused spiritual resources, a community, and time. Developing and living with missional wisdom takes time. It cannot be hurried. For a beautiful classic on the way in which persons can become wounded healers see Henri J. M. Nouwen, *The Wounded Healer: Ministry in Contemporary Society* (New York: Doubleday, 1972).

exploitive, violent forms of Christendom—the church functioning as empire. These are not simply historic voices. All around us there are living souls who cry out to be liberated from religiously framed violence, from exclusion, labeling, shaming, attacking, and dehumanizing violence done blasphemously in the name of Jesus. We must heed what they say and repent. Otherwise we cannot become the face of Jesus to our neighbors, nor will we recognize the face of Jesus in them.

One of the saddest realities we must face as a church is the way that mission and evangelism have been hijacked to serve the interests of empire. By empire I mean the church functioning in collusion with secular and military power to get what it wants. Historically this has meant the domination of indigenous people and "others" of any kind in order to exploit and subjugate people and steal their resources. It has at times meant genocide.

By empire I also mean the church structuring itself as a fiercely hierarchical institution modeled after the Roman Empire. This has happened throughout much of Christian history.[8] We cannot faithfully bear witness to the real gospel as a church unless we come to terms with what has happened along these lines. We must actively work to heal the wounds caused by destructive, colonial, imperialistic forms of "mission" and "evangelism." That healing begins with our own repentance, moves into an awakening theological imagination, and continues to move outward in ever-widening circles into a world torn apart by religious violence. Our theology and practice of the Eucharist are at the absolute center of this work.[9] At the holy Table we act out everything we believe about ourselves, our neighbors, and our God. All of our secret beliefs about power, privilege, status, and control are laid bare with the bread and wine. How much of what we tell at the Table accords with the actual life and practice of Jesus?

To be a eucharistic people is to be a kenotic people, which requires a reversal of our usual hierarchies of privilege and power. This is the theme of the Kenotic Hymn. If we truly comprehend and accept the imperative of Saint Paul, to "let the same mind be in you that was in Christ Jesus," we cannot justify using the Eucharist, or any other sacrament, as a means of building hierarchies of power in the manner of a broken world. The Table must become the sign of an altogether different kingdom with its

---

8   For more about the church and empire, see Joerg Rieger, *Christ and Empire: From Paul to Postcolonial Times* (Minneapolis: Fortress Press, 2007).

9   The six paragraphs that end with this footnote are found in chap. 2 of my book coauthored with Larry Duggins, *Missional. Monastic. Mainline. A Guide to Starting Missional Micro-Communities in Historically Mainline Traditions* (Eugene, OR: Cascade, 2014), and are used with permission.

upside-down meaning of "Lord." The kenotic Table has profound political meanings along with everything else.

Who is qualified to serve Communion in a kenotic church? Is it the one with titles, robes, and stoles, the one called Reverend or better yet, the Reverend Doctor? Is it the one who often literally presides from an elevated position in order to look down upon the congregation? Are these trappings the "one thing necessary"?

Or is the sacred nonnegotiable a person who is being emptied in the manner and name of Christ, a person bearing witness to the love of God in the world? When all is said and done, is it not the presence of the Holy Spirit who anoints the bread and wine, making them become for us the body and blood of Christ? Should not both clergy and laity, assuming both are Spirit-filled, be capable of learning and practicing eucharistic theology? Should not the ordained person's unique role be more than simply able to serve the sacrament? Should it rather be one of serving, modeling, teaching, and companioning Spirit-filled laypersons as to the deep meaning of eucharistic theology so that when the laypersons serve the bread and wine they do so in a manner befitting Jesus?

To celebrate the Eucharist, to bless, break, and distribute the bread and wine is to identify oneself as a recipient of evangelistic grace and to commit to becoming a willing vessel of that same grace to others. Such grace is healing, forgiving, liberating, and renewing. It has spiritual, personal, relational, economic, and political dimensions. Baptism by water and the Spirit ought to be our credentials for distributing this grace. With these credentials, Jesus said, we shall receive power to become his witnesses in our city, our region, our nation, and the world (Acts 1:8). He gave this promise to a motley group of 120 women and men, none of whom was ordained.

A Service of Word and Table

In "A Service of Word and Table I," found on pages 6–11 of *The United Methodist Hymnal*, let us consider the language of the liturgy to see what the liturgy might tell us about authority and service, politics and grace. First, note how mutually inclusive the prayers and injunctions are for all who are gathered. From the opening prayer with its confession through all the prayers to the sending forth, both celebrant and congregants confess to sin and ask forgiveness. The entire assembly prays for illumination of the scriptures used. Either clergy or laity may read the scriptures. All persons gathered share in the recitation of the Apostle's Creed. No one is exempt. All persons give and receive signs of reconciliation and peace. All are invited to share in the offering. There is, throughout the liturgy, mutuality of hunger and reception of grace.

The language of the Great Thanksgiving is also inclusive, with the celebrant using "we" language to adore God, to remember the story of creation, Fall, and redemption. We all declare the holiness of God, we all announce the good news of Easter, that "Christ has died; Christ is risen; Christ will come again." We all pray the Our Father with confidence as children of God.

In the breaking of the bread the celebrant offers the prophetic words of inclusion, "Because there is one loaf, we, who are many, are one body, for we all partake of the one loaf. The bread which we break is a sharing in the body of Christ." And the celebrant continues, "The cup over which we give thanks is a sharing in the blood of Christ." That is, all of us, whether laity or clergy, ordained or not, are inseparably part of the body and blood of Christ. There is but one body, with one Head, who is Christ. According to the teaching of Saint Paul in 1 Corinthians 12:12-30, there is no hierarchy of importance or power in the body of Christ. Every member is irreplaceable, precious, and unrepeatable. Indeed, applying kenotic emphasis, the apostle states that, "the parts of the body that people think are the weakest are the most necessary. The parts of the body that we think are less honorable are the ones we honor the most. The private parts of our body that aren't presentable are the ones that are given the most dignity" (1 Cor 12:22-23, CEB). Our own eucharistic liturgy reminds us of the entire corpus of St. Paul's kenotic teaching. The kingdom of God is one in which our notions of power, privilege, and hierarchy are turned on their heads so that a little child—one in whom there is no status or privilege—may lead us.

Transcripts of the Trinity

Within our Wesleyan hymnody we also find resources to open our missional imagination about who is qualified to preside at Table and the political ramifications thereof. As Paul Chilcote notes, Charles Wesley writes repeatedly of the Christian as one who is a "transcript of the Trinity."[10] Using the language of perichoretic,[11] mystical union, Charles describes the

---

10 I am indebted to Professor Chilcote for his wonderful work in Wesleyan hymnody, and for sharing this list of Charles Wesley's songs. Professor Chilcote has written extensively about the spirituality of Wesleyan hymnody and is the past president of the Charles Wesley Society.

11 Perichoresis is the concept of the mutual, kenotic self-giving, self-emptying, and interpenetration of the Father, Son, and Spirit. The word *perichoresis* means "circle dance," and is an ancient metaphor for the Trinity.

worshiping, baptized believer as one who is in God and in whom God abides, so much so that to a watching world the ordinary Christian becomes a transcript, an icon, a facsimile of the Triune God. Notice the non-italicized lines in the following hymns:[12]

A Morning Hymn

"See the day-spring from afar
Usher'd by the morning-star!"
Haste; to him who sends the light,
Hallow the remains of night.
Souls, put on your glorious dress,
Waking into righteousness:
Cloath'd with Christ aspire to shine,
Radiance he of light divine;
Beam of the eternal beam,
He in God, and God in him!
Strive we him in us to see,
Transcript of the deity.[13]

The Communion of Saints. Part I.

Father, Son, and Spirit, hear
Faith's effectual, fervent prayer,
Hear, and our petitions seal;
Let us now the answer feel,
Mystically one with thee,
Transcript of the Trinity,
Thee let all our nature own
One in Three, and Three in One.[14]

---

12   Italics are my addition for emphasis.
13   "A Morning Hymn," *Hymns and Sacred Poems.* Published by John Wesley, M. A. Fellow of Lincoln College, Oxford; and Charles Wesley, M. A. Student of Christ-Church, Oxford, 2nd ed. (London: 1739), 178.
14   John Wesley, *Hymns and Sacred Poems* (1740), 138.

Hymn XV. "Why will ye die, O house of Israel." Ezek[iel] xviii. 31.

[7]*You, whom he ordain'd to be*
Transcript of the Trinity,
You, whom he in life doth hold,
You, for whom himself was sold,
You, on whom he still doth wait,
Whom he would again create,
Made by him, and purchas'd, why,
Why will you for ever die?[15]

Psalm VIII.

[6] *Him with glorious majesty*
Thy grace vouchsaf'd to crown,
Transcript of the One in Three,
He in thine image shone:
All thy works for him were made,
All did to his sway submit,
Fishes, birds, and beasts obey'd,
And bow'd beneath his feet.[16]

[CXCIII.] [Hymns for Christian Friends.] Hymn III.

[5] *Made like the first happy pair,*
Let us here thy nature share,
Holy, pure, and perfect be,
Transcript of the Trinity.[17]

---

15   John Wesley and Charles Wesley, *Hymns on God's Everlasting Love*, Hymn XV. "Why will ye die, O house of Israel" Ezek[iel] xviii. 31 (London: W. Strahan, [1742]), 44.

16   John Wesley and Charles Wesley, *A Collection of Psalms and Hymns.* 2nd ed. "Psalm VIII" (London: W. Strahan, [1743]), 66.

17   Charles Wesley, *Hymns and Sacred Poems*, vol. 2, [CXCIII. Hymns for Christian Friends.] (Bristol: Felix Farley, 17[39]), Hymn III, 264.

Hymn XXVIII. On the Death of Mrs. L[efevre], July 6, 1756. [Part I.]

[5] *She was (what words can never paint)*
A spotless soul, a sinless saint,
In perfect love renew'd,
A mirror of the deity,
A transcript of the One in Three,
A temple fill'd with God.[18]

XCVII. "Remember thy CREATOR (Heb., CREATORS) in the days of thy youth."—Eccles. xii. 1.

[2] *He challenges thy youthful days*
Who did thy being give:
Created for his only praise,
For him rejoice to live;

Transcript of holiness divine,
The Triune God proclaim,
And spirit, and soul, and flesh resign
To glorify his name.[19]

To become a follower of Jesus is to become an icon of the liberating, healing, making-all-things-new God. Who could possibly be more qualified to bless the sacrament, than a "transcript of the Trinity"?

Will Ordination Lose Its Meaning?

The hallmark of John Wesley's doctrine of perfection is that all Christians are called to enter into the fullest possible experience of love of God and neighbor. This process of sanctification is a lifelong progression that he calls "going on to perfection." In Wesleyan theology love of God always manifests in love of neighbor, for holiness always has both individual and

---

18 John and Charles Wesley, *Funeral Hymns* (London: Strahan, [1759]). Hymn XXVIII. "On the Death of Mrs. L[efevre]," July 6, 1756. [Part I.], 47.

19 Charles Wesley, *Hymns On The Trinity*, XCVII., Eccles. xii. 1, "Remember thy Creator (Heb., CREATORS) in the days of thy youth" (Bristol: William Pine [1767]), 63.

social dimensions. Every Christian is to be in union with God's missional purposes in the world, an ideal that few Christians reached in Wesley's day or in ours. Indeed, the detailed description of the "Almost Christian" in Wesley's sermon of the same name, puts to shame most clergy today.[20] For both John and Charles Wesley the normal Christian life for lay or clergy is one in which the believer is "ordain'd to be, transcript of the Trinity."[21]

While ordinands in the United Methodist Church must answer a question as to whether they expect to be made perfect in this life—and the correct answer is yes—Wesley makes no argument that going on to Christian perfection is only a prerogative of the ordained. Holiness of heart and life are normative for every baptized Christian. The Holy Spirit in plenitude, the One who is the giver of grace at the sacred Table, is just as available to laity as to the ordained in Wesley's theology.

Inevitably, though, the question arises: If laity are authorized to preside at Table, what will become of clergy? Why even have clergy if ordinary Christians are just as capable as clergy of kenotic leadership and service?[22]

Though I have many clergy colleagues who believe that properly trained laity should be given sacramental authority, sometimes anxious clergy say, "If laypeople can serve Communion there won't be anything unique or special about being ordained. Ordination will lose its meaning." This sentiment baffles me, partly because I am myself ordained, and the percentage of time that I spend blessing the Eucharist in my little community is quite small, approximately ten minutes per week. While I cherish that time, I know that there is a lot more involved in ordained ministry than serving the sacraments. The majority of my pastoral service has to do with helping people live their baptismal vows—resisting evil and injustice in whatever form it presents itself, trusting Jesus, and joining the *missio Dei*.

The primary role of the ordained person is chief equipper of the saints, who then become the distributed "body of Christ, redeemed by his blood." This is a much deeper, more rigorous understanding of both ordination and of eucharistic authority. An "equipper of the saints" orientation in ordained

---

20   John Wesley, "The Almost Christian," available at http://www.umcmission. org/Find-Resources/John-Wesley-Sermons/Sermon-2-The-Almost-Christian. For more on Wesley's doctrine of Christian Perfection see William J. Abraham, "Christian Perfection," *The Oxford Handbook of Methodist Studies*, ed. William J. Abraham and James E. Kirby (Oxford: Oxford University Press, 2009), 587–601.

21   Charles Wesley, Hymn XV. "Why will ye die, O house of Israel." Ezek[iel] xviii. 31. *Hymns on God's Everlasting Love* (1742), 44.

22   This is an interesting question in light of certain Anabaptist and Quaker traditions that eschew the tradition of ordination, but it is beyond the scope of our current discussion.

ministry requires skill in spiritual direction and community organizing, among other things. If in fact we rethink the role of the clergy as that of developing people who *become* broken bread and poured-out wine, who can also *serve* broken bread and poured-out wine, then we will have a far more robust understanding of "administration of the sacrament" by the clergy. This meaning of "administration" is one with profoundly missional, evangelistic, social, and political implications.

According to Ephesians 4:11-16, the work of the pastor/teacher is that of equipping the church for ministry, not doing the ministry for a passive and dependent church. The goal of pastoral ministry in this epistle is that the church can fully participate with God in the work of redemption and healing of the cosmos. By growing up into full stature in Christ, believers are able to "live as children of light," mediating grace and divine love to the world. Here again we are mindful of Charles Wesley's lovely phrase, "transcript of the Trinity." Notice the injunction of the author to pastors to nurture the church so that it grows in love and fullness, unity and knowledge of God's Son:

> He gave some apostles, some prophets, some evangelists, and some pastors and teachers. His purpose was to equip God's people for the work of serving and building up the body of Christ until we all reach the unity of faith and knowledge of God's Son. God's goal is for us to become mature adults—to be fully grown, measured by the standard of the fullness of Christ. As a result, we aren't supposed to be infants any longer who can be tossed and blown around by every wind that comes from teaching with deceitful scheming and the tricks people play to deliberately mislead others. Instead, by speaking the truth with love, let's grow in every way into Christ, who is the head. The whole body grows from him, as it is joined and held together by all the supporting ligaments. The body makes itself grow in that it builds itself up with love as each one does their part. (Eph 4:11-16, CEB)

Notice also that nothing is said in this text about the Eucharist, or who is qualified to administer it. One would think that if the most distinctive role of an ordained person is to serve the Eucharist, it would say so in the most explicit text in the New Testament that describes the work of a pastor. But the fact remains that nowhere in the New Testament are there rules about who is qualified to serve the sacrament. The only rules about the Eucharist have to do with receiving it, coming to the Table with one's heart prepared, rightly discerning and respecting the body of Christ in our community as well as in the bread and cup (1 Cor 11:17-24). Those rules apply to everyone.

According to *The Book of Discipline of The United Methodist Church*, the overarching purpose of ordination is to affirm and continue "the apostolic ministry through persons empowered by the Holy Spirit. As such, those who are ordained make a commitment to conscious living of the whole gospel and to the proclamation of that gospel to the end that the world may be saved."[23] The fulfillment of the ordained person's duties includes "leadership of the people of God through ministries of Service, Word, Sacrament, Order, Compassion, and Justice."[24] As I read these compelling words, the inarguable focus of ordination is *the apostolic life*, the life lived in utter devotion and surrender to God, the life that is *sent out in the name of Jesus* (that is the meaning of *apostle*) to equip others who will also be sent out in the *missio Dei*.

The Tradition behind the Tradition

Every beginner reading Wesley's work quickly comes to realize that Wesley had no intention of causing schism or creating a new denomination. Yet as Methodism came to North America and flourished, it eventually became a missional and evangelistic necessity to Wesley to authorize persons within the Methodist movement to serve the sacraments. He was unable to imagine laity serving in this manner—after all, he was a product of the eighteenth-century church. So all he could think of was ordaining people to the ministry so that sacraments could be served. After a protracted and painful struggle and the resistance of a local Anglican bishop toward ordaining people for the ministry in North America, Wesley broke with his own tradition and did just that. He appointed Thomas Coke, an Anglican priest, to become the superintendent of Methodists in the New World. Wesley also appointed "presbyters." Coke's co-superintendent was Francis Asbury, both of whom later came to be known as the first bishops of the Methodist Episcopal Church. Wesley was unauthorized to appoint or ordain anyone, yet he did it because it became a missional imperative. That is how our Methodist church began.

It was more important to the father of Methodism that new Christians be baptized and have access to the Lord's Supper than to follow the established tradition. It is time for us to take our cue from our own founder with regard to the tradition behind our tradition.

The soul of Methodism is holistic evangelism, what Wesley called spreading scriptural holiness across the land for the transformation of the world. Evangelism is the tradition behind our tradition. As was true in the beginning of our movement, Methodists today find ourselves at a critical

---

23   *The Book of Discipline of the United Methodist Church* (Nashville: The United Methodist Publishing House, 2012), ¶303.1.

24   Ibid., ¶303.2.

juncture in history. The Western church is in steep decline, mostly unable and often unwilling to reach its secular neighbors.

In the past century The United Methodist Church, along with every other denomination in North America, has declined. According to a 2012 Pew Forum on Religion in America, 28 percent of Americans have left the church in which they were raised.[25] One in four persons ages 18–29 claim no religious affiliation at all. Of these, 13 percent were raised in nonreligious homes.[26] Many studies indicate that the shrinkage of the mainline church will continue and escalate, much as the Anglican Church has dwindled in the UK. In the midst of steady numeric and financial decline many churches are closing, reducing the number of available clergy for the population. There is also the fact that numbers of young clergy have radically fallen in The United Methodist Church in the past thirty years. The reduction of clergy on the near horizon brought about by these and other factors led the 2012 General Conference to designate seven million dollars to a Young Clergy Initiative Fund, to try to stem the loss of future ordained leaders.[27] Denominational leaders are hard pressed to attract into old patterns and expectations a younger generation that frankly does not care if the institution fails. As many of my divinity students have said, "We are tired of being told we need to save the institution. What we want to do is answer God's call to mission."

A truly Wesleyan renewal of the church to its mission is going to require the gifts and call of ordinary Christians. Early Methodism grew rapidly in North America not because of clergy, but because of laity. Methodism in the future will rise or fall based upon how we equip and deploy lay Christians.

Missional and New Monastic Fresh Expressions

As the institution of Methodism is in decline, however, a grassroots movement in multiple expressions is growing to empower laity to start and lead different kinds of faith communities. Several initiatives are emerging within Methodism, including the Lay Missionary Planting Network developed by

---

25   "U.S. Religious Landscape Survey," Pew Forum on Religion and Public Life, 2012, http://religions.pewforum.org/reports.

26   Daniel Cox, "Born and Raised: More Americans Are Being Raised Without Religion and Choosing to Stay that Way," *Huffington Post*, July 31, 2013, http://www.huffingtonpost.com/daniel-cox/born-and-raised-more-amer_b_3682847.html?utm_hp_ref=fb&src=sp&comm_ref=false#sb=971572b=facebook.

27   Jay Voorhees, "Young Clergy Summit: Focusing on a New Generation of Church Leaders," *The United Methodist Reporter*, September 7, 2012, http://www.unitedmethodistreporter.com/2012/09/young-clergy-summit-focusing-on-a-new-generation-of-church-leaders/.

Rev. Sam Rodriguez, the missional community training and coaching that Rev. Paul Nixon of the Epicenter Group is doing with Path One (the church planting arm of The United Methodist Church),[28] and the Missional Wisdom Foundation, which resources annual conferences and other groups to start and lead missional and new monastic communities that are led primarily and permanently by teams of laity.[29] No doubt others will also emerge and evolve.

These Wesleyan expressions of the missional and new monastic movement have much in common with early Methodism, which was in many ways a lay monastic movement.[30] While the Lay Missionary Planting Network is designed to help Hispanic laity plant faith communities that eventually result in traditional, clergy-led congregations, Missional Wisdom communities are designed to be led permanently by teams of laypersons who follow a disciplined rule of life based upon United Methodist membership vows. These communities are located in diverse social contexts where they practice incarnational ministry. By anchoring these smaller house churches with established congregations, the missional communities can have some oversight and participation of clergy and impact the church with their evangelistic practices of prayer, hospitality, and justice. And the missional communities can find in the anchor church a strong partner in prayer and encouragement and other forms of support. Here and in other fresh expres-sions of Wesleyan, missional, lay-led communities, thoroughly equipped and accountable laypersons could be authorized to serve the Eucharist. Because these kinds of communities are practicing a eucharistic life, incarnating the gospel in a life of prayer, hospitality, and justice, the addition of sacramental authority would be not only reasonable, but in keeping with John Wesley's example of choosing the tradition behind the tradition.

Breaking Down Sinful Walls

In our rapidly changing world that marks the end of Christendom in the West, can we comprehend that the flattening of power, the move toward democratization, and the rejection of dictatorships globally is a blessing and not a curse? These tectonic shifts are spiritual and political movements extrinsic to the church that in some ways embody the radical teaching of Galatians 3:28: "There is neither Jew nor Greek; there is neither slave nor

---

28   http://www.epicentergroup.org/#/about-our-team.

29   www.missionalwisdom.com.

30   By "lay monastic movement" I refer to ordinary laity following a disciplined rule of life involving personal and corporate acts of piety and charity, and especially engaging systemic social injustice.

free; nor is there male and female, for you are all one in Christ Jesus" (CEB). The breaking down of sinful hierarchies of power based on gender, race, and class that war against the fundamental dignity of humans and the sanctity of human life is fundamental to God's work of redemption. This is true outside the church and inside the church. The most shocking aspect of Pentecost was the radical inclusion of women and diverse nationalities in the receiving and giving of the Spirit, the telling and hearing of the good news. Pentecost breaks down every wall that sin has built.

In our postcolonial world the only kind of Christian witness that can speak with moral authority or believability to persons who have suffered much at the hands of Christendom is the apostolic, kenotic, eucharistic, pentecostal gospel of Jesus Christ. This apostolic gospel is the one that the powers and principalities fear, for it brings down strongholds and sets the captives free.[31]

This apostolic, evangelistic witness must first be welcomed into our own hearts and lived in community among our own neighbors. It must be spoken of lovingly and humbly wherever wider opportunity is given. And it must be manifest in the way we conduct our worship. For at the Table of Christ we enact everything we believe about ourselves, our neighbors, and our God.

---

31 Ephesians 6:10-20 is the text that tells Christians as a community how to resist organized forces of wickedness that oppress people and attack the work of God. In 2 Corinthians 10:4-6 the apostolic work is described as potent warfare against spiritual forces. Both of these texts have deeply political, economic, and spiritual dimensions.

TWELVE

Eucharist and Formation

Paul W. Chilcote

Meals form people, and in the practice of the Christian community, no meal shapes those who follow Jesus more than the Eucharist. Meals shape identity, situate communities in a particular place in the world, and establish ways of being and doing in relation to God and others. It is not too much to say that the Eucharist is the primary sign-act through which God forms both individual believers and the community of faith. In his exploration of the liturgical formation of Christian identity, Albert Walsh observes:

> Word and Sacrament together form the essential and most influential liturgical matrix for the transformation and maintenance of a distinctive Christian identity. ... the eucharistic-evangel, as a "means of grace" and as a worship experience in which the "real presence" of Jesus Christ is most clearly revealed, brings clarity to the identity of Jesus Christ as the crucified, risen, returning Lord, and that this revelation of Christ's particular identity and presence encounters, transforms, and maintains in grace the distinctive identity of the Christian.[1]

The issue of Eucharist and formation, then, reaches deeply into the very heart of the gospel and the way in which God both transforms and forms beloved children through the most intimate means of a meal. Several critical issues revolve around this theme viewed through the lens of the Wesleyan tradition, including the centrality and formative nature of meals, the Eucharist as a primary means of grace, the way in which this meal forms both the interior and exterior life of the participants, and the formative power of the fourfold action of the Eucharist as a paradigm for the Christian life.

The Centrality and Formative Nature of Meals

By the time we arrived in Zimbabwe in 1992, a terrible drought had decimated the entire southern region of Africa. My wife, working with nurses and health-care providers at the hospital nearby, soon identified five

---

1   Albert J. D. Walsh, *The Eucharist's Biographer: The Liturgical Formation of Christian Identity* (Eugene, OR: Pickwick Publications, 2012), 1–2.

hundred critically malnourished children in the large commercial farms that normally produced an abundance of crops for that nation and beyond. Every family we visited in one particular area revealed unbelievable levels of deprivation and despair. The scenario was the same at every turn. "Where is your food?" we would ask. "We have no food," came the response. "Only God can save us now." God provided an opportunity for us to serve those dear, hungry brothers and sisters in Africa. Widows and orphans were most at risk. Whenever we made a delivery of basic food items and supplies to those who needed it most, the women would fall to the ground, weeping, and then they would spring to their feet, singing the praises of God. They all looked to God who used us as instruments to provide them with food. Our common dependence on God made us one and enabled us to celebrate God's amazing grace and provision together.

Our African friends taught us the significance of a meal. Experienced thousands of times in our own culture, the meal took on heightened significance in that African context. For the African, meals establish relationships as well as sustain the life of a community. The sharing of food consummates the interaction of people in the home. The meal shapes the participants—forms a bond—makes them one. The more we reflected upon these realities, the more clearly we discerned the connections between meals and formation in the biblical witness. Elliott Wright discusses the significance of the meal and its power to shape communities of faith:

> Faith and food are inextricably linked in human experience and belief. This includes the act of eating as well as the natural cycles of planting and harvest. One reason is the obvious importance of nourishment to life. Food is so essential that the activities involved in obtaining, preparing, and enjoying it are closely related to basic human concerns: happiness and sadness, want and plenty, life and death—even God.[2]

It is not too much to say that the Passover Meal, celebrating the deliverance of the people of Israel from bondage in Egypt, has shaped the Jewish community through its history more than any other single act. This meal established their identity and shaped them into the delivered people of Yahweh. In the New Testament, meals play an equally important role in terms of forming the people of Jesus' way. Jesus' first miracle involves the changing of water into wine at a wedding feast in Cana (John 2:1-11). His feeding of the five thousand is recorded in every Gospel. A

---

2   Elliott Wright, "Faith and Food: Biblical Perspectives," *New World Outlook* (September/October 2001): 8.

feast consummates the parable of the prodigal son and the celebration of forgiveness and homecoming (Luke 15:23-27). Jesus and his disciples celebrate the Passover Meal on the threshold of his death (Mark 14:12-25), and the meal at Emmaus celebrates the power of resurrected life (Luke 24:13-32). Parallel to the Passover Meal for the Jewish community, the Eucharist establishes the identity of the followers of Jesus and fashions them into the New Israel. This meal shapes them into a community of grace through the reception of God's grace in a meal, *re*-members them through the remembrance (*anamnesis*) of God's mighty acts in Jesus Christ, and forms them into a covenant community through the celebration of a New Covenant meal.

Eucharist as a Primary Means of Grace

The term *means of grace* can be defined as those outward signs, words, or actions ordained by God to be the ordinary channels by which persons in search of life encounter God's grace.[3] Wesley described prayer and fasting, Bible study, Christian fellowship, and participation in the Sacrament of Holy Communion as "instituted" means of grace, as opposed to "prudential" means, such as doing all the good you can. The instituted means, in particular, not only nurtured and sustained growth in grace among the early Methodist people, but formed them into a powerful religious movement, and the founders of this movement believed that the Eucharist played a particular role in the process of this formation. Not only does the Sacred Meal enable the community to remember the past event of the cross and Christ's redemptive work for all, it celebrates the presence of the living Lord in a feast of thanksgiving and orients the community in hope toward the consummation of all things in the great heavenly banquet to come. No means of grace was as important to the Wesleys, in terms of its shaping influence, as this Holy Meal.[4]

In her work on *Wesleyan Eucharistic Spirituality*, Lorna Khoo explores the model of "forming lives through the eucharist" in the early Methodist movement.[5] The program of the Wesleys entailed both structured and unstructured formation. The simple fact that the Lord's Supper was

---

3   John Wesley employs this basic definition in his sermon on "The Means of Grace," in *The Works of John Wesley*, vol. 1, ed. Albert C. Outler (Nashville: Abingdon Press, 1984), 395.

4   The following paragraphs are drawn in larger measure from one of my earlier articles, "Eucharist among the Means of Grace," *Word and Deed: A Journal of Salvation Army Theology and Ministry* 8, no. 2 (May 2006): 5–22.

5   Lorna Khoo, *Wesleyan Eucharistic Spirituality* (Adelaide: ATF Press, 2005), 179–92.

celebrated regularly and that "constant communion" was modeled by the
Wesleys themselves, deepened the shaping influence of these events:

> Formation in Wesleyan eucharistic spirituality did not address merely the
> intellect. It sought to touch both head and heart, affection and imagination.
> A very important element in eucharistic formation was the use of the eucha-
> ristic hymns. . . . The hymns helped Methodists to focus on Christ and his
> cross. This is the secret of Wesleyan eucharistic spirituality: the singing of the
> hymns during the long communion services.[6]

The *Hymns on the Lord's Supper*, a collection of 166 hymns for use at
the Sacrament, published jointly by the Wesley brothers in 1745, affords a
particularly rich iconic landscape to explore, an intersection of Eucharist and
formation well worth scrutiny.[7] These hymns elicit a vision of the Sacrament
as a memorial of the sufferings and death of Christ, as a sign and means
of grace, and as a pledge of heaven, as well as explore the meaning of
sacrifice, both that of Christ and of the believer. With regard to these various
dimensions of the Sacrament, the Lord's Supper as a sign and means of grace
played a particularly significant formative role in the lives of the Methodists.

The Eucharist celebrates the presence of the living Christ. This present
dimension interfaces directly with the concept of the Sacrament as a sign
and means of grace. Without any question, the earliest Eucharistic feasts of
the Christian community, at which the disciples of Jesus "ate their food with
glad and generous hearts" (Acts 2:46, NRSV), were characterized by joy and
thanksgiving. The term *Eucharist* itself comes directly from the Greek word
eucharistia meaning "thanksgiving." This was the "Thanksgiving Feast" of
the early Christians; a celebration of the Resurrection and the presence of
the living Lord. Charles Wesley captures that primitive Christian spirit:

> *Jesu, we thus obey*
> *Thy last and kindest word,*
> *Here in thine own appointed way*
> *We come to meet our Lord;*

---

6   Ibid., 185–86.
7   Given the fact that the Wesleyan Revival in eighteenth-century Britain was
     both evangelical and sacramental, it should not be surprising that the eucha-
     ristic hymns of John and Charles Wesley have received much attention over
     the years. See the groundbreaking work of J. Ernest Rattenbury, *The Eucharistic
     Hymns of John and Charles Wesley* (London: Epworth Press, 1948) and the more
     recent study by Daniel B. Stevick, *The Altar's Fire: Charles Wesley's Hymns on
     the Lord's Supper* (London: Epworth Press, 2005). This essay is not intended to
     be an exhaustive analysis of the hymns in terms of the theme—Eucharist and
     formation; rather, the hymns will illustrate various facets of the theme.

> The way thou hast injoin'd
> Thou wilt therein appear:
>> We come with confidence to find
> Thy special presence here.
>
> Our hearts we open wide
> To make the Saviour room:
>> And lo! The Lamb, the crucified,
> The sinner's friend is come!
> His presence makes the feast,
> And now our bosoms feel
>> The glory not to be exprest,
> The joy unspeakable.[8]

In one of his most powerful hymns, he plumbs the depths of this mystery of faith:

> O the depth of love divine,
>> Th' unfathomable grace!
> Who shall say how bread and wine
>> God into man conveys?
> How the bread his flesh imparts,
>> How the wine transmits his blood,
> Fills his faithful people's hearts
>> With all the life of God!
>
> Sure and real is the grace,
>> The manner be unknown;
> Only meet us in thy ways
>> And perfect us in one,
> Let us taste the heavenly powers,
>> Lord, we ask for nothing more;
> Thine to bless, 'tis only ours
>> To wonder, and adore.[9]

---

8   John and Charles Wesley, *Hymns on the Lord's Supper* (Bristol: Farley, 1745), Hymn XXXI, st. 1–2, 69. Referred to as HLS hereafter. The texts used throughout are from the critical edition available online through *Wesley and Methodist Texts and Research Resources,* Center for Studies in the Wesleyan Tradition, Duke Divinity School. https://divinity.duke.edu/initiatives/cswt/charles-published-verse.
9   Wesley, HLS, Hymn LVII, st. 1 & 4, 41.

Through faith, the outward sign transmits the signified. Since the Wesleys always conceived grace in relational categories, in their view, God applies grace to those who believe through the restoration or sustaining of a covenant bond. And the heights to which faith can move and depths to which this relationship can reach are immeasurable:

> Communion closer far I feel,
>   And deeper drink th' atoning blood,
> The joy is more unspeakable,
>   And yields me larger draughts of God,
> 'Till nature faints beneath the power,
> And faith fill'd up can hold no more.[10]

Formation through eucharistic practice entails both the interior life of believers—their attitudes and deepest qualities of character—and the way in which they live in relation to others—their exterior life. Personal formation through participation in the Meal (who one is) connects intimately with the shaping of behavior (what one does) through the sign-act of Eucharist. While interiority and exteriority cohere on such a deep level and should not be separated in an artificial way, it is helpful to think about them as separate categories.

Interior, Personal Formation

All meals have an intimate quality, and the Sacrament touches people at the deepest personal level, shaping them in the deepest possible ways. Two particular aspects of interior formation inform a Wesleyan view of the Sacrament.

The Sacrament *forms believers through spiritual nourishment related to God's grace*. The primary purpose of any meal is to provide nourishment for those who are hungry. The dimensions of this shaping influence are more complex than immediately meets the eye. One eats when one is hungry, so participation in the meal, first, and perhaps foremost, acknowledges a need. Individuals gather around the Table in recognition of their need of grace and God's provision. The meal shapes a healthy sense of vulnerability—of acknowledgment—in the hearts and minds of those who receive. Charles Wesley sings:

> Come to the feast, for Christ invites,
>   And promises to feed,

---

10   Wesley, HLS, Hymn LIV, st. 5, 39.

'Tis here his closest love unites
The members to their head.

'Tis here he nourishes his own
   With living bread from heaven,
Or makes himself to mourners known,
   And shews their sins forgiven.[11]

Those who are hungry and thirsty come to the Feast. Wesley associates the spiritual needs of God's children with the primary physical needs of life in a simple, two-stanza hymn:

Lord of life, thy followers see
Hungring, thirsting after thee,
At thy sacred table feed,
Nourish us with living bread.

Chear us with immortal wine,
Heavenly sustenance divine,
Grant us now a fresh supply,
Now relieve us, or we die.[12]

"This eucharistic feast," claims Wesley, "Our every want supplies."[13] The Holy Meal forms a true self-understanding in the hearts and minds of God's people who recognize their need and have the assurance of God's provision in Christ. In an article entitled "Worship as Acknowledgment," Robert Cushman maintained that authentic worship

> is a choice between apparent fulfillment through self-assertion or true fulfillment through acknowledgment of responsible dependency. . . . it is the glad and eager acknowledgment of the claims of the Kingdom. . . . It cries, "O God, Thou art my God; early will I seek Thee; my soul thirsteth for Thee . . ." (Ps 63:1). The language of worship is prayer; it is a sign of man's apprehension that he stands in the higher Presence.[14]

---

11   Wesley, HLS, Hymn LX, 43–44.
12   Wesley, HLS, Hymn XXXIV, 26.
13   Wesley, HLS, Hymn IV, st. 2, 4.
14   Robert E. Cushman, *Faith Seeking Understanding: Essays Theological and Critical* (Durham, NC: Duke University Press, 1981), 181–83.

The Eucharist inculcates this spirit in the believer.

Second, Holy Communion *conforms believers to the image of Christ*. In the Wesleyan theological tradition, the fundamental goal of the Christian life is the fullest possible growth into the love of Christ—an ongoing restoration of the *imago Dei* in the life of the believer. "In Wesleyan eucharistic spirituality," writes Lorna Khoo, "Christ is the one who calls us, enabling us by his grace and through his Spirit to grow toward the goal: Christian perfection. The calling and the goal would form the character of the Methodists and also colour their perceptions of life."[15] Perhaps the most critical question in this regard, as David Lowes Watson has pointed out, is "how to permit God's grace to foster a maturity of constant obedience, so that sanctifying grace might work with an unimpeded love."[16] John Wesley had learned from Thomas à Kempis that humility and purity of intention were the most critical keys in this regard. These two interior qualities shape the primary contours of the work for which he was most famous and that influenced Wesley most deeply, the *Imitation of Christ*.[17] Purity of intention implies a will attuned to God's own will and holiness—having God first and foremost in thought, feeling, and action. When Thomas describes simplicity and purity as the two wings that enable the soul to soar (II.4), he directs the reader's attention to the heights of holiness achieved by those whose hearts and wills are firmly fixed on God. Eucharist shapes these desires and aspirations in the heart.

It is this connection between the Eucharist and growth toward the *telos* of perfect love that is so distinctive with regard to formation through Eucharist in the Wesleyan tradition. An examination of the writings of the early Methodist people, as well as the Wesleys, reveals constant reference to participation in the Sacrament as the way to facilitate growth toward maturity in Christ. The Methodists simply affirmed that participation in the Eucharist shapes the fullest possible love in the disciple of Jesus.

> *O what a soul-transporting feast*
> *Doth this communion yield!*
> *Remembering here thy Passion past*
> *We with thy love are fill'd.*

---

15   Khoo, *Wesleyan Eucharistic Spirituality*, 179.

16   David Lowes Watson, *Accountable Discipleship* (Nashville: Discipleship Resources, 1985), 34.

17   See my edition of this work, *The Imitation of Christ: Selections Annotated & Explained* (Woodstock, VT: SkyLight Paths Publications, 2012).

Sure instrument of present grace
Thy sacrament we find,
Yet higher blessings it displays,
And raptures still behind.[18]

Conformity to Christ entails a second dimension intimately bound to the Sacrament of the Lord's Supper; the fullest possible infilling of love ultimately means conformity to the cross as well. The Holy Mystery demonstrates with absolute clarity that the cross-shaped life is the only authentic Christian existence. The "suffering servants" of God are called to take up their crosses daily in multifarious acts of self-sacrificial love.[19] Nowhere do the images of self-emptying, service, and sacrifice—the signs of the cruciform life—converge more poignantly than in the *Hymns on the Lord's Supper*. The thirty hymns of section 5 in this collection, "Concerning the Sacrifice of our Persons," focus upon this living oblation of the church and all who seek to be faithful disciples of their Lord. The desire to "be all like Thee," inevitably leads to the heartfelt prayer, "Grant us full conformity, / Plunge us deep into thy death."[20] Wesley describes the full extent of solidarity with the crucified Lord:

His servants shall be
With Him on the tree,
Where Jesus was slain
His crucified servants shall always remain.[21]

In a profoundly anamnetic hymn placing the believer at the foot of the cross, Wesley asks the rhetorical question, "Would the Saviour of mankind / Without His people die?" The question elicits one of the most powerful images in the Eucharistic hymns: "No, to Him we all are join'd / As more than standers by." Given the fact that Christ took the suffering of the world freely upon himself, even to the point of death on a cross, "We attend the slaughter'd Lamb, / And suffer for His cause.[22] The Eucharist shapes the followers of Jesus into a community that suffers with others for the sake of love. Lester Ruth has summarized this vision of Eucharistic formation well:

---

18 Wesley, HLS, Hymn XCIV, st. 1 and 2, 82.
19 I have explored this theme more fully in "'Claim Me for Thy Service': Charles Wesley's Vision of Servant Vocation," Proceedings of The Charles Wesley Society 11 (2006–2007): 69–85.
20 Wesley, HLS, Hymn CLIV, st. 3, 129.
21 Wesley, HLS, Hymn CXLII, st. 3, 120.
22 Wesley, HLS, Hymn CXXXI, st. 1, 112.

The Wesleys did not intend a merely ritualized, formal concept of sacrifice in the Lord's Supper. They intended that the Lord's Supper would show how we actually live by taking up the cross daily, dying to sin, denying ourselves, and enduring suffering that we might do good in the world. The Lord's Supper reveals that we are both priests and sacrifices like Christ is. This is the essence of what it means to be God's people.[23]

The Eucharist "forms the Savior in the soul," to use a phrase of Charles Wesley, by reminding the disciples of Jesus of their true identity—children of God shaped by grace. It also facilitates the process by which they are conformed to the image of Christ by setting before them a goal toward which to strive under the grace of God. The Meal that proclaims Christ's death until he comes establishes a cruciform pattern of life in the faithful disciple and draws all the followers of Jesus into a community shaped by the cross and resurrection as well.

Exterior, Communal Formation

All meals also have a profound communal dimension, and the Sacrament creates a particular community with a peculiar vocation in the world. Two aspects of exterior formation are parallel to the interior, personal shaping influence of the Sacrament.

First, the Eucharist *unites believers with Christ in a community of joy.* It is not too much to say that the Sacrament forms the church—the one, holy, apostolic community of God's grace. In stanza 1 of the first hymn cited above with regard to interior formation, the singer confesses "'Tis here his closest love unites / The members to their head."[24] As Saint Paul observes in his First Letter to the Corinthians: "Because there is one bread, we who are many are one body, for we all partake of the one bread" (10:17, NRSV). *The Dogmatic Constitution on the Church (Lumen Gentium)*, promulgated by Pope Paul VI, provides eloquent reflection on this particular shaping quality of the Sacrament:

> Really partaking of the body of the Lord in the breaking of the Eucharistic bread, we are taken up into communion with Him and with one another. . . . All the members ought to be molded in the likeness of Him, until Christ be formed in them. For this reason we, who have been made to

---

23   Lester Ruth, "Word and Table," in *The Wesleyan Tradition: A Paradigm for Renewal*, ed. Paul W. Chilcote (Nashville: Abingdon Press, 2002), 146.

24   Wesley, HLS, Hymn LX, p. 43.

conform with Him, who have died with Him and risen with Him, are taken up into the mysteries of His life, until we will reign together with Him.[25]

The Eucharist *re*-members the body of Christ, brings together its constitutive parts, and recreates the church for the purpose of its mission in the world. Michael Lawler maintains:

> Sacraments do not merely manifest some reality, they also realize it and make it concretely real. Eucharist, therefore, does not merely manifest communion in the body of Christ, it also effects communion. In eucharist the Holy Spirit moves believers to communion, thus constituting the *koinonia*-communion that is the church of Christ and of God. Where eucharist is celebrated in communion, there is wholly church. . . . it is in the eucharistic meal, above all, that the Spirit of God makes believers-in-communion, thus constituting the church.[26]

The act of sharing together in the Sacrament forms the church—the body of Christ—and the keynote of their *koinonia* is joy.

> *Our hearts we open wide*
> *To make the Saviour room:*
> *   And lo! The Lamb, the crucified,*
> *The sinner's friend is come!*
> *His presence makes the feast,*
> *And now our bosoms feel*
> *   The glory not to be exprest,*
> *The joy unspeakable.*[27]

Joy originates from union with Christ. The Sacrament celebrates the headship of Christ over the body and creates a new fellowship within one family, redeemed by his blood.

> *Come dear Redeemer of mankind,*
> *   We long thy open face to see,*
> *Appear, and all who seek shall find*
> *   Their bliss consummated in thee.*[28]

25 Pope Paul VI, *Lumen Gentium: The Dogmatic Constitution on the Church* (New York: Pauline Books, 1965), I.7.
26 Michael G. Lawler, *What Is and What Ought to Be: The Dialectic of Experience, Theology, and Church* (New York: Continuum, 2005), 102.
27 Wesley, HLS, Hymn LXXXI, st. 2, 69.
28 Wesley, HLS, Hymn XXXVIII, st. 5, 29.

Charles Wesley envisaged the Heavenly Banquet as the ultimate expression and fulfillment of God's joy in the heart of the believer. Seldom does he reach the lyrical heights of the following ecstatic affirmation:

> *How glorious is the life above*
>   *Which in this ordinance we taste;*
> *That fulness of celestial love,*
>   *That joy which shall for ever last!*
>
> *That heavenly life in Christ conceal'd*
>   *These earthen vessels could not bear,*
> *The part which now we find reveal'd*
>   *No tongue of angels can declare.*
>
> *The light of life eternal darts*
>   *Into our souls a dazling ray,*
> *A drop of heav'n o'reflows our hearts,*
>   *And deluges the house of clay.*
>
> *Sure pledge of extacies unknown*
>   *Shall this divine communion be,*
> *The ray shall rise into a sun,*
>   *The drop shall swell into a sea.*[29]

Second, the Holy Mystery *forms a missional community for witness and service in the world.*[30] Frank Andersen articulates this vision in a fresh way for the contemporary church: "Each Sunday, then, we gather to symbolize our identity in Christ. We gather to *build the holy* community and to keep alive the vision that impelled Jesus. What he achieved in his short, redemptive life is now being completed by us. On us has been conferred his consciousness and mission: we are his contemporary presence."[31] The connection between mission and the Sacrament was not lost on the Wesleys and can be discerned most clearly in their concept of eucharistic sacrifice. We have already seen how the Sacrament shapes

---

29   Wesley, HLS, Hymn CI, 87.
30   The following paragraphs are based in part on my article, "The Integral Nature of Worship and Evangelism: Insights from the Wesleyan Tradition," *Asbury Theological Journal* 61, no. 1 (Spring 2006): 7–23.
31   Frank Andersen, *Making the Eucharist Matter* (Notre Dame, IN: Ave Maria Press, 1998), 64.

a cruciform spirit of self-sacrifice in the interior life of the believer. But this spirit finds profoundly communal expression through the Eucharist as well. Charles Wesley's sermon on Acts 20:7 articulates a concept of sacrifice consonant with the view he espouses in his *Hymns on the Lord's Supper* devoted to this theme. He views the Lord's Supper as a "re-presentation" of the sacrifice of Christ.[32] A half century ago, J. Ernest Rattenbury demonstrated that Wesley's emphasis falls on the twofold oblation of the church in the Sacrament. The body of Christ offered is not merely a sacred symbol of Christ's "once-for-all" act of redemption; the Sacrament shapes the people of God into a living sacrifice for the life of the world.[33]

Charles Wesley's hymns help to clarify the relationship between the redemptive sacrifice of Christ and the missional, sacrificial character of the Christian community, a connection actualized in the lives of those who participate repeatedly in eucharistic worship. In this regard, he adheres very closely to the position articulated in Daniel Brevint's *The Christian Sacrament and Sacrifice*, namely, "The main intention of Christ herein was not the bare *remembrance* of His Passion; but over and above, to invite us to His Sacrifice":[34]

> *While faith th' atoning blood applies,*
> *Ourselves a living sacrifice*
> *We freely offer up to God:*
> *And none but those his glory share*
> *Who crucified with Jesus are,*
> *And follow where their Saviour trod.*

> *Saviour, to thee our lives we give,*
> *Our meanest sacrifice receive,*
> *And to thy own oblation join,*
> *Our suffering and triumphant head,*
> *Thro' all thy states thy members lead,*
> *And seat us on the throne divine.*[35]

---

32 Kenneth G. C. Newport, ed., *The Sermons of Charles Wesley* (Oxford: Oxford University Press, 2001), 277–86.

33 See Rattenbury, *Eucharistic Hymns*, 123–47.

34 Quoted in Rattenbury, *Eucharistic Hymns*, 178. This Anglican tract functioned as a preface to the Wesleys' collection of eucharistic hymns.

35 Wesley, HLS, Hymn CXXVIII, st. 3, 110.

More than anything else, the church expresses this sacrifice through its commitment to justice in the world.

A Latin American Methodist leader shared a poignant story with me some years ago that expresses this formational aspect of the Eucharist dramatically. During a period of horrendous oppression on the part of his government, he and many of the members of his congregation found themselves in prison on an Easter Sunday morning. Many within their community had been killed and many of them feared for their own lives. Despite the fact that they had no provisions for a celebration of Holy Communion, they sang resurrection hymns together, prayed, and the pastor led them through the liturgy. When it came time to consecrate the elements, he elevated his empty hands and said: "The bread which we do not have today is a reminder of those who are hungry, for those who are oppressed, and for those who yearn for the provision that only God can give." After consecrating the bread, he took an invisible cup in his hands, and said: "The wine which we do not have today is a reminder of those who, with Jesus, have shed their blood for the sake of righteousness. Through their sacrifice, they join with Jesus in witness to the triumph of God's love over all those forces that seek to destroy life. Through our participation in this sacred meal we promise to seek righteousness, justice, and peace in all we do." The Eucharist *re*-forms the church—the community of God's faithful people who are committed to God's will and God's way. It constitutes a righteous fellowship that moves ineluctably from the Table into the world to proclaim and live God's vision of shalom for the world.

Shaped by the Fourfold Action of the Eucharist

In the Methodist tradition, Jim White was one of the first to describe the Sacrament as a "sign-act of love." "Sacramental worship is distinguished by its use of sign-acts," he observed, "that is acts that convey meaning. . . . These sign-acts have signified sacred things and have become ways of expressing through the senses what no physical sense could perceive, God's self-giving."[36] According to White, God acts in the sacraments as love made visible through relationships of love within the community. In the Prayer of Great Thanksgiving—the prayer that consecrates the sacramental elements for sacred use—words and actions combine to provide a powerful manifestation of God's love. The sign-act embodied through this prayer shapes the hearts and minds of those who participate in the Table, and at the center of this prayer lies

---

36   James F. White, *Introduction to Christian Worship*, 3rd ed. (Nashville: Abingdon Press, 2000), 175–76.

what Dom Gregory Dix described as the fourfold action of the Eucharist.[37] As the faithful repeatedly participate in the Eucharistic actions of taking, blessing, breaking, and giving—the constitutive elements of an authentic, Christian life—God conforms them to the image of Christ. Their lives become truly eucharistic as faith working by love leads to holiness of heart and life.

Just as Jesus *takes* the bread and the cup into his hands, he takes the lives of the faithful, if they have the courage to relinquish them into the care of the Lord, to be used for God's purposes. As disciples witness the repeated action of the celebrant taking the elements into her or his hands, they are reminded of the need to resign themselves to Christ so that God, through the power of the Spirit, can shape them into fit instruments of God's love. "Yes, Lord, we are Thine," confesses Wesley, "And gladly resign / Our souls to be fill'd with the fulness Divine."[38] Whenever the faithful put themselves in the hands of God, the offering is holistic, involving both soul and body. It is nothing less than permitting God to take what God has already freely given. "Now, O God, Thine own I am," affirms the servant of the Lord, "Now I give Thee back Thy own."[39] Eucharist embodies the two concomitant actions—the faithful present themselves to God; Jesus takes the faithful in his hands for divine purpose. Wesley expressed these themes eloquently in a hymn of supplication echoing the words of the prayer after Communion in the liturgy of the Book of Common Prayer:

> *Father, on us the Spirit bestow,*
>   *Thro' which thine everlasting Son*
> *Offer'd himself for man below,*
>   *That we, ev'n we before thy throne*
> *Our souls and bodies may present,*
> *And pay thee all thy grace hath lent.*
>
> *O let thy Spirit sanctify*
>   *Whate'er to thee we now restore,*
> *And make us with thy will comply,*
>   *With all our mind and soul and*
> *power, Obey thee as thy saints above*
> *In perfect innocence and love.*[40]

---

37   Gregory Dix, *The Shape of the Liturgy* (New York: Seabury Press, 1982), 48–50. Compare my discussion of the Prayer of Great Thanksgiving and these four actions in *Changed from Glory into Glory: Wesleyan Prayer for Transformation* (Nashville: Upper Room Books, 2005), 118–21.

38   Wesley, HLS, Hymn CLVI, st. 4, 131.

39   Wesley, HLS, Hymn CLV, st. 5, 130.

40   Wesley, HLS, Hymn CL, st. 5, 126.

In the Eucharist, God shapes believers into a community of those who are taken into the hands of God for a divine purpose.

Just as Jesus *blesses* the bread and the cup, he consecrates and commissions the community of faith for their work in the world. Jesus gives thanks to God by blessing his disciples. In Jesus' hands, the community of faith becomes the beloved community of God. In the blessed act of Holy Communion, the community that blesses God through words and actions receives the reciprocal blessing of God.

> *Here all thy blessings we receive,*
> *Here all thy gifts are given;*
> *To those that would in thee believe,*
> *Pardon, and grace, and heaven.*

> *Thus may we still in thee be blest*
> *'Till all from earth remove,*
> *And share with thee the marriage-feast,*
> *And drink the wine above.*[41]

Those upon whom a blessing is conferred are called to be a blessing themselves. In a wonderful little book entitled *Teaching as Eucharist*, Sister Joanmarie Smith writes:

> We experience blessings as gifts of divine origin. As such, we can hardly "work" on being a gift of God. . . . God wants to imbue us with the fruits of the Spirit: love, joy, peace, patience, kindness, generosity, faithfulness, gentleness and self control (Gal 5:22-23). In fact, we can claim these fruits as the effects of our baptism. They are blessings in our lives that make us blessings in the lives of others.[42]

In the Eucharist, God shapes believers into *a community of those who are blessed to be a blessing.*

Just as Jesus *breaks* the bread, he liberates the hearts of his faithful followers and sets them free. Early in the history of the church, even within the early strata of the New Testament, the term "the breaking of bread" became closely associated with the eucharistic meal. The account of Pentecost provides an amazing window through which to see the life of the earliest Christian community: "They devoted themselves to the apostles'

---

41   Wesley, HLS, Hymn XLII, st. 5 & 6, 31.
42   Joanmarie Smith, *Teaching as Eucharist* (Mineola, NY: Resurrection Press, 1999), 48.

teaching and fellowship, to *the breaking of bread* and the prayers. . . . Day by day, as they spent much time together in the temple, they *broke bread* at home and ate their food with glad and generous hearts" (Acts 2:42, 46, NRSV, my emphasis). Charles Wesley makes the connection between the breaking of bread and the opening of eyes and hearts:

> *O thou who this mysterious bread*
> *Didst in Emmaus break,*
> *Return herewith our souls to feed*
> *And to thy followers speak.*

> *Unseal the volume of thy grace,*
> *Apply the gospel-word,*
> *Open our eyes to see thy face,*
> *Our hearts to know the Lord.*[43]

If we apply this image of breaking to the community of faith, the action can hardly mean the breaking of children of God; rather, this action is intimately connected to the next action of giving. This breaking is done for the purpose of sharing. The disciples of Jesus Christ can only offer themselves to others if their eyes and hearts have been opened—if they have been liberated by the vision of God's grace offered freely for all. In the Eucharist, God shapes believers into *a community of those who are broken so they can share their lives freely.*

Just as Jesus *gives* the bread and the cup to those gathered at the Table, he gives his coheirs as gospel-bearers for the sake of God's reign. In the Sacrament, Jesus gives himself to us. He offers all that he is. He lays himself before each of his followers and says, "I am yours, and you are mine forever." Through this sign-act of love, he establishes his new covenant with all who put their trust in him. In the same way that he gave himself to God and gave his life for others and gives us bread as a token of these actions, also he gives us the opportunity to offer our lives as a sacrifice of praise to God. Charles Wesley celebrated the fullest possible measure of this service and witness in the world and prayed that, in his self-giving, God would be glorified:

> *Claim me for Thy service, claim*
> *All I have and all I am.*

---

43   Wesley, HLS, Hymn XXIX, st. 1 & 2, 22–23.

Take my soul and body's powers,
  Take my memory, mind, and will,
All my goods, and all my hours,
  All I know, and all I feel,
All I think, and speak, and do;
Take my heart—but make it new.[44]

In similar fashion, John Wesley's "Covenant Prayer" expresses poignantly what it means, in the words of the liturgy, for us "to give ourselves to Christ, as he has given himself to us":

I am no longer my own, but thine.
Put me to what thou wilt, rank me with whom thou wilt.
Put me to doing, put me to suffering.
Let me be employed by thee or laid aside for thee,
exalted for thee or brought low by thee.
Let me be full, let me be empty.
Let me have all things, let me have nothing.
I freely and heartily yield all things
to thy pleasure and disposal.
And now, O glorious and blessed God,
Father, Son, and Holy Spirit,
thou art mine, and I am thine. So be it.
And the covenant which I have made on earth,
let it be ratified in heaven. Amen.[45]

In the Eucharist, God shapes believers into a community of those who are given, like Jesus, for the life of the world.

Taken. Blessed. Broken. Given. The following story illustrates how these actions, experienced time and time again, shape the lives of faithful Christians. Jürgen Moltmann will go down in history as the founder of the "theology of hope." I first met Professor Moltmann when I was a graduate student at Duke University. During one of his visits to campus, I timidly invited him to lunch and we enjoyed a wonderful meal together. While introducing myself to him more fully, I explained that I was working in my doctoral studies with Frank Baker. "Oh," he interrupted, "I'd like to share a story with you about Frank and Nellie Baker."

---

44   Wesley, HLS, Hymn CLV, st. 3 and 4, 129–30.
45   "A Covenant Prayer in the Wesleyan Tradition," in *The United Methodist Hymnal* (Nashville: The United Methodist Publishing House, 1989), no. 607.

He said that during the war there was a German prisoner of war camp on the northeast coast of England. A young pastor and his wife served a small Methodist circuit close by. They were filled with compassion and compelled to do something to reach out to these men. So they went to the commander and asked permission to take a prisoner with them to church each Sunday and then to their home where they would eat their Sunday dinner together. It was agreed. So Sunday after Sunday, a steady flow of German soldiers worshiped and ate with the Bakers in their home throughout the course of the war. This world-famous theologian paused, looked at me intently, and said, "One of those soldiers was a young man by the name of Jürgen Moltmann. And I want you to know that the seed of hope was planted in my heart around Frank and Nellie Baker's dinner table." The Eucharist shapes the interior life of the disciples of Christ—faithful people with glad and generous hearts—and molds them into a community of hope that shares God's love among all people with joy.

THIRTEEN

Eucharist and Ethics

Rebekah Miles

Julia Foote, a nineteenth-century evangelist of the African Methodist Episcopal Zion Church, wrote about attending the death of a sister in Christ. Mrs. Simpson knew that the end was near and asked those gathered to join in singing Charles Wesley's "Oh, For a Thousand Tongues to Sing":

> As we sang the last verse, she raised herself up in bed, clapped her hands and cried: "He sets the prisoners free! Glory! glory! I am free! They have come for me!" She pointed toward the east. Her mother asked her who had come. She said: "Don't you see the chariot and horses? Glory! glory to the blood!" She dropped back upon her pillow, and was gone. She had stepped aboard the chariot. Lee, reflecting on her own limited perception of what had happened at the deathbed, wrote, "we could not see [the chariot], but we felt the fire."[1]

The Lord's Supper is one of those extraordinary moments in this life—not unlike the deathbed—where the veil becomes thin, and we approach and have partial access to realities that are ordinarily beyond the reach of our senses. These moments carry enormous power for the transformation of our lives, our churches, and our world. We do not see the chariot in all its glory, but we feel and are refined by the fire.

I will center our attention primarily on the Wesleys' *Hymns on the Lord's Supper* (HLS).[2] I am particularly interested in the way the hymns themselves draw in

---

1   William Andrews, ed., *Sisters of the Spirit: Three Black Women's Autobiographies of the 19th Century* (Bloomington: Indiana University Press, 1986), 195.

2   Throughout this essay, I rely primarily on the 1825 edition. John and Charles Wesley, *Hymns on the Lord's Supper* (HLS) (London: J. Kershaw, 1825). References to the hymns will be given parenthetically in the text. For more about the hymns and Wesleyan eucharistic theology, see Daniel B. Stevick, *The Altar's Fire: Charles Wesley's Hymns on the Lord's Supper, 1745: Introduction and Comment* (Peterborough, Eng.: Epworth Press, 2004); Lorna Lock-Nah Khoo, *Wesleyan Eucharistic Spirituality: Its Nature, Sources, and Future*, ATF Dissertation Series 2 (Adelaide, Australia: ATF Press, 2005); Stephen Sours, "Eucharist and Anthropology: Seeking Convergence on Eucharistic Sacrifice between Catholics and Methodists."(PhD diss., Duke University, 2011); Aaron Kerr, "John and Charles Wesley's Hymns on the Lord's Supper (1745): Their Meaning for Methodist Ecclesial Identity and Ecumenical Dialogue." (PhD diss., Duquesne University, 2007); and Geoffrey Moore, "'Of all who to Thy wounds would

the listener, shaping the religious and moral imagination, sharpening the spiritual senses, giving believers new eyes to see things beyond their normal vision, and encouraging them to make a complete offering of themselves at the Lord's Table and beyond. If the hymns are to be believed, the extraordinary realities of the Lord's Supper have the capacity to transform the most ordinary parts of our lives and to propel us into ministries of transformation in the world.

Several autobiographical experiences shape my reading both of the hymns and our current context. Some years ago I began to have ecstatic religious experiences that often come during Communion services. Perhaps through what Charles Wesley called "faith's interior eye," I came to experience vividly for myself that the Lord's Supper is one of those rare—and even singular—places where, because the veil is thin, one can feel in extraordinary ways the presence of Christ and the communion of the saints. It isn't so much that my theology of the Lord's Supper changed; I simply came to a new felt sense confirming what I already believed about Christ's extraordinary presence in the Lord's Supper. These experiences, though infrequent, have created a careful attentiveness in me, a watchful eye, not for the extraordinary experiences but for the underlying reality that I know is there whether I feel it or not.

Second, my mother died in 2009 several weeks before the beginning of Lent. The simple tasks of caring for her dying body and then preparing her dead body for burial transformed my experience of the broken body of Christ. I also learned for myself that near the time of death, as at the Lord's Supper, the veil between the visible and invisible realms is thin and one can feel in extraordinary ways the presence of Christ and the communion of the saints.

I mention these two factors because I am convinced that the hymns were shaped not only by Daniel Brevint's essay, but also by two aspects in the Wesleys' lives that mirror the two parts of my own just described: (1) the ecstatic experiences of early Methodists in Communion services; and (2) their experience with the bodies of the dying. If you read Charles's journal entries around the time of the writing and publication of the hymns, he is not only offering Communion in larger worship settings, but he is also, sometimes on the same days, visiting, and even serving Communion to, the gravely ill and dying. He knew about suffering and wounded bodies. Both the Lord's Supper and the deathbed provided a place where the veil between the visible and the invisible realms became thin, and both Christ and the communion of the saints were made powerfully present.

---

fly': Sacrifice, Suffering, and Sanctification,' in *Hymns on the Lord's Supper* (1745)." Paper presented at the 48th annual conference of the Wesleyan Theological Society, Seattle, Washington, March 21–23, 2013.

A Basic Wesleyan Understanding of the Eucharist and the Means of Grace

For the Wesleys, the Lord's Supper was the chief means of God's grace, the primary therapy for human sin and sickness. John would later describe it as the "grand channel for conveying God's grace to human souls."[3] It is, wrote Charles, Christ's "richest legacy" to humanity (HLS 42:4). Its regular practice over time helps to pattern the Christian life, shaping Christians in conformity to Christ and helping them to transform the world.[4]

Throughout many of John Wesley's writings and Charles Wesley's hymns and poems you see the centrality of all the means of grace in the Christian life, including the moral life. The means are often recommended in both deontological and teleological terms. On the deontological side, John Wesley speaks of the instituted means of grace as ways we fulfill our duty by obeying divine commands (for example, to care for the poor, to pray, to fast). On the teleological side, they are not only commands but also means for great benefit leading us toward the end of holiness. They can be channels of God's grace offering pardon for sin, power over sin, and par-ticipation in God. God's grace, offered through these means, forms us over time, bringing transformation to our tempers, our habits, and our character. On the other hand, the neglect of these means can, over time, have serious consequences—the decline of faith, the lessening of conformity to Christ, and the increase of sin and vice.[5] As Charles wrote,

> *Why is the faithful seed decreased,*
> *The life of God extinct and dead?*
> *The daily sacrifice is ceased, And*
> *charity to heaven is fled.*

---

3   John Wesley, "Upon our Lord's Sermon on the Mount." See also, "Work-ing Out Our Own Salvation," http://www.umcmission.org/Find-Resources/ John-Wesley-Sermons. All sermons referred to here can be found at this website and also in *The Works of John Wesley: Sermons,* ed. Albert C. Outler (Nashville: Abingdon Press, 1984–1987).

4   For more on Wesleyan understandings of the Lord's Supper, see John Wesley, "On the Duty of Constant Communion," and Gayle Carlton Felton, *This Holy Mystery: A United Methodist Understanding of Holy Communion* (Nashville: Disci-pleship Resources, 2005). For a basic, if dated, introduction to John Wesley's un-derstanding of the sacraments, see Ole E. Borgen, *John Wesley on the Sacraments: A Theological Study.* (Grand Rapids: Francis Asbury Press, n.d.; Grand Rapids: Zondervan, 1986.).

5   See, for example, John Wesley's sermons "The Means of Grace" and "On Zeal."

Sad mutual causes of decay,
Slackness and vice together move;
Grown cold, we cast the means away,
And quench the latest spark of love. (HLS 166:11–12)

This same two-part framework plays out in Wesley's sermon "The Duty of Constant Communion."[6] A Christian should receive Communion as often as possible for two reasons. First, because it is the Christian's duty to obey the "plain command of Christ." (This imperative to obey Christ's command is expressed in *The Hymns on the Lord's Supper* in one of my favorite lines of the collection: "If Jesus bid me lick the dust, I bow at his command" [HLS 86:7]. Moreover, Christ's injunction "do this in remembrance of me" was not an ordinary, run of the mill, divine command but Christ's "dying words to all his followers."[7]

Second, we receive Communion because it brings great benefits that move us toward the ultimate goal of sanctification. The Lord's Supper is a means of grace offering not only pardon for sin but also power over sin and strength to love and obey God and to "perform our duty." It can lead us toward perfection, offer refreshment to our soul, and reveal the hope of heaven. The Lord's Supper is a means toward becoming happy in God by growing more into his likeness (i.e., sanctification). This includes the transformation of our tempers, habits, virtue, and character as well as our work for the social transformation of the world around us.

The Hymns on the Lord's Supper

This brings us to the Wesleys' *Hymns on the Lord's Supper*. Together the hymns offer a view of the Lord's Supper and its place in the Christian life, including the moral life, that is presented in full color and that moves well beyond the arguments offered in "Duty of Constant Communion." The Wesley brothers published *The Hymns on the Lord's Supper* in the spring of 1745. The volume included 166 hymns (almost all of which are thought to be Charles's)[8] as well

---

6   The sermon "The Duty of Constant Communion" was originally adapted by John Wesley in 1732 from a 1707 text by fellow Anglican Robert Nelson. The perspective expressed in this sermon is consistent with other Wesleyan texts on the means of grace.

7   Wesley, "The Duty of Constant Communion."

8   I will refer throughout to Charles Wesley, because I am only using the hymns that are widely thought to be his work. Hymns 9 and 160 are revisions of George Herbert poems. Hymn 85 is a translation—probably John's—of a Zinzendorf hymn. In addition, at least three hymns—58, 62, 114–are disputed. It is widely thought that most of the hymns are Charles's and that John Wesley's role in the hymns was primarily editorial.

as a preface—John Wesley's abridgment of Daniel Brevint's seventeenth-century text *The Christian Sacrament and Sacrifice*.[9]

Historical Context for the Hymns and Their Purposes

The volume was likely prepared in response to an immediate pastoral need. The Wesleys were advising their people to attend Communion regularly. As the Methodist revival took on steam, crowds would sometimes gather for worship, including Communion (often at local Anglican churches that were sympathetic). Early Methodists reported large gatherings, sometimes over a thousand.

As so many people began to come to Communion services, the Wesleys were faced with a problem. It was common practice at the time for members of the congregation to come forward and kneel at the chancel rail to be served and dismissed in groups. Early Methodists reported Communion services sometimes lasting five and six hours. To make things even more challenging, weekly Communion was a novelty for many members of their societies. People needed help interpreting what they were doing. Just as important, they needed assistance in bringing their Sunday devotions at the altar into the rest of their lives, whether their daily devotional practices, works of mercy, employment, family life, and so on.

The hymns, then, served several purposes. They could be sung as the congregation came forward for Communion.[10] They provided a devotional resource for individuals in preparation for Communion and as a part of their regular prayers. And they helped to teach people about Communion and its transformative power. Geoffrey Wainwright has referred to these three as the liturgical, devotional, and catechetical purposes of *The Hymns on the Lord's Supper*.[11]

I am convinced that the hymns also served an additional purpose as a kind of training manual for the spiritual senses, pointing to and then

---

9   Although it is sometimes very hard to separate out the voices of Brevint, Charles Wesley, and John Wesley, I will focus here on the hymns themselves and not on John Wesley's abridgment of Brevint or the Brevint text itself. Although many of the hymns, though by no means all, follow the themes of the Brevint text (and not simply Wesley's shorter abridgement), they become something very different in Charles's hands.

10 Although congregational hymn singing was not a regular worship practice among most Anglicans at that time, the Wesleys were an exception. Out of step with practices of the time, John had incorporated singing into Communion services as early as his time as a priest in Savannah, Georgia, and this became a regular practice among the Methodists.

11 Geoffrey Wainwright, introduction, *The Hymns on the Lord's Supper* (Madison, NJ: Charles Wesley Society, 1995), vi. This edition is a facsimile of the first edition of the hymns from 1745.

helping people to see and feel spiritual realities not evident to the ordinary senses. Clearly this goes far beyond what we normally think of as catechesis and what we ordinarily find in catechetical materials. This function is more epistemological than catechetical. Various labels could be assigned to this fourth purpose or function: the awakening and enhancement of the spiritual senses, the opening of the eyes of faith, or simply the mystical.

This additional purpose is linked, I believe, to the rash of ecstatic experiences in the Lord's Supper during this period. In many ways, the hymns grew out of, reflected, interpreted, and fostered those experiences. Journal entries from the Wesleys and others in their societies described powerful experiences of the Spirit in Communion at corporate worship as well as in pastoral visits with the dying. Here are a few excerpts from Charles' journals.

Around the time of the publication of the hymns, Charles described a service of Communion: "I administered the sacrament to all the Society; and the God, the consolation of Israel, visited us. Members of the whole congregation were moved to cry after him, either through sorrow or through joy."[12]

The following Sunday, he wrote: "I found the great blessing after the sacrament, an ordinance which God always magnifies, and honours with his special presence. I prayed by our sister Rogers, just on the wing for paradise. It was a solemn season at the Society, while I spake of death, and the glory which shall follow" (April 7, 1745).

A few months later he noted in his journal: "In our prayer after the sacrament, the heavens dropped down from above, nay, and the skies seemed even to pour down righteousness" (ibid., July 21, 1745). The next day he visited a woman who was dying. "I gave the sacrament to our sister H., who is coming to the grave as a ripe shock of corn. A poor trembling, tempted soul she has been; but, at the approach of death, all her fears are vanished; and she lies gasping for the fulness of eternal life" (ibid., July 22, 1745).

Several years earlier he had written of a similar experience in which he referenced the "thin veil." "I gave the sacrament to one whom I had left waiting for Christ. She was now full of His Spirit, ready for the Bridegroom. No cloud interposed between her Beloved and her; only the thin veil of flesh and blood, which was well-nigh rent asunder. What would I give to be on that death-bed!" (ibid., November 4, 1739).

Charles had also written of an extraordinary personal experience in a Communion service in May of 1738 when he saw a vision of Christ's

---

12   Sunday, March 31, 1745, *The Manuscript Journal of the Reverend Charles Wesley,* M.A., vol. 2, ed. S .T. Kimbrough Jr. and Kenneth G.C. Newport (Nashville: Abingdon Press [Kingswood Books], 2007), 437.

crucified body. (This was only a few days after Charles's pivotal May 21st experience where he felt the gift of peace in Christ and a few days before John's Aldersgate experience.) Charles wrote, "Before communicating, I left it to Christ, whether, or in what measure, he would please to manifest himself to me, in this breaking of bread. I had no particular attention to the prayers: but in the prayer of consecration I saw, by the eye of faith, or rather, had a glimpse of, Christ's broken, mangled body, as taking down from the cross. [I could] only repeat with tears, 'O love, love!'" (ibid., May 25, 1738).

The hymns were written, then, not only out of a practical need for a resource to be used liturgically during Communion as well as devotionally and catechetically. They were also conceived in the midst of these ecstatic moments in Communion. Moreover, they provided a way to draw Christians, by means of all their senses, into the experience of the Lord's Supper and to help them be open to whatever might be illuminated or revealed through "the eye of faith." The hymns become, in a strange way, a kind of training manual or prompt for developing the spiritual senses and seeing, with the eyes of faith, the real presence of Christ at the Lord's Supper and, subsequently, for moving beyond the table and into the community to care for others.

The Hymns on the Lord's Supper became an important part of Methodist life and through the remainder of the eighteenth century was reprinted nine times, more often than any other Wesley hymn collection. Then the collection as a whole was largely forgotten through the nineteenth and early twentieth centuries, especially in the United States. There was a British reprint in 1825 and over the years a few hymns were picked up and used in other Methodist hymnals (though often not in the Communion sections), but there was little direct use of the work as a whole, especially in the US context. This is not all that surprising given the lesser focus on the Lord's Supper among many nineteenth-century American Methodists.[13]

In the last half of the twentieth century, the hymns (including the Brevint abridgment) became more widely available.[14] Moreover, we have seen scores of scholarly articles, books, and dissertations on the collection (often focusing more on Brevint and on John's abstract rather than on Charles's

---

13 In addition, the emergence of theological liberalism among Methodists in the nineteenth century would have made these bloody, sacrificial hymns seem even less attractive. See Geoffrey Moore, "Eucharistic Piety in American Methodist Hymnody (1786–1889)" in *Music and the Wesleys*, ed. Nicholas Temperley and Stephen Banfield (Urbana: University of Illinois Press, 2010), 88–102. ,

14 J. Ernest Rattenbury, *The Eucharistic Hymns of John and Charles Wesley: To Which Is Appended Wesley's Preface Extracted from Brevint's Christian Sacrament and Sacrifice Together with Hymns on the Lord's Supper*, 3rd American ed. (Akron, OH: OSL Publications, 2006).

hymns). We have not, however, seen a widespread resurgence of devotional interest in the hymns among ordinary Wesleyans.[15]

The Hymns as Invitation

On some points, *The Hymns on the Lord's Supper* are similar in argument to "The Duty of Constant Communion" and other sources. The Lord's Supper is the highest and richest of the means of grace (HLS 42:4 and 99:1). Christians are commanded by Christ to receive the Lord's Supper; indeed it is his "dying bequest" (Hymn 95:1, see also Hymns 1:1 and 90:1). Moreover, in *The Hymns*, the Lord's Supper offers many benefits for growth that are often summarized in pairs—e.g., pardon and holiness (HLS 31:2) or groups of threes—e.g., "pardon, and holiness, and heaven" (HLS 1:2 and 38:3); "pardon, and power, and perfect peace" (HLS 56:4 and 39:3); and "pardon, grace, and glory" (HLS 164:2). These benefits are central for all parts of the Christian life, including the moral life.

If I stopped there, however, I would be doing the hymns a great disservice. The hymns are also a lure, an invitation. They invite the listeners to enter, through the Lord's Supper and the singing of the hymns themselves, into various moments of salvation history, particularly the cross. Using vivid language and all of the senses, hearers are drawn to feel themselves a part of the biblical story—especially Good Friday—in a way that transforms their hearts, character, and actions. The hymns use various means to this end.[16]

First, the hymns are made up of vivid, sensual details. Charles is painting a picture with words and drawing the listener/singer into the canvas, emphasizing colors and sounds, and prompting the imagination. To underline this point, Charles uses phrases that make the connection explicit. For example, the phrase "call to mind" (or variants) is used ten times. Charles also draws heavily on the language of the senses. Words like *see, show, hear,* and *taste* are much higher on the word frequency lists for Charles's hymns than for Daniel Brevint's essay or John Wesley's abridgment.

---

15 Although this new interest in the hymns has not had widespread devotional or liturgical impact, there are connections with contemporary liturgical renewal. The 1948 Rattenbury edition was published in the United States in 1990 by the Order of St. Luke, which is dedicated to liturgical renewal.

16 Joanna Cruickshank writes of Charles Wesley's hymns on suffering as a tool to train early Methodists to imaginatively see Christ's suffering, which then, in turn, prompts powerful feelings that are transformative. My interests are similar, although I, unlike Cruickshank, am focused on the place of the hymns in training the spiritual senses so that believers actually see something that exists independently of their imagination. See *Journal of Religious History* (October 2006):311–30.

Second, the hymns pull on the emotions of those singing them, drawing heavily on language of emotion, feeling, and heart. In a word frequency search comparing Brevint's essay and Charles's hymns taken alone, I found that the words *heart* and *feel* both made Charles Wesley's list of top one hundred most frequently used words but ranked only in the 300s and 500s for Brevint.

Third, the hymns also have the singer/reader articulate different needs from various points of view in the Christian life. For example, there are hymns for those who are engaged in active sin and need repentance and forgiveness. There are hymns for mature Christians who are weary of using the means of grace—especially the Lord's Supper—when they don't feel anything. By singing these verses, congregants who were facing these different problems were able to give voice to their own experiences.

Fourth, the hymns also place the readers/singers in the biblical narrative, having them speak/sing as if they were a particular character. There are verses from the perspective of the thief on the cross, Jesus' mother, a disciple at the foot of the cross, a person who seeks healing from Jesus, and a disciple who seeks Jesus himself after the Resurrection.

Fifth, the hymns make many references to death and suffering bodies—primarily Christ's body. Charles uses the words *death, dying, pain, suffering,* and *wounds* very frequently—much more often than they are used in the Brevint text, John's abridgment, or *Hymns for the People Called Methodists*. He writes also of tortured, torn, mangled, rent, and broken bodies. Many of the most vivid, graphic details in the hymns are about Christ's suffering and death, which some have criticized as valorizing suffering. While I'm sympathetic to those concerns, I am also convinced that the language of suffering and death plays a crucial role in the hymns and cannot be ignored. This language is important not only for obvious historical reasons—that is, the Lord's Supper is inevitably linked with Christ's death on the cross—but also for the role this language plays as it draws in readers/singers and helps them to enter the story of the cross with a depth of feeling and compassion.

In many cultures today—certainly the United States—most people have little direct contact with the care of the bodies of the dying and the dead. People are much more likely to survive into old age. Moreover, when people are dying we usually give over their care to medical professionals, and when they are dead to mortuary professionals.

By contrast, when Charles was writing these hymns, he was visiting the sick and dying. Many of the people who were singing the hymns also had similar experiences—either in their families or with people they visited as a part of their ministries. If a person has intimate experience with the suffering and death of a loved one—particularly care for suffering bodies and dead bodies—the language of Christ's suffering and death takes on richer meaning. In addition, the language of the bodily suffering and death of Christ in the hymns is overlaid on the singer/reader's experiences of the physical trauma at the suffering and death of loved ones. In a culture where dying and death are a part of ordinary life, this language is emotionally evocative and carries great power.

These five factors join to draw the singers/readers into the experience of the Lord's Supper, to stir up strong emotions, and to help them imagine themselves in the experience. At the same time, Charles seems to be up to something more than an exercise in imagination.

When Charles describes Christ's broken body in vivid language and asks his listeners to see, he is not simply prompting their imagination; he is urging Christians to strain beyond their ordinary senses and to see, with the eyes of faith, something beyond the ordinary range of vision. He is giving them tools for opening the spiritual senses. And he is also inviting them to pray for that opening, for eyes that can see these other, substantial realities.

The Lord's Supper as a Wrinkle in Time

Throughout the hymns, then, hearers are not merely imagining themselves present at the cross. In the Lord's Supper, communicants become, through faith, participants in what Christ has done. In some way, time collapses at the Lord's Table. In the Lord's Supper, the Spirit gives believers the capacity to see, hear, and feel what Christ has done. We see the Father through the sacrifice, wounds, and blood of the son; the Father sees us through the wounds of Christ; the Father hears us through the groans of Christ.

In the hymns, Charles presents the Lord's Supper as a kind of wrinkle in time or wormhole, that is, a moment and place that offers partial access to and limited participation in other moments and places both in the past and future. By the power of the Holy Spirit, the eyes of faith are opened and the communicant is able to see and experience, as the Lord's Supper is celebrated, Christ's suffering. Charles writes, "Christ revives his sufferings here, / Still exposes them to view; / See the Crucified appear. / Now believe he died for you!" (HLS 8:2).[17]

---

17   Although the issues of sacrifice and offering or oblation are very complicated and beyond the scope of this paper, note that Wesley is careful to avoid language of repeated sacrifice. The Lord's Supper offers us access to something eternal instead of a contemporary repetition of what was done in the past.

This wrinkle in time is made possible by virtue of our oneness with the eternal Christ who is uniquely present at the Lord's Supper. Charles, like Daniel Brevint and John Wesley in his abridgment, calls to mind Aaron, who never went before God without bearing the twelve stones for the twelve tribes of Israel. By virtue of the stones, Aaron always comes before God with his people. Likewise, Christ as priest always bears with him his church, his body. In that sense, even at the cross itself, Christ's people are present.

Charles places the communicants, those singing and hearing these hymns, at the cross. They are there not merely by the power of their imaginations and the vividness of the pictures Charles creates—but also by virtue of their oneness with Christ.

> Would the Saviour of mankind
> Without his people die?
> No; to him we all are join'd,
> As more than standers by.
> . . .
>
> We attend the slaughter'd Lamb,
> And suffer for his cause.
>
> Him e'en now by faith we see:
> Before our eyes he stands!
> On the suffering Deity
> We lay our trembling hands:
> Lay our sins upon his head;
> Wait on the dread sacrifice;
> Feel the lovely victim bleed,
> And die while Jesus dies! (HLS 131:1 and 2)

Or again, in hymn 140:

> He dies, as now for us he dies!
> That all-sufficient sacrifice
> Subsists, eternal as the Lamb,
> In every time and place the same:
> To all alike it co-extends.
> Its saving virtue never ends.
> . . .

> *And all who could not see him die*
> *May now with faith's interior eye*
> *Behold him stand as slaughter'd there,*
> *And feel the answer to his prayer.* (HLS 140:1 and 2)

By God's grace, Christians are offered at the Lord's Table "evidence of things unseen." By faith, they are able to see this evidence. In hymn 123, Charles writes "by faith we see thy suffering past, in this mysterious rite brought back" (HLS 123:3).

These themes recur throughout the hymns. In hymn 5, Charles writes of the strangeness of time at the Lord's Supper.

> *Thy offering still continues new;*
> *Thy vesture keeps its bloody hue:*
> *Thou stand'st the ever-slaughter'd Lamb*
> *Thy priesthood still remains the same.*
>
> *Now let it pass the years between,*
> *And view Thee bleeding on the tree.* (HLS 5:2 and 3)

This wrinkle in time does a lot of work in *The Hymns on the Lord's Supper*. In addition to the overall benefits brought by God's grace through the Lord's Supper, which were described above, there are several particular benefits to the wrinkle in time itself. When in the Lord's Supper we have, through the eyes of faith, access to Christ on the cross, several interesting and powerful things happen.

First, just as the Lord's Supper opens up for believers an intimate view of Christ on the cross, it also shapes God's perspective on things. The Father sees us through Christ and his suffering. At the Lord's Table, the suffering Christ becomes a lens for the Father's gaze on us. In the hymns, the believer addresses the Father, calling attention to the Lord's Table where Christ's suffering is presented.

> *Father, God, who seest in me*
> *Only sin and misery;*
> *See thine own anointed one;*
> *Look on thy beloved Son.*
>
> *Turn from me thy gracious eyes,*
> *To that bloody sacrifice . . .*

Here exhibited beneath.

. . . Then through him the sinner see;
Then in Jesus look on me. (HLS 119:1–4)

Theologian Geoffrey Moore argues that scholars examining *The Hymns on the Lord's Supper* tend to ignore a crucial aspect of these hymns, that is, that this encounter with Christ's suffering makes a difference, not only to us but also to God. He writes,

> The eucharistic sacrifice . . . makes a difference to God by "placing us in the wounds of Christ." By virtue of our placement inside Christ's wounds, God "looks on us" through Christ, our sin being "covered" by Christ's sacrifice, and we are once again reconciled to God. For the believer . . . the eucharistic sacrifice as our participation in Christ's sacrifice is manifest in our own sanctification and holy living.[18]

Second, just as the Father looks at us through Christ and his suffering, we look back and see into the Father's gaze through Christ. In other words, the face of God that we see looking at us is the face of God looking at Christ. Charles Wesley wrote about our approach to the Father at the Lord's Table:

To thee, through Jesus, we draw near.
Thy suffering, well-beloved Son,
In whom thy smiling face we see,
In whom thou art well pleased with me. (HLS 125:1)

Third, through this shifting of ordinary time and space, the Lord's Supper, as described in the hymns, opens up, by the power of the Spirit, a view not only of the Father and the Son but also of the communion of saints. Charles wrote, "Lift your eyes of faith, and see / Saints and angels join'd in one!" (HLS 105:1)

Fourth, in the hymns the Lord's Supper, as a wrinkle in time, offers glimpses not only of the cross but also of other moments and places in salvation history—especially those still to come. When Charles refers in the hymns to the Lord's Supper as a foretaste of heaven, he seems to be referring to an actual present participation in a future reality.

Fifth, communicants, experiencing Christ and his suffering at the Lord's Table, are brought to greater compassion for him and greater desire to serve him, to follow him, and to offer themselves up with him.

---

18   Geoffrey Moore, "Of all who to Thy wounds would fly." (See n.2 for full reference.)

Sixth, this wrinkle in time provides a way to make our offerings, our sacrifices, jointly with Christ's offering. The next to the last section of the hymn collection focuses on our sacrifices. In the Lord's Supper, we offer all that we have and are. We place our offering on Christ and it is made acceptable as it is joined with Christ's sacrifice. We offer ourselves, our souls, our actions, our sin, our goods, our friends, our praise, our prayers, our bodies, our thoughts, our desires—basically everything we are and have and feel.

In hymn 141, Charles calls to mind those fortunate souls who stood beneath the cross.

> *O what a time for offering up*
> *Their souls upon thy sacrifice!* . . .
>
> *Not all the days before or since,*
> *An hour so solemn could afford,*
> *For suffering with our bleeding Prince,*
> *For dying with our slaughter'd Lord.* (HLS 141:3–4)

If the foot of the cross is the most opportune time and place for Christ's followers to make their offering, then the Lord's Supper, by giving the believer access to the cross, becomes a place of offering. Charles continues in this same hymn:

> *Yet in this ordinance divine,*
> *We still the sacred load may bear;*
> *And now we in thy offering join,*
> *Thy sacramental passion share.*
>
> *We cast our sins into that fire,*
> *Which did thy sacrifice consume,*
> *And every base and vain desire*
> *To daily crucifixion doom.*
>
> *Thou art with all thy members here.*
> *In this tremendous mystery:*
> *We jointly before God appear,*
> *To offer up ourselves with Thee.* (HLS 141:5–7)

According to the hymns, in the Lord's Supper we offer not only our sins and praises, but everything we are, have, and do. We give over ourselves, our souls, bodies, prayers, sin, deaths, desires, and "imperfect efforts." We offer all property, goods, fame, vows, friends, actions, words, thoughts, memory, mind, will, time, health, and freedom. At the altar we give everything we have, know, feel, think, speak, or do. We place everything on the altar, and "the altar sanctifies the gift." (It is hard to read this section of the hymns and not think of Phoebe Palmer, a nineteenth-century evangelist and leader in the Holiness movement who is known for her altar theology. It looks like there is an influence here, but I have not been able to trace the genealogy.)

This brings us to the final benefit of the wrinkle in time. As we make this offering in the Lord's Supper, the Father is able to receive our offerings with Christ's offerings. Just as the Father's gaze on Christ shapes his view of us, so the Father's acceptance of Christ's offering makes possible his acceptance of ours. And the Spirit gives us the capacity to attend to this divine giving and receiving.

By virtue of Christ's offering, our offering—including the offering of ourselves—is made holy. Drawing on the language "the altar sanctifies the gift" from the Gospel of Matthew (23:19, NKJV), Charles writes in Hymn 137,

> Whate'er we cast on him alone
> Is with his great oblation one,
> His sacrifice doth ours sustain,
> And favour and acceptance gain.
>
> ....
>
> Mean are our noblest offerings,
> Poor, feeble, unsubstantial things;
> But when to him our souls we lift,
> The altar sanctities the gift.
>
> Our persons and our deeds aspire,
> When cast into that hallow'd fire;
> Our most imperfect efforts please,
> When join'd to Christ our Righteousness.
>
> Mix'd with the sacred smoke we rise,
> The smoke of his burnt-sacrifice;
> By the eternal Spirit driven
> From earth, in Christ we mount to heaven. (HLS 137:3, 5–7)

In The Hymns on the Lord's Supper, Charles Wesley is not simply playing to our emotions or stirring up our imagination. He is not merely helping to create a sensory rich tapestry of Christ's offering of himself on the cross that then prompts us to offer ourselves as well. Charles is inviting us to pay attention in new ways, to see something real that stands beyond the ordinary, to strain to open our spiritual senses, and to ask the Spirit for eyes to see Christ present with us and for the courage to offer all of ourselves and everything else in communion with Christ's offering. He calls us to pay attention to something that is really happening. We are encountering the suffering of Christ and this encounter is changing everything. He calls us not only to see this reality and to offer all that we are and have to God, but also, by the power of the Holy Spirit and the presence of the crucified Christ, to encounter and even participate in the divine life. It is this encounter and participation that is the ground of our life and growth as Christians and the wellspring of whatever good we might do or whatever transformation we help to make in the world. The ethical and social impulses grow, in part, from the Lord's Table.

In the opening of this article, I described the way that both deathbeds and the Lord's Table can be thin places where the veil between the visible and invisible realms is thin and where one can experience in extraordinary ways the presence of Christ and the communion of the saints.

I've written previously about early Methodists and deathbed narratives. [19] John Wesley's *Arminian Magazine* often ran stories about the deaths of the faithful and their last hours as friends and family gathered around, singing and praying them through the passage from life to death. Historian Richard Bell noticed that over time the deathbed stories in the *Arminian Magazine* began to follow a certain pattern. Bell suggests that witnesses were trained, by these previous deathbed accounts, to write the stories in a certain way. I read the same accounts and come to a completely different conclusion. Methodists were learning not so much how to write about death as how to die and how to bear witness to another's dying. They learned to see things in a different way and even to look for things that might not be apparent to the ordinary senses. The stories themselves became a kind of training manual for the faithful.

Perhaps *The Hymns on the Lord's Supper* served a similar role among eighteenth-century Methodists. They were not merely a prompt to the imagination or a descriptive theology in verse. They became a kind of training

---

19   Rebekah Miles, "We Have This Treasure in Earthen Vessels," in *Reflections on Grief and Spiritual Growth*, ed. Andrew Weaver and Howard Stone (Nashville: Abingdon Press, 2005). See also Richard Bell, "'Our People die well': Death-bed Scenes in Methodist Magazines in Eighteenth-century Britain" (unpublished manuscript, The Annual Meeting of the Association of Education in Journalism and Mass Communication, 2003). Used with permission.

manual or an invitation to see things in a new way and to pay attention to what might otherwise be overlooked. They provided a lens through which the believer might see beyond the ordinary.

Moreover, the experience evoked by the hymns was not merely about sight but also about knowledge, about epistemology. People were being trained how to understand the world, God, and Christ's sacrifice in a new way. As they saw in new ways they also came to know in new ways, to know what happened on Calvary, who God is, and what God calls his people to do and be in a fuller and more intimate way. And the new vision and knowledge that arose as believers learned to experience the Lord's Supper began to shape more fully a people and their experience of God and the world.

Poetic Meaning and Experience

Scholars reflecting on these hymns and on the treatise on which they are based often try to discern—and just as often disagree about—what, according to the texts, is or is not happening in the Lord's Supper. How is the Lord's Supper a means of grace? In what manner does it convey benefits to communicants? Where and how is Christ present? In what sense is Christ's suffering a present reality and what work does it do?

The hymns themselves offer one way to approach these kinds of questions. Several hymns emphasize the partial, limited nature of our knowledge and perception. By the power of the Holy Spirit, we are given eyes to see a part of this invisible reality, but never the whole. We are given the grace to see and know and feel enough. We do not see the chariot, but we feel the fire. Or maybe we don't even feel the fire, but we are in the company of others who do and of a tradition that bears witness to its reality. And that fire, whether it is ever fully seen or understood or even felt, still carries power—power to change our lives and our worlds.

> O the depth of love divine.
> Th' unfathomable grace!
> Who shall say how bread and wine,
> God into man conveys?
> How the bread his flesh imparts;
> How the wine transmits his blood;
> Fills his faithful people's hearts
> With all the life of God? . . .
> Sure and real is the grace.

The manner be unknown;
Only meet us in thy ways
And perfect us in one:
Let us taste the heavenly powers.
Lord, we ask for nothing more;
Thine to bless, 'tis only ours
To wonder and adore. (HLS 57:1 and 4) (See also Hymn 59.)

"Sure and real is the grace, the manner be unknown." We are given the means to know what we need to know; some things may simply lie beyond our ken.

As I read the hymns, there are moments when I'm not exactly sure what Charles Wesley believes. When are the vivid images a description of reality as it is and when are they pointing to something beyond themselves, to something perhaps even indescribable or at least not describable with exact precision?[20]

Of course this is poetry we are talking about. One of the great advantages of hymns and poems over descriptive essays is that exact precision is not the point. Poems can be more open-ended. They can be richer in color and sound than in precision. This may especially be true of hymns and religious poetry that are often pointing to an encounter with a God who is not fully describable. Poems and hymns have a way of drawing people into a reality that we cannot adequately or even accurately describe, pointing to something beyond themselves, and even prompting a kind of participation.

This does not mean that doctrine does not matter or that reasoned reflection on the things of God is unnecessary. On the contrary, doctrine and theological reflection are at the heart of our shared Christian life. Even so, there are cases where our capacities for understanding are outstripped by our questions and the mystery of the subject at hand.

Perhaps we don't have to understand fully. Indeed, maybe our desire to understand fully is one of the things we must sometimes place on the altar. And maybe there are times when our sight is limited but we can be guided

---

20   This is true elsewhere for the Wesleys. In other of Charles's hymns and John's sermons, it is hard to know for sure what parts are truth claims about how things are and what parts are playing some other role, for example, persuasive, rhetorical, symbolic, or invitational. I make this point about John in my article, "John Wesley as Interreligious Resource: Would You Take This Man to an Interfaith Dialogue?" in *A Great Commission: Christian Hope and Religious Diversity,* ed. Martin Forward, Stephen Plant, and Susan White (New York: Peter Lang Publishing, 2000).

by the sight and understanding of others. Maybe this is one of the reasons we belong to a body with many members; we can rely on one another.

More often than not, we don't fully get what we are doing in the Eucharist, but we live in a tradition and in the company of others who have tried to make sense of things. More often than not, we get no full sighting of the chariot; we don't even feel the heat of fire. But we belong to a community where people on occasion see the chariot and feel the fire. When it comes to the things of God, it often doesn't take a complete understanding or exact clarity to get us where we need to be. Maybe on some days and some topics, it takes ordinary Christians in community witnessing to what they do see and know and feel; for example, a dying woman shouting glory and pointing to the chariots bearing down from the east; a faithful witness, Jarena, who feels the fire goes on to write about it; a young Charles who catches a glimpse of the crucified Christ at the Lord's Table and is driven to write hymns about what he has felt and seen.

At the Lord's Table we don't have to know exactly what's happening and how. We simply need this commandment from a crucified Christ to "do this in remembrance of me." We also need the witness of a community through theology, doctrine, and story. We need a community of interpretation, helping us to understand as far as we can and to learn to watch attentively and to strain to see with new eyes, and to let go of things that are not fully within our ken.

Responding in Our Time

I worked on this paper before and during the 2012 United Methodist General Conference, where I was a clergy delegate. So I've been thinking about the Lord's Supper and the Wesleys in relation to the polity and mission of The United Methodist Church.

At General Conference, I thought a lot about church renewal. In many ways, I've never been more pessimistic about renewal; even so, I also have less anxiety about it now. Things are so bad that it is clearly beyond our power to fix it.

In the face of failure and decline, you have to wonder if the Lord's Supper becomes the most transformative thing we could do for the renewal of the church—even more transformative than restructuring, even more transformative than changing the social principles, even more transformative than creating new systems for clergy accountability. Moreover, the point of Christian transformation is not merely the renewal of the church, but the renewal of human lives and societies in their entirety and, ultimately, the renewal of the whole of creation.

What made *the Hymns on the Lord's Supper* so effective for eighteenth-century Methodists and how do we offer comparable resources for our time? How do we encourage the faithful to enter into the space of the Lord's Supper and be attentive to what is happening around them? How do we create texts and experiences that help people come to the Table of the Lord to see and be transformed by the crucified and risen Christ? How do we help people if not to see the burning chariot then to feel and be transformed by its refining fire?

Of course, to bring people in great numbers and fervor to the Lord's Table, we cannot simply tell them they need it. The challenge is to help them—and ourselves—want it. To meet that challenge, we may need not merely (or even primarily) study commissions, legislative proposals, or even academic papers, but also the doxology of hymnody, the imagery of poetry, the power of testimony, and liturgy, which is, of course, the work of the people.

FOURTEEN

Eucharist and Money

L. Edward Phillips

The discussion of the report of the Committee on Revision of the Ritual of the Methodist Episcopal Church at the General Conference of 1888 was vigorous and contentious. The Address of the Bishops, which opened the conference, explicitly called for "a form of public worship which shall be uniform and imperative in its essential features."[1] Yet many Methodists resisted the idea of uniformity. W. S. Urmy, delegate from California, suggested a compromise that added the words, "as far as possible" to the committee's proposal:

> Let the morning service be ordered *as far as possible* in the following manner: 1. Singing one of the hymns of our hymn-book, the people standing. 2. Prayer, concluding with the Lord's Prayer, audibly repeated by the congregation, the people kneeling. 3. The reading of a lesson from the Old Testament and another from the New, either of which may be read responsively. 4. Singing another of our hymns, the people sitting. 5. Preaching. 6. A short prayer for a blessing on the word. 7. Singing, closing with a Doxology, the people standing. 8. The pronouncing of the apostolic Benediction.[2]

Critics from both sides attacked the report and Urmy's resolution.[3] Finally, however, Urmy's substitute for the report was adopted with one final amendment inserting a collection of money. Despite the debate over the report and its substitute, as far as the record shows, the General Conference accepted the addition of a collection to the order without objection. The *Daily Christian Advocate* did not even bother to record the name of the delegate who made the amendment.

The omission of a collection from the original order may seem surprising to United Methodists of the twenty-first century, for despite the tremendous

---

1 Journal of the General Conference of the Methodist Episcopal Church (New York: Phillips & Hunt, 1888), 56–57, https://ia801405.us.archive.org/10/items/journalnewyork00meth.

2 *Daily Christian Advocate*, The Methodist Episcopal Church, May 31, 1888, General Conference (Atlantic City, N.J.: Methodist Book Concern, 1860–1936). Available at Pitts Theology Library Reference (BX8201.D3).

3 Ibid.

variety of liturgical orders followed by Methodist congregations today, the great majority of them contain an offering of money as a high point of the Sunday morning service. In the late nineteenth century, however, the collection of money was not consistently associated with Sunday worship. American Methodists, of course, collected money, but they did not routinely understand the collection as an essential, regular component of Sunday worship.

Background: Collections in the Church in England

The collection of money in worship is a well-documented practice in the English Church prior to the Reformation. Contributions of money occurred at Mass, and the use of the word *oblationes* ("offerings") to describe these gifts is not uncommon.[4] Originally these collections included both alms for the poor and gifts devoted to the clergy. The gifts to the clergy (or to other material aspects of church maintenance) were specifically denoted as "offerings," while alms were a separate category. Moreover, churches collected these alms and offerings above the expected "tithes," which were assessed as rent on land or the agricultural produce of land over which the church had some claim.[5] Alms were considered voluntary, but by the later Middle Ages, the gifts to the clergy were considered to be obligatory dues paid four times a year.[6] On these "appointed offering days," the priest would face the people and ask for his offering, collecting the money in a paten or basin held by an attending minister or by taking it in his own hand.[7] There are firsthand reports of priests refusing to give Communion to parishioners who did not bring their "dues."[8]

At the time of the Reformation, the English Church retained the practice of offering money and collecting alms, and the Book of Common Prayer

---

4   For examples see, John Dowden "'Our Alms and Oblations': An Historical Study," *Journal of Theological Studies* 1 (1900), 326–27.

5   Christopher Hill, *Economic Problems of the Church from Archbishop Whitgift to the Long Parliament* (London: Oxford/Clarendon Press, 1956).

6   While offerings could be made at other times, the four standard, required times were Christmas, Easter, the Feast Day for the dedication of the Church, plus one other. Henry VIII stipulated that these later two offering days were to fall on the Nativity of John the Baptist and the Feast of Michael the Archangel. See Francis Procter, *A New History of The Book of Common Prayer with a Rationale of Its Offices*, rev. Walter Howard Frere (London: Macmillan and Co., 1901), 480; Dowden, "'Our Alms and Oblations': An Historical Study," 328.

7   In the sixteenth century, the standard Easter dues seem to have been two pennies for the priest and one for the clerk (Hill, *Economic Problems*, 169).

8   Dowden, "'Our Alms and Oblations': An Historical Study," 328. He cites *Statuta Ecclesiae Scoticanae*, vol. ii. P. 40 addresses this abuse.

makes explicit what had been the common practice of the medieval Catholics. The 1559 Book of Common Prayer (which was the third edition of the prayer book, but the one in use for the several decades following), included rubrics that direct the taking up of alms at Holy Communion during the offertory:

> Then shal the Churchewardens, or some other by them appoyncted, gather the devocion of the people, and put the same into the poore mens boxe,[9] and upon the offeryng daies appointed, every man and woman shal pay to the Curate the due and accustomed offerings, after whiche done, the Priest shal saie . . .[10]

The 1559 Book of Common Prayer clearly differentiated the devotions of the people (referred to in the Prayer for the Church Militant as "alms"), which are collected and placed in the Poor Men's Box, and the "due and accustomed offerings" which everyone "shall pay to the Curate" on the "appointed days," four times each year.

By the time of the formulation of the 1559 Book of Common Prayer, however, more severe anti–Roman Catholic strains of Puritanism were already taking root. Puritans were suspicious of all ceremonial as latent Romanism, especially those ceremonies that did not have a clear justification from Scripture. While the offering of money appeared to have scriptural precedents (the Offertory Sentences illustrated this), Puritans feared that the giving of alms or offerings could become a form of works righteousness.[11] They retained the giving of alms at the Lord's Supper, but placed this at the very end of the service, so that it would clearly *not* be an offering to God.[12] The alms were specifically dedicated for the poor and therefore did not include a collection for the clergy. Indeed, Puritans preferred to treat the clergy as salaried workers who were paid for their services to congregations.[13]

The Puritan Revolution of 1640 succeeded in banning the Book of Common Prayer, and at that time the House of Lords appointed a committee

---

9   The Injunctions of 1547 declared that a Poor Men's Box be placed in every church.

10   For the text: http://books.google.com/books?id=qWRNAAAAYAAJ&printsec=-frontcover&source=gbs_ge_summary_r&cad=0#v=onepage&q=communion&f=-false. fol. 82.

11   Horton Davies, *Worship and Theology in England Vol. 1: From Cranmer to Hooker* (Grand Rapids: Eerdmans, 1996 [1970]), 260.

12   Arlo D. Duba, "Offering and Collection in the Reformed Tradition," *Reformed Liturgy and Music*, vol. 15:1 (1982), 27. Duba cites John Calvin, *Institutes*, IV, xviii, 7: "No assembly of the church should be held without the word being preached, prayers being offered, the Lord's Supper administered and alms given."

13   Hill, *Economic Problems*, 23–27.

to investigate irregular liturgical practices. Among other irregularities the committee found the practice of "introducing an offertory before the communion, distinct from the giving of alms to the poor."[14] To address the abuse, the *Directory for Public Worship* (1644) standardized the practice of almsgiving and further stipulated "The Collection for the poore is so to be ordered, that no part of the publique worship be thereby hindred."[15] The typical location for this collection was at the conclusion of the service as had been the earlier Puritan observance. The *Directory* also called for collections for the poor on declared days of fast and days of public thanksgiving. Nowhere, however, does the *Directory* allow for an offering in worship other than the collection of alms.

With the reestablishment of the monarchy in 1660, plans began for the reinstatement of a Book of Common Prayer, which were finalized in 1662. Several ceremonial revisions concerned collections. The revised rubric for the offertory sentences read:

> When these [offertory] Sentences are in reading, the Deacons, Church-wardens, or other fit persons appointed for that purpose, shall receive the Alms for the Poor, and other devotions of the people, in a decent bason to be provided by the Parish for that purpose; and reverently bring it to the Priest, who shall humbly present and place it upon the holy Table.[16]

No longer were the alms gathered and then placed into the Poor Men's Box as in 1559, but were presented and placed on the "holy Table." The regular, quarterly, "accustomed" dues no longer applied. An additional rubric at the conclusion of the service indicated more than alms for the poor are intended by the phrase "devotions of the people":

> After the Divine Service ended, the money given at the Offertory shall be disposed of to such pious and charitable uses, as the Minister and Church-wardens shall think fit. Wherein if they disagree, it shall be disposed of as the Ordinary shall appoint.[17]

This left open a rather wide interpretation of "pious and charitable uses." Furthermore, the 1662 Book of Common Prayer placed more ritual emphasis

---

14   Cardwell's Conferences &c. p. 273, cited by Dowden, 335. See also Procter, *A New History of the Book of Common Prayer*, 152.
15   The text may be found at http://www.reformed.org/documents/wcf_stan-dards/index.html.
16   The text may be found at http://justus.anglican.org/resources/bcp/bcp.htm.
17   Ibid.

on both alms and "devotions of the people," by requiring, for the first time in history, these offerings be placed "upon the Holy Table."

Yet, even with these clarifying rubrics, it is not clear how often a collection of alms and devotions would take place. In a good many, if not the majority, of the parishes of the Church of England in the seventeenth and eighteenth centuries, Holy Communion was celebrated quarterly or even less frequently. It was not uncommon for the Sunday services in the established church to conclude immediately after the sermon, without the Offertory Sentences or Prayer for the Church Militant.[18] In other words, the Puritans may have lost the debate about the place of a ritual offering of money in worship, but they won the debate that such an offering must be voluntary rather than "accustomed."

This very brief description of the collection illustrates several complex intuitions within the English church concerning the practical and ritual uses of money. First of all, the church always maintained some sort of distinction between alms for the poor and money offerings used for church maintenance or clergy support. Alms were a sort of "perpetual" collection (the Poor Box was always available), while collections for church and clergy support were occasional. Second, the church showed reticence in the ritualization of the collection. Before 1662, collections were not placed on the Communion table, but even when the 1662 Book of Common Prayer directed that the "alms and oblations" be placed on the "holy Table," the rubric also directed the priest to do so "humbly." Finally, the collection of alms had associations with the Holy Communion that other collections did not, and even the ritually austere Westminster Directory associated alms with the order of Holy Communion.

Wesley on the Use of Money

Wesley's sermon "The Use of Money" provides a summary of his understanding of the role of material wealth in the Christian life. He exhorted the Christian to "gain all you can, save all you can, give all you

---

18   At least, this was the case by the early nineteenth century. See James Burns, *The Moral Effect of Irregularities in the Ritual* (London: R. Clay, Printer, 1843), 14. On Sundays when Communion was not celebrated, the service was to include "all that is appointed at the Communion, until the end of the general Prayer [For the whole state of Christ's Church militant here in earth] together with one or more of these Collects last before rehearsed, concluding with the Blessing." This should include the offertory sentences and the collection, if taken. That is why omission of the offering would be "irregular," even if it were a common practice.

can," but Christians should understand their use of wealth as a primary responsibility before God. Much like the Puritans, Wesley taught that to fulfill this obligation one should take a rational, as opposed to a sentimental, approach to giving. Everything belonged to God for sacred use, and this sacred use included all bona fide human need—personal or otherwise.

With the Puritans, Wesley preached that providing money for human need per se, was not sufficient, for the Christian must do this with the right intention. But Wesley also maintained that concerns about right intention should not become an excuse to avoid doing good to others. As his General Rules stated, Methodists "continue to evidence their desire for salvation . . . By doing good . . . trampling under foot that enthusiastic doctrine that 'we are not to do good unless *our hearts be free to it.'"

According to Wesley, therefore, all proper Christian "giving" was merely using God's own wealth for God's own purposes. Giving could not be in any way a "supererogation" since God had claim to everything anyway. The question was not whether Christians ought to give, but when, how, and to whom. This required prayerful discernment of a rational ordering of priorities, without sentimentality: it was a matter of personal and communal discipline.

Since early Methodism was a movement rather than a church proper, the practice of monetary collections among early Methodists was, largely, designated giving, that is, giving toward specific needs identified by the movement. It is a well-known fact that the original purpose of the class meetings was to raise money for the building of a chapel in Bristol. Wesley's journal records numerous examples of collections for particular purposes: for the poor or clothing for the poor or for buildings or to aid a church family in distress, and so on. Wesley also asked for "subscriptions" (i.e., pledges) for particular purposes. The classes were encouraged to collect money for the general expenses of the society. The collections at public meetings for preaching and worship, however, were not ordinarily used for operating expenses; rather, they were alms or other charitable gifts for ministry to the poor.

Wesley does not usually comment on the place of these collections in the order of service. An entry in Wesley's journal for Sunday, May 7, 1758, indicates what may have been typical of such collections, at least as they were received in the established church:

> I preached at eight and at five. Afterward I was desired to make a collection for a distressed family. Mr. Booker, the Minister of the parish willingly stood at the door to receive it; and encouraged all that went by to be merciful after their power.[19]

---

19   Various editions of Wesley's journal are available online.

As noted above, the Poor Man's Box was placed by the door in most parish churches, and prior to 1662, the alms collected in the service were placed in the box. It seems likely that ad hoc collections were typically received at the door.

Early Methodists in America

Methodism took root in the British colonies without the organic connection to the established church that John Wesley could assume for British Methodism. Yet well before the Christmas Conference of 1784, Methodists had organized their preachers and had already built their first meeting places, beginning with John Street Church in New York City. These actions required financial support. In December of 1772, a conference of preachers in Maryland discussed the matter of collections for "the preacher's board and expenses." The conference decided there was no need to take up these collections weekly, which suggests that collections were not a part of the preaching services or even the weekly class meetings.[20]

"The Order for the Administration of the Lord's Supper" in Wesley's *Sunday Service of the Methodists of North America*, sent with Thomas Coke in 1784, lightly revised the order in the Book of Common Prayer. It contained the offertory sentences and the rubric directing "some fit person" to "receive the alms for the poor, and other devotion of the people, in a decent Bason [sic], to be provided for that purpose; and then bring it to the elder, who shall place it upon the Table."[21] Even when the Americans revised the ritual in 1792 (a year after Wesley's death) by dropping most of the Ante-Communion, the rite retained the offertory sentences and the collection of alms, including the rubric directing the "basin" to be placed on the table.[22]

Holy Communion, however, would not become the standard weekly practice, though Methodists would continue to make a collection of alms for the poor at their occasional Communion services, as well as at their love feasts.[23] Rather, American Methodists made regular collections at weekly class meetings and brought these funds to their quarterly meetings. Methodists would also on occasion take up a collection at preaching services

---

20 Nathan Bangs, *A History of the Methodist Episcopal Church*, vol. 1, 3rd ed. rev. and corrected (New York: T. Masao and G. Lang, 1839), 60–61.

21 *John Wesley's Sunday Service of the Methodists in North America* (Nashville: The United Methodist Publishing House, 1984), 130.

22 For an account of these revisions, see Karen B. Westerfield Tucker, *American Methodist Worship* (New York: Oxford University Press, 2001), 119–27.

23 British Methodists also took up alms at love feasts. See Horton Davies, *Worship and Theology in England, Vol. 3, From Watts and Wesley to Maurice, 1690–1850* (Princeton, NJ: Princeton University Press, 1961), 200.

at which persons who were not members of the society might be in attendance. Lester Ruth, in his study of early Methodist quarterly conferences, notes that these public collections "although made sporadically, could be a significant source of revenue for a circuit" and could provide "10 to 20 percent of the money available for a circuit during a quarter."[24] Indeed, "sporadic" is an apt description of almost every element of American Methodist patterns of worship on the frontier, except, possibly, preaching.[25] If there were to be any hope of consistent financial support of the traveling pastors, it would have to come from the classes and quarterly meetings of the society.

The Development of "Stewardship" in American Churches

The sporadic giving patterns of Methodists may have sufficed during the early days of frontier Methodism, but this kind of giving could not sustain the increasing need for institutional stability. Over the course of the nineteenth century, moreover, congregational ministries became increasingly more expensive. For example, the Sunday school barely existed at the beginning of the century, but by 1828, the Methodist Episcopal Church (MEC) recommended that elders promote Sunday schools in all of their circuits.[26] Sunday schools required resources of time, print material, and meeting space, obviously adding to the expense of congregational life.

Methodists, of course, were not alone among the churches in the United States trying to develop appropriate methods for financing the church. James Hudnut-Beumler's study of the evolution of church finance demonstrates the difficult choices faced by churches in the new competitive and entrepreneurial ethos of nineteenth-century American religion: "As they moved from the public sector into the private sphere, American churches had available two broad models for support: the private club and voluntary member-supported institution."[27] The private club model "charged pew rents and ostracized those who used the 'free' pews in the back of the church." The "member-supported institution," on the other hand,

24   Lester Ruth, *A Little Heaven Below: Worship at Early Methodist Quarterly Meetings* (Nashville: Abingdon Press [Kingswood Books], 2000), 51.

25   William N. Wade, "A History of Public Worship in the Methodist Episcopal Church and Methodist Episcopal Church, South, from 1784 to 1905," (unpublished PhD diss., University of Notre Dame, 1981), 219–22.

26   James E. Kirby, Russell E. Richey, and Kenneth E. Rowe, *The Methodists*, Denominations in America no. 8 (Westport, Conn.: Greenwood Press, 1996), 172.

27   James David Hudnut-Beumler, *In Pursuit of the Almighty's Dollar: a History of Money and American Protestantism* (Chapel Hill: University of North Carolina Press, 2007), 11.

depended on moral appeal to those users of it to contribute voluntarily, all the while knowing that many would not.[28] Most Methodist congregations in the nineteenth century used the second method, though larger, more affluent congregations often used the pew-rent system with its un-subtle class bias.

To address the increasing expense of ministry, American congregations sought a middle way between the obvert classism of the pew-rental system and the fickleness of the voluntary ad hoc collection system. Protestants would, in Hudnut-Beumler's description, "reinvent the tithe" as the fundamental biblical principle of Christian giving, often connecting this to another biblical principle, "stewardship." This entailed the rise of "planned giving." But churches also continued to take up collections, particularly in the weekly Sunday schools, for various causes. Thus, we see the development of the shape of Protestant church life in the United States today: yearly pledge drives for "planned giving"; special ad hoc collections for various needs.[29]

From Collection to Offering

Gradually, historically "non-liturgical" Protestants began to institute the shift in approach to collections in their official orders of worship. The eighteenth-century *Directory for Worship* of the Presbyterians, for example, referred to a "collection for the poor, or other purposes of the church" just before the apostolic benediction, keeping the traditional Puritan order.[30] By 1886, the *Directory for Worship* added a chapter entitled, "On the Worship of God by Offerings," which encouraged liberal giving by designating it "a solemn act of worship to Almighty God."[31] As Hudnut-Beumler describes this change:

> What the magisterial Reformers had tried to purge—the idea that human beings independently possessed anything they could offer God—was restored to a central place of significance. . . . The liturgical orders of the 1890s manifested the acceptance of this new essential element in American worship.[32]

So when the Methodist Episcopal Church added a collection to the official order of service in 1888, this was a tacit acceptance of a development in church finance among Protestants generally.

---

28   Ibid., 12.
29   Ibid., specifically, 59.
30   Cited in Duba, "Offering and Collection in the Reformed Tradition," 28.
31   Ibid., 29.
32   Hudnut-Beumler, *In Pursuit of the Almighty's Dollar*, 58.

Like the Presbyterians, Methodists gradually began to apply ritual language to the collection. The joint *Methodist Hymnal* of 1905 added an "offertory" to the collection, though this referred to a musical piece, rather than the presentation of the collection per se.[33] By 1920, the *Doctrines and Discipline of the Methodist Episcopal Church* included under paragraph 71, regarding "Christian Stewardship," the principle that "Weekly payments, as far as possible, should be offered as an act of worship at the public service."[34] The *Discipline* also made a change to the "Order of Public Worship" that specified "Worship in the presentation of tithes and offerings, during or after which an Offertory may be rendered."[35] In short, by the early twentieth century there was an increasing ritualization of the money in Methodist worship: what had formerly been "the collection" had now become "the offering" along with ritual resonance of that term.[36] But while "tithes and offerings" might include money specifically designated to care for the poor, alms as an especially significant and separate category of giving receded into the background.

In 1932, the revisions of the Order of Worship (which were accepted almost entirely at the merger of the MEC, the MECS, and the Methodist Protestants in 1939), provided three orders, all of which contained a presentation of "offerings." The third of these orders, entitled, "An order for Morning or Evening Prayer" contained even more explicit rubrics regarding the offering: "Here, when convenient, may be sung an anthem: the offering also being received and reverently brought to the Minister, the congregation meantime rising; and it should be placed upon the Table with singing or prayer."[37] There is no missing the intended ritual importance of rubrics that go so far as to comment on the reverence of the ushers (but without the request for the minister to "humbly present and place it on the holy Table" as in the Book of Common Prayer). This is quite a shift from 1888.

With increasing ritualization came a naïve theology of the sacramental power of money. A column in the *Northwestern Christian Advocate* in 1903

---

33   *The Doctrines and Disciplines of the Methodist Episcopal Church, 1904* (New York: Eaton & Mains, 1904), par. 70; *The Doctrines and Disciplines of the Methodist Episcopal Church, South, 1910* (Nashville: Publishing House of the Methodist Episcopal Church, South, 1910), para. 224.

34   *The Doctrines and Disciplines of the Methodist Episcopal Church, 1920* (New York: The Methodist Book Concern, 1920), para. 71.

35   Ibid., para. 72.

36   Stephen Perry, "The Revival of Stewardship and the Creation of the World Service Commission in the Methodist Episcopal Church, 1912–1924," in Russell E. Richey et al., *Perspectives on American Methodism, Interpretive Essays* (Nashville: Abingdon Press [Kingswood Books], 1993), 410.

37   *The Doctrines and Disciplines of the Methodist Episcopal Church, 1932* (New York: The Methodist Book Concern), para. 511.

observed that for the "man" whose life is consecrated to God, "There is a wonderful thing about money—it can be transmuted into a living spiritual power."[38] Fifteen years later, a column in the Methodist magazine *Men and Money* complained about the irreverent and distracting use of organ music during the pastor's prayer for the money offering:

> No, it was not an accident. The minister and the organist planned the thing together. It was a stunt—a prayer staged to soft music! The masters of liturgy and form, who follow the reverent ceremonial of the past, may teach the rest of us how to avoid the bizarre. Music is there that thrills and haunts. But the moment the Host is exalted at the mass—silence. Shall it not be so when the offering is made? Does it not symbolize our acknowledgment of God's ownership over all that we have?[39]

Stephen Perry suggests that such interpretations were an attempt by Methodists "to establish wealth as a virtue" and "to sanctify the social and economic life of the world."[40] But they clearly also addressed the need of churches to have generous givers in order to fund the increasingly expensive cost of doing church.

The Money Offering as the Objective Core of Protestant Worship

The ritualization of money, moreover, addressed a concern about the fundamental significance of Christian worship that had been developing over the final decades of the nineteenth century. Nineteenth-century revivalism and the Sunday school had promoted worship as a method for conversion and religious education. By the beginning of the twentieth century, Protestant leaders began to show a great deal of anxiety about these subjective, instrumental approaches. In 1920, the pragmatist philosopher and psychologist of religion James Bissett Pratt gave a provocative analysis of the problem of contemporary Protestant worship:

> Religion is not so much theology as life; it is to be *lived* rather than reasoned about. In short, religion is not a theory about reality; it *is* reality. . . . It takes itself seriously, and is not satisfied with being simply comforting and "useful"; it means to be also *true*. . . . And if it be said that the *value* of religion at any rate

---

38   *Northwestern Christian Advocate* (Jan. 14, 1903): 32.
39   *Men and Money* 1, no. 4 (June 1918): 164.
40   See Perry, "The Revival of Stewardship and the Creation of the World Service Commission in the Methodist Episcopal Church, 1912–1924," 41 and following pages.

> is subjective only [a position Pratt identifies with modern Protestantism] then at least religion must not know that this is the case; for if it learned the secret both its value and it would cease to be even subjective.[41]

In other words, Pratt argued that in order for modern Protestant Christianity to do what it places the highest value on—namely, shaping the subjective faith and moral values of the modern person—it must not lose its objective core, that which is true and real. Yet, regarding worship, Pratt saw that this was the precise danger of Protestant worship of his day:

> The attempt to produce merely subjective religious effects is always in danger of defeating itself. For religion, as we have seen, involves a belief which means to have objective validity. . . . The worshiper in the Protestant Church must be made to feel, as the Catholic feels at the mass, that *something is really being done*—something in addition to the subjective change in his own consciousness. . . . In other words, what the Protestant service needs more than anything else is the development of the objective side of its worship.[42]

Pratt was not optimistic about the future of Protestantism if it did not reclaim its objective core to worship.

Not a few Christian leaders began to take notice of this problem. Von Ogden Vogt,[43] William Sperry,[44] and Methodists J. Hastie Odgers and Edward G. Schutz[45] wrote books or articles that attempted to reclaim an objective core to religious experience for Protestants. These authors, along with Pratt, were widely referenced among Methodists, and their works appeared on Course of Study book lists in the Methodist Episcopal Church and the Methodist Episcopal Church, South. All of these books argued that Protestant worship must reclaim a genuine experience of awe as a response to the objective truth of religion if it were to thrive in the modern world.

Modern, enlightened Protestants, of course, (so they argued) could not accept with integrity the crude realism of the Catholic Mass or the unsophisticated emotionalism of the camp meeting as a source of religious awe. But modern Protestants *could* find awe in dignified ritual form and beautiful

---

41   James Bissett Pratt, *The Religious Consciousness: A Psychological Study* (New York: Macmillan, 1920), 7.

42   Ibid., 307.

43   Von Ogden Vogt, *Art and Religion* (New Haven: Yale University Press, 1921).

44   Willard L. Sperry, *Reality in Worship: A Study of Public Worship and Private Religion* (New York: Macmillan, 1925).

45   J. Hastie Odgers and Edward G. Schutz, *The Technique of Public Worship* (New York: The Methodist Book Concern, 1928.)

architecture. What sort of architecture would be appropriate? Modern worship needed, in their opinion, the awe-inspiring architecture of the Gothic church. Protestant leaders began to promote Gothic Revival architecture, not merely for the facades of churches, but also for interiors. This meant divided chancels, with imposing pulpits and vestments, and it meant a high altar table against a reredos. Regarding this aesthetic appropriation of Gothic chancels, Vogt remarked: "One expects an Episcopal Church to be beautiful and one looks for an altar in it. The noteworthy thing is the number of free churches which have revived the ancient setting for the communion table at the head of an apse or chancel."[46] Inspired by this new aesthetic movement, the Architectural Bureau of the Methodist Episcopal Church advocated Gothic-style chancels with altar tables for Methodist church buildings.[47] Methodists, like most Protestants, of course, did not need this as a place to celebrate the Eucharist every Sunday, since few mainline Protestants held their Lord's Supper more than four times a year. Rather, the altar functioned as a visual focal point and reminder of Christ.[48] On it would be placed candles, a cross, and plates full of money (much of it used to finance the new Gothic buildings!) brought forward by ushers during an elaborate procession, imitating the offertory processions of Episcopalians.

The irony of this appropriation of Anglican/Episcopal ceremonial by Methodist and other "non-liturgical" churches in the early twentieth century is that Anglican liturgical theologians were uncertain about the ritual presentation of the money offering. There is not room here to describe in detail the developments concerning the collection in Episcopal churches, but at the beginning of the nineteenth century, Episcopal churches in the United States (like most Protestant churches) did not regularly have a money offering at the Sunday service. As late as 1870, Bishop Richard Hooker Wilmer in an address to the Alabama Diocese enthused, "It gratifies me greatly to be able to say that offerings are now presented by the people, on every Lord's Day, in almost all the Churches of the Diocese."[49] But despite the increasing frequency of Lord's Day offerings, the ceremonial appropriate to the collection of "Alms and Oblations" was heatedly debated among Episcopalians. By the early twentieth century, the great Anglican liturgist Percy Dearmer commented:

---

46   Vogt, *Art and Religion*, x.
47   James F. White, *Protestant Worship: Traditions in Transition* (Louisville: Westminster/John Knox Press, 1989), 165–66.
48   Vogt, *Art and Religion*, 211–15.
49   Journal of the Proceedings of the Protestant Episcopal Church in the Diocese of Alabama (Mobile, AL: Henry Farrow & Co, 1871), 43. See: https://play.google.com/store/books/details?id=ZGoQAAAAIAAJ&rdid=book-ZGoQAAAAIAAJ&rdot=1.

One even hears of "Offertories" at Evensong, and one even sees the clergy make wave offerings of the alms (some carry them in solemn procession) at choir offices, as if they were in a conspiracy to rob the Mass of its meaning. . . . The priest is then to present the bason [sic] and place it upon the holy Table: this he is to do, not ostentatiously, but "humbly", slightly raising it: there is no authority for the solemn elevation of the alms-bason, nor for signing the coins, while to hand the bason to the server after the presentation is simply a defiance of the rubric, "shall humbly present and place it upon the holy Table."[50]

In Dearmer's account, an elaborate presentation of the "alms and oblations" obscured the ritual preparation of the table for the celebration of the Lord's Supper.

The development of the highly ritualized pattern of offertory in Methodism, as in mainline Protestantism generally, moved in the opposite direction: money was *definitely* a proper offering deserving the high ritual expression. Absent the "really" real of the Catholic Eucharist (as Pratt described it), modern Protestants turned to an aestheticized presentation of the "really" real of money, the desperate need of churches in the competitive religious market in the United States and the singular marker of value in the capitalist West. By the middle of the twentieth century, Methodist churches urban and rural, small and large, formal or folksy, ritualized the weekly collection by singing a doxology as a regimen of ushers in procession brought plates of cash and personal checks to be "offered" to God with all the pomp of a Medieval high mass. There could be little doubt that this was the ritual high point of the service.

Alms, Offerings, and the Lord's Supper

The development of the highly ritualized offering of money, however, was not the entire story of Methodist collections, for Methodists continued to receive alms for the poor at the Lord's Supper whenever they celebrated the sacrament. As noted above, the American Methodist revision of the ritual in 1792 retained the rubric directing "some fit person appointed for that purpose, shall receive the alms for the poor and other devotions of the people."[51] At the same time, the 1792 revision dropped the four offertory sentences that alluded to a collection for the ministers (1 Cor 9:7, 11, 13-14; and Gal 6:6-7). In his commentary on the ritual, Thomas O. Summers remarked of the collection at the Lord's Supper:

---

50   Percy Dearmer, *The Parson's Handbook* (Oxford: Horace Hart, 1907), 374–75.
51   Nolan B. Harmon, *The Rites and Ritual of Episcopal Methodism* (Nashville: Publishing House of the Methodist Episcopal Church, South, 1926), 100.

The rubric speaks of "the alms for the poor, and other devotions of the people"—the latter referring to contributions for the ministry. These were liberal in ancient times, as the clergy were largely supported by such offerings. But the English clergy rarely, if ever, realize any thing from this source—and Methodist ministers have no interest in these contributions hence the sentences in question are omitted from our book.[52]

In 1854 the Methodist Episcopal Church, South, moved the rubric concerning the collection to the beginning of the offertory and dropped the reference to "other devotions of the people" to emphasize the alms: "The elder shall read one or more of these sentences during the reading of which the stewards shall take up the collection for the poor." In 1864, the Methodist Episcopal Church made a similar change.[53] Indeed, an explicit call for a collection for the poor at services of Holy Communion was part of the ritual for Holy Communion until *The Methodist Hymnal* of 1964, which ostensibly continued the practice, but without explicit mention of "the needy": "Where custom prevails, an offering may be left by the people at the chancel when they come forward to receive the elements."[54] This second collection was distinct from the "offering from the people" before the Great Thanksgiving, and it was clearly a remnant of the collection for the poor. Thus the Methodist Ritual of Holy Communion continued to manifest two intuitions going back to the 1559 Book of Common Prayer: (1) alms for the poor are distinct from other offerings of money and (2) alms fittingly belong to the service of Holy Communion.

This tradition ended with the authorized ritual with services of "Word and Table" in *The United Methodist Hymnal* of 1989, which no longer distinguished a collection for the poor from other offerings of money. This more recent change reflects the influence of the ecumenical liturgical movement of the twentieth century.[55] Drawing on the practices of the patristic era, the liturgical movement sought to reclaim an offertory procession during which men and women brought their charitable gifts to the altar, including bread and wine for the offering of the Eucharist.

---

52 Thomas Osmond Summers, *Commentary on the Ritual of the Methodist Episcopal Church, South* (Nashville: A. H. Redford, 1873), 11. Also referenced by Harmon, *Rites and Ritual*, 134.

53 See Harmon, *Rites and Ritual*, 101.

54 *The Methodist Hymnal* (Nashville: The Methodist Publishing House, 1964), no. 830 (p. 14).

55 Similar changes occurred, for example, in the 1979 Episcopal Book of Common Prayer, which dropped all reference to alms during the offertory.

The degree to which the modern attempt to reclaim this ancient practice has succeeded is beyond the scope of this essay, though anecdotal evidence of colleagues and students suggest that United Methodists have not understood the change. Even when bread and wine are brought forward with the collection plates, most United Methodists continue to understand the money collection alone as the actual "offering." Given that the Lord's Supper is still an occasional service for most United Methodists, while money offerings occur weekly, this is not surprising. Indeed, it is testimony to the formative power of regular liturgical practice. But this raises the question as to whether the money offering as typically performed is a wholesome ritual. Liberal sharing of one's financial resources is surely a sound Wesleyan virtue. One may, however, wonder if elaborately ceremonial giving of money enacts more than Christian liberality. Without maligning the intentions of individual worshipers, is it possible that the money offering ritually displays our modern enthrallment to wealth?

Yet among older Methodists one still finds the habit of placing alms on the communion rail whenever they celebrate Holy Communion. Old liturgical habits die hard, and, as Summers noted, this one has much deeper roots in Methodist tradition. It reaches back to the Christian intuitions that grasped an essential connection between remembering the poor in our community and meeting Jesus at his table. Perhaps this humble action, almost unnoticed today and in danger of disappearing altogether, enacts a challenge to the pretentions of elaborate rituals surrounding the money offering, the widow's mite, if you will, shaming the Pharisees. It is a response to Paul's challenge to the Corinthians that whatever they may think they are doing, if they do not honor the poor, it is not the Lord's Supper.[56]

---

56   The author would like to acknowledge that the groundwork for the study leading to the contents of this chapter was funded by The Louisville Institute Sabbatical Grant for Researchers.

FIFTEEN

Eucharist and Pastoral Care

Edward P. Wimberly

Introduction

The forces of secularism and economics have triumphed, leaving us with an anxiety that isolates us, cutting us off from what we most need. We live in a world that equates having wealth, status, prestige, position, and power with being loved and truly happy. We have confused having with being— having things with being in significant relationships with the power of real presence. This anxiety comes from believing that personal worth and value is based on one's social status and leads to an insidious form of narcissism, a malignant self-love, which creates relational refugees or disconnected, fractured people who are cut off from God, the authentic source of life, love, and happiness. Behind the human thirst for status and the unrelenting need to give and receive love as members of a beloved community is an unresolvable conflict that cannot be mediated but by the grace of God.

Relational Refugees

While for some the need for love and true happiness appears to have taken a backseat to a lust for wealth, power, and status, culture itself encourages us at every turn to invest our efforts in things that will never completely fulfill their promises to make us whole persons. In other words we live in an age where anxiety prevails because we equate status with love.[1] The result is that relationships and those practices that authentically connect us to relationships with others are trivialized and discounted. As more people invest their resources in a futile and selfish quest for more, more for themselves and others like them at the expense of caring for others (and, most especially, strangers), the more emphasis there is on a self-love that rests solely on appearances, rather than on reciprocal face-to-face relationships and communal practices, such as the Eucharist. Consequently, a facade of

---

1   Alaine Botton, *Status Anxiety* (New York: Vintage, 2005), 6.

happiness replaces happiness and masks persons' ability to enter into satisfying relationships. The facade blocks the possibility of being truly present with and to others, including, and most tragically, with God.

The selfish search for love is an epidemic, symbolized by a series of self-deceptive and phony practices. These practices result in a persona that reflects only one's status related to one's wealth and prosperity, rather than reflecting the image of God and our true purpose. As we experience the need to appear prosperous for attracting admiration and love, we become disconnected from genuine and loving community. We become relational refugees who may want to be genuinely loved for who we are; but, rather, we find ourselves measuring our worth by what we have or what we can buy.

In a context where there is a plethora of online dating and Facebook friends, people are also lonelier than ever before. Paradoxically, we continue to put less value on tangible human presence and therefore exacerbate the problem. We begin to wonder: What is wrong with me? Why do I feel so alone? These questions come out of feelings of shame. When we feel shame, we see ourselves as defective or stained and not worthy of being loved, making us even more susceptible to the lure of what some have called "shiny gods."[2]

Given a pursuit of love and happiness in the wrong places, people typically don't turn to the traditional religious resources to help them connect to community. Instead they ignore or minimalize the church and what the church can be for them. Thus, the end result is a further deepening of the hunger for self-worth as well as alienation from faith communities. The gulf between selfish desires and our need for authentic relationships widens, and we become relationally and spiritually homeless. Only real, face-to-face presence can anchor our sense of wholeness and well-being, but we have become a restless people unable to satisfy our most basic relational needs, resulting in shame and loss—loss of meaning, loss of purpose, loss of love, loss of faith, and sometimes loss of our selves.[3]

Because of our refugee status, practical engagement in religious practices slips far down on our priority list. But when we eventually tire of running after things that don't deliver on their promises to fulfill our needs, we are ready to consider alternatives, perhaps like turning to God and the church. When our pursuit of happiness and love based on transitory wealth, position, status, and power becomes futile, we can be motivated to look for something more lasting. If the community of faith is welcoming, we

---

2   See Mike Slaughter's *Shiny Gods: Finding Freedom from Things That Distract Us* (Nashville: Abingdon Press, 2013).

3   Cornel West, *Race Matters* (New York: Vintage, 1993), 19–20.

might then begin to consider it and seek love in a secure relationship with God and the members of Christ's body, the church, which is grounded and sustained by sacramental practices such as Holy Communion. However, if we profess faith in God and do not live out our faith, we can become what John Wesley called practical atheists.

Holy Communion as a Salve for Anxiety

This chapter focuses on the relevance of and the need to recover John Wesley's practical theology of happiness that comes from participating in the Eucharist as a means by which we can ameliorate the effects of the anxiety that isolates us and cuts us off from our humanity and the power of significant relationships. I concur wholeheartedly with Sarah H. Lancaster that Wesley's practical theology, which is centered in his concept of relational happiness as a gift given by God, has supreme salience for our hunger for love[4] and can be a salve for our anxiety.

Lancaster defines North American culture as a happiness culture, and this means that happiness, as defined by psychology, is seeking life satisfaction and the absence of pain.[5] In other words, happiness is seen as an end in itself and not a by-product or result of significant relationships fostered in the presence of other people or God. Thus divorced from relationships, happiness, as it is culturally defined, becomes just another status object—something we have to have—something that we strive to possess as a good, a thing. In other words, we have emptied happiness of its value and meaning. Wesley's understanding of happiness, on the other hand, rests in his understanding of what I call "eschatological banking." In Wesley's Sermon 89, "The More Excellent Way," Wesley references the future hope of heaven, and he emphasizes the proper human attribute needed to prepare to participate in the heavenly future. He says:

> But suppose it were not forbidden, how can you on principles of reason, spend your money in a way which God may possibly forgive, instead of spending it in a manner which he will certainly reward? You will have no reward in heaven

---

4   Sarah Heaner Lancaster, *The Pursuit of Happiness: Blessing and Fulfillment in Christian Faith* (Eugene, OR: Wipf and Stock, 2011), 98–99. For her, the theme of happiness has made a comeback in our culture today, and Wesley's understanding of happiness as a gift from God has contemporary salience in the public marketplace.

5   Ibid., 96–99.

for what you lay up; you will, for what you lay out. Every pound you put into the earthly bank is sunk: it brings no interest above. But every pound you give to the poor is into the bank of heaven. And it will bring glorious interest; yea, and as such, will be accumulating to all eternity.[6]

Wesley's reference is clearly about the future, but it is also about the source of true happiness. He references the benefit and reward focused on the future in heaven. Contemporarily, however, Lancaster is accurate about present-day people being concerned about the immediacy of happiness.

So Wesley's concept of the practice of constant communion emphasizing engagement in a significant practice, which I have referred to as "eschatological banking," is an investment, a hope, in God's rule, reign, and the unfolding story of the transformation of God's world. Through God's prevenient grace we are called; and through our participation with God in the sacraments, we can fulfill our need to be loved and valued and find happiness in being part of God's narrative. The practice of partaking the Eucharist is a way we can stay in constant communion with God and keep recalling our memory of God's mighty acts of salvation and continue celebrating God's loving presence and provision for us. According to Wesley, communing with God brings happiness. Through God's presence, God brings us the joy of our salvation.

Wesley's Pastoral Theology

The hope and healing found in participating in the Eucharist is part of Wesley's pastoral theology. Wesley's pastoral care involved his effort to help people enter into a satisfying and loving personal relationship with God and others as they participated in God's unfolding story of transformation. Wesley's theology emphasizes that real love, joy, and happiness come as a result of accepting God's grace through practices designed to help us stay focused on God's transformative presence. The benefit of these practices (1) come as a result of having a personal and hopeful relationship with God through Jesus Christ, (2) help us share that hope through participation in God's faithful community within the framework of congregations and small groups, and (3) enable us to abide in God's eternal presence through the sacrament of the Eucharist.

---

6   John Wesley, "The More Excellent Way," in *The Works of John Wesley: Sermons*, vol. 3, ed. Albert Outler (Nashville: Abingdon Press, 1986), 276.

Practical Atheists

The Works of Wesley says that some of Wesley's thinking on Holy Community is found in Sermon 101 and, written fifty years later, in Sermon 130. The thinking reflected in Sermon 101, "The Duty of Constant Communion," is based on the work of Robert Nelson, who was an Anglican liturgist.[7] Later in 1787, Wesley revised Nelson further, resulting in Sermon 130, which represents the fullest development of Wesley's eucharistic doctrine. Sermon 101 and Sermon 130 focus on the benefits and virtues that accrue to a person from being in intimate connection with the Triune God, through participation in Holy Communion.

In both sermons, the benefits of participating in the Eucharist are vertical (with God) and horizontal (with others), and spiritually there is pardon for sin, the "strengthening of the soul and refreshing it with the hope of glory."[8] Obeying the command to communicate and fellowship constantly, in Wesley's mind, was a path to being eternally happy. Taking the Eucharist was a way of receiving God's mercy and grace for obtaining "holiness on earth and everlasting glory in heaven."

While the benefits of Holy Communion seem obvious, at least to Wesley, he addresses why people don't avail themselves of the gift of God's presence and are, instead, practical atheists. He does this in Sermon 130, entitled "On Living without God." The sermon was written in 1791 and is based on Ephesians 2:12,[9] which addresses the hopelessness of living in the world without God. Wesley's sermon comes from his concern that the people of his day, although they might say they were Christian, didn't live following the precepts and principles of Christ. Therefore they sought salvation where it would never be found and consequently lived in hopelessness. They were baptized, but it made no difference in their day-to-day living. They were not following the order of salvation as proclaimed by Christ and set forth in the Bible. Specifically they were neglecting the observance of Holy Communion, and Wesley sought to challenge them.

What Wesley called "practical atheism" was not people's refusal to believe in God, but rather their failing to avail themselves of the practices, activities, and exercises that can connect us to God's resources and gracious gift of love, which results in happiness. Historically, one such practice has

---

7   An Introductory Comment to John Wesley, "The Duty of Constant Communion," *The Works of John Wesley*, vol. 3, ed. Outler, 427.

8   Wesley, "The Duty of Constant Communion," *The Works of John Wesley*: Sermons, vol. 3, ed. Outler, 429.

9   Wesley, "On Living without God," *The Works of John Wesley*, vol. 4, ed. Outler, 168–76.

been Holy Communion. Holy Communion acts as a counter to today's practical atheism and our chasing after false idols of wealth and status. Participating in Holy Communion gives us an entry point into a present and not-yet world that is God's realm. It is into this existence we are called, and when we embrace the sacraments we discover our ultimate purpose and find satisfying ways to help us give and receive authentic love in God's presence.

Wesley wanted people to understand that Christ was present in the Eucharist and that it offered a person the real opportunity to commune with God, experience God's love and grace, live in hope, and find happiness. In addressing the some people's objection to partaking the Eucharist because they did not experience the benefits of Communion that were promised, Wesley's first response is that it is our duty to be obedient to God's command to "Do this in remembrance of me." But if doing our duty to be obedient is not enough, Wesley adds the promise that "we shall find benefit sooner or later." He also insists that taking Communion regularly will prevent people from "falling back in their growth and falling into temptation.[10]

But by neglecting participating in Holy Communion, people became practical atheists despite their excuses and protests to the contrary. People today still use many of these same reasons. They include feeling unworthy and fearing damnation because they aren't good enough—shame and anxiety. Another reason for not participating in Holy Communion is the disappointment of not finding what they are looking for. They don't see the benefit, so they continue to chase idols, which yields hopelessness. Wesley says,

> But undoubtedly we shall find benefit sooner or later, though perhaps insensibly. We shall be insensibly strengthened, made fitter for service of God, and more constant in it. At least we are kept from falling back, and preserved from many sins and temptations. And surely this should be enough to make us receive this food as often as we can; though we do not presently feel the happy effect of it, as some have done, and we ourselves may when God see best.[11]

It is as though what we would call anxiety dulls our senses, preventing us from perceiving the full benefit of being with God. In psychological circles it is well known that the presence of anxiety cuts off foresight and prevents people from making rational decisions. The presence of anxiety clouds and dulls our senses and clouds our judgment. Wesley's remedy is to obey God,

---

10   John Wesley, *The Works of John Wesley:* Journal and Diaries, vol. 19, ed. W. Reginald Ward and Richard Heitzenrater (Nashville: Abingdon Press, 1990), 98.

11   Wesley, "The Duty of Constant Communion," *The Works of John Wesley*, vol. 3, ed. Outler, 437–38.

who only has our best interests at heart. Slowly by being in God's presence, the anxiety will be dispelled, and the light of God's love will become visible.

In Sermon 130, Wesley proclaims the good news that comes from God breaking through our practical atheism by transforming our dulled physical existence into eternal life. When people enter into communion and fellowship with God, Jesus Christ, and the Holy Spirit, Wesley preached, human beings see, hear, taste, and feel differently. Wesley says,

> He feels the love of God shed abroad in his heart by the Holy Ghost which is given unto him or, as our Church expresses it, feels the workings of the Spirit of God in his heart. Meantime it may easily be observed that the substance of all these figurative expressions is comprised in that one word "faith," taken in its widest sense; being enjoyed, more or less, by everyone that believes in the name of the Son of God. This change from spiritual death to spiritual life is properly the new birth.[12]

Wesley is referring to Romans 5:5, which says: "Hope does not disappoint us, because God's love has been poured into our hearts through the Holy Spirit that has been given to us" (NRSV). In short, through our communing with God through Holy Communion, God's Spirit communicates that we are beloved children of God and that there is hope for us and the world. This not only dispels our anxiety, but keeps us on the road that leads to perfection, where we are able through spiritual senses to hear, see, touch, and feel God's love permeating our lives—giving us hope, purpose, and meaning.

Another benefit of taking Communion for Wesley was not just happiness now but eternal happiness. At this point it is sufficient to say that Wesley believed that the benefit of eternal happiness was obvious, but there is also some indication in his sermon "The Duty of Constant Communion" that he envisaged happiness as the joy that came from being empowered to live holy lives of love.

It is clear from his sermons that Wesley's practical theology focuses on constant communing through celebrating Holy Communion and that this experience of God's presence speaks to our basic desire for the assurance that we are loved. Moreover, this love is manifest and available within communities of faith, which support and reinforce the work that God is already doing. Assuredly, as Wesley would say, we will eventually experience God's love in our lives. We can be assured of God's love. Our hope can heal us of our shame of not being worthy of love and the anxiety of feeling worthless.

---

12 Wesley, "On Living without God," *The Works of John Wesley*, vol. 4, ed. Outler, 173.

Holy Communion and Pastoral Care

Wesley's emphasis on Holy Communion grows out of his understanding of the therapeutic function of the sacraments, and Wesley's theological orientation makes his pastoral work compatible with what takes place in modern pastoral care. That is to say that Wesley emphasized using Christian practices to help human beings experience God's love and then share that love through acts of mercy and justice with others and thereby find authentic happiness.[13] Indeed, happiness is a gift of God's grace communicated through practices such as Holy Communion.[14]

Historically, pastoral care has had four foci, all of which point persons to wholeness in the context of face-to-face relationships; namely, healing, sustaining, guiding, and reconciling.[15] Healing includes restoring people's brokenness, whether emotional, physical, spiritual, or relational. Sustaining concerns holding the line, supporting, and preventing further damage or hardship when healing or restoration may not be possible. Guiding has to do with teaching or leading the person toward wholeness. And reconciling deals with restoring relationships with justice and mercy. Wesley's notion of the efficacy of the Eucharist includes all four foci of pastoral care. For Wesley, these foci are interwoven into all the functions or tasks of ministry including preaching and worship, visiting and caring for the sick and imprisoned, teaching and discipleship formation, and social witness.[16]

The Eucharist reinforces all these aspects of ministry. A central theological function of these different dimensions of ministry is to draw persons and the faith community into a vital relationship to God for the sake of conforming persons to Christ's image and through grace, guiding persons toward justification and sanctification. More precisely, the Eucharist assists the working of God's grace through the Holy Spirit to form human beings and Christian community, so "scriptural holiness can

---

13   Ellen Charry, *By the Renewal of Your Minds: The Pastoral Function of Christian Doctrine* (New York: Oxford University Press, 1997).

14   See Lancaster, *The Pursuit of Happiness*, 109–10, and Edward Wimberly, *No Shame in Wesley's Gospel: A Twenty-First Century Pastoral Theology* (Eugene, OR: Wipf and Stock, 2011), 70–77.

15   William A. Clebsch and Charles R. Jaekle, *Pastoral Care in Historical Perspective* (Englewood Cliffs, NJ: 1964).

16   The definitions of worship, nurture, care, and witness can be found in Edward Wimberly, *Pastoral Care in the Black Church* (Nashville: Abingdon Press, 1979), 80. For the definitions of formation and discipline see Wimberly, *No Shame in Wesley's Gospel*, 62–63.

be spread throughout the land."[17] Ultimately, Wesley's understanding of the Eucharist is that it guides human beings into a relationship with God and sustains them as whole persons in God's unfolding story of salvation, thereby healing their lives and reconciling them with God. By experiencing the presence of God in the Eucharist, people could find assurance of their status before God as God's beloved children and the sustenance to be God's witnesses in the world.

Worship, disciple formation, care, and witness are important because these concepts embrace a holistic understanding of the Eucharist in Wesley's thinking. More specifically, worship is an expression of the church's understanding of its mission in relation to God's great purpose. Nurture and opportunities for witness address how the church assists individuals and families to draw on faith resources as they are formed and shaped communally in their faith. Witness has everything to do with sanctifying love as Christians grapple with social injustices such as slavery, which Wesley profoundly ad-dressed. Worship, disciple formation, care, and witness, each and all of these contain aspects of healing, guiding, sustaining, and reconciliation, which are the ingredients of traditional pastoral care. The major point is that Holy Com-munion, for Wesley, was an essential practice that supported all the tasks of ministry, and through the power of the Holy Spirit enabled Christians to holistically participate in God's unfolding narrative.

Following are a few examples from Wesley's sermons and diaries about how these practices of pastoral care look. In Sermon 101, "The Duty of Constant Communion," he says:

> A second reason why every Christian should do this [partake of Holy Communion] as often as he [or she] can is because the benefits of doing it are so great to all that do it in obedience to him; namely, the forgiveness of our past sins and the present strengthening and refreshing of our souls. In this world we are never free from temptation. Whatever way of life we are in, whatever our condition be, whether we are to sick or well, in trouble or at ease, the enemies of our souls are watching to lead us into sin. And too often they prevail over us.[18]

Wesley believed that human beings who took every opportunity to commune with God would experience and be nourished by God's grace as

---

17 John Wesley, "The Character of a Methodist," in *The Works of John Wesley: The Methodist Societies*, vol. 9, ed. Rupert E. Davies (Nashville: Abingdon Press, 1989), 31–46.

18 Wesley, "The Duty of Constant Communion," *The Works of John Wesley*, vol. 3, ed. Outler, 429.

well as be strengthened for life's twists and turns. This constant communing was part of disciplined Christian living, and it reflects Wesley's holistic understanding of the sacrament of Holy Communion.

In Sermon 77, "Spiritual Worship," Wesley discusses the benefits of being significantly related to God. He points out that since there was only one God in heaven so there was only one happiness. "God made our heart for God's self," wrote Wesley, echoing Saint Augustine. As a result, there is "happy knowledge of the true God," and the result is "knowledge and love of God," which was manifested in Jesus. Wesley also believed that "real" Christians were happy, because Christians seek happiness in God and not in fellow-creatures. There is no happiness for Wesley, however, in the pleasures of the world. He wrote, "Turn to him in whom are hid all the treasures of happiness." Only by being in union with God will we find the fountain of happiness.

In this same sermon, Wesley also exhorts his listeners to maintain their happiness, and "expect a continual growth in grace, in the loving knowledge of our Lord Jesus Christ." He writes that Christians can expect the "power of the Highest shall suddenly overshadow you." Moreover, union and communion with God is the sure path to holiness. The combination of hearing the gospel preached and experiencing Holy Communion makes worship especially efficacious. Holiness and happiness go together.

Reinforcing his understanding of God's miraculous presence in Holy Communion, Wesley records in his *Journal and Diaries of 1735–1738* miraculous healings that took place when people took Holy Communion. He wrote: "One who was big with child, in a high fever, and almost wasted away with a violent cough, desired to receive the Holy Communion before she died. At the hour of her receiving she began to recover, and in a few days was entirely out of danger."[19] Citing another example, Wesley reported about a Mrs. Crouch who had some real spiritual concerns and, consequently, was advised not to take Communion until her spiritual turmoil was solved. Wesley reports:

> Being in deep heaviness, [she] had desired me to meet her this afternoon. She had long earnestly desired to receive the Holy Communion, having unaccountably strong persuasion that God would manifest himself to her therein and give rest to her soul. But her heaviness being now greatly increased, Mr. Delamott gave her that fatal advice not to communicate till she had living faith. This still added to her perplexity. Yet at length she resolved God rather than man. And "he was made known unto her in breaking of bread." In that moment she felt

---

19 John Wesley, *The Works of John Wesley:* Journal and Diaries, vol. 18, ed. W. Reginald Ward and Richard Heitzenrater, (Nashville: Abingdon Press, 1990) 141.

her load removed; she knew she was accepted in the Beloved, and all the time I
was expounding at Mr. Bray's was full of that peace which cannot be uttered.[20]

Although we don't know what the problem was, it involved a need for
spiritual healing and perhaps reconciliation with God. Her need for healing
prompted the offering of the Eucharist, and by partaking of the elements,
God communed with her and healed her by God's presence.

It is also important to see Holy Communion within Wesley's understanding of the pastoral care involved in worship. In Sermon 77, Wesley
connects happiness with the worship of God.[21] He indicates that he wants
to expound on the "marks of communion with God." Based on 1 John 5, he
points out that communion (as experienced in Holy Communion) is with
the Triune God, the Father, Son, and Holy Spirit. In addition, knowledge
of being significantly related to God as children of God is conveyed by the
Holy Spirit, which also promotes the fruits of the Spirit. Our life, our joy,
and our happiness come as we live and dwell with the Father, Jesus Christ,
and the Holy Spirit. By being in communion with God, the true Vine, we
become the branches, as Christ taught. We become God's true heirs and
God's extensions into the world as whole people.

Wesley's understanding of the benefits of Communion varies depending
on the unique and idiosyncratic needs of people. The care of the souls always
varies with individual experiences. Moreover, Wesley believed that by offering
the opportunity to commune with God through the Eucharist, the pastor was
addressing these profound problems in the best way possible. Wesley reports:

> I was born (said Zacharias Neisser) on the borders of Moravia, and was first
> awakened by my cousin Wenzel, who soon after carried me to hear Mr. Steimetz,
> a Lutheran minister about thirty (English) miles off. I was utterly astonished. The
> next week I went again. After which, going to him in private, I opened my heart,
> and told him all my doubts, those especially concerning popery. He offered to
> receive me into communion with him, which I gladly accepted of; and in a short
> time after I received the Lord's Supper from his hands. While I was receiving I
> felt Christ had died for me. I knew I was reconciled to God. And all the day I was
> overwhelmed with joy, having those words continually on my mind, "this day is
> salvation come to my house: I also am a son of Abraham." This joy I had continu-
> ally for a year and a half, and my heart was full of love to Christ.[22]

---

20   Wesley, *The Works of John Wesley:* Journal and Diaries, vol. 19, ed. Ward and
     Heitzenrater, 98.
21   Wesley, "Spiritual Worship," *The Works of John Wesley,* vol. 3, ed. Outler, 88–102.
22   Wesley, *The Works of John Wesley:* Journal and Diaries, vol. 18, ed. Ward and
     Heitzenrater, 287.

Wesley's pastoral theology demonstrates how the presence of God through Holy Communion ministers to the many different needs of people and that it goes right to the source of the problem, and a tangible result of personal healing and wholeness is being happy. In today's language, we might call this ministry of the Holy Spirit in Communion "inner healing," which is based on the conviction that the Holy Spirit discerns and offers healing where it is needed most.[23]

Wesley's Orthopathy and Orthonarrative

In Wesley's notion, happiness as a sign of wholeness brings into the discussion the issue of right feeling or orthopathy. Ted Runyon says that Wesley's philosophical thinking was grounded in John Locke's epistemology. Runyon concludes that Wesley's right feeling rested in a transcendent subjectivism that came from outside the person and originated from God.[24] Reflecting on Runyon's assessment of Wesley's eschatology, it seems clear that Wesley's view of happiness rests on his orthopathy, which is rooted in orthonarrative or right story or right plot.[25] That is to say that our happiness comes when we give ourselves over to God's present but not yet fulfilled story of transformation and reconciliation. The source of our true happiness in Wesley's thinking is being connected to God's unfolding story where we participate in God's narrative plot for our lives. It is there we will find our calling and purpose for life. It is there that we will find hope and love.

> We are transformed when our personal stories are connected to God's unfolding story of God's establishing God's reign. It is when our inner histories encounter God's outer or external history unfolding in our lives that we confront the generative source of all human transformation. Thus, transformation is a process of surrendering to a source of happiness and virtue that has its origin outside the self.[26]

Happiness in Wesley's thinking becomes possible when we encounter God's real presence in God's unfolding story, which is enacted in Holy Communion, and we give ourselves over to that story and its implications for our

---

23 Agnes Sanford, *The Healing Light* (New York: Macalester Park, 1947, rev. 1972).

24 Theodore Runyon, "Orthopathy: Wesleyan Criteria for Religious Experience," in *Heart Religion in the Methodist and Related Movement*, ed. Richard B. Steele (Lanham, MD: Scarecrow, 2003), 296.

25 Wimberly, *No Shame in Wesley's Gospel*, 56–61.

26 Ibid., 59.

own life. Indeed, the experience of happiness and the continued renewal of our participation in God's unfolding story are benefits of receiving God's grace by participating in Holy Communion. Wesley's emphasis on our duty and commitment to "Do this in remembrance of me" speaks directly to the benefits of attending to our Communion with God consistently. Rather than being practical atheists, we will grow to experience God, not just for our own sake, but so that we can show and proclaim God's love for others in our daily living. Happiness in God is not the end, it is the beginning of our eternal life, and it can provide hope and healing now for a world obsessed with selfish pursuits for status and crippled by anxiety.

SIXTEEN

Eucharist and Prayer

E. Byron Anderson

> *Here our children find a welcome in the shepherd's flock and fold;*
> *here as bread and wine are taken, Christ sustains us, as of old.*
> *Here the servants of the Servant seek in worship to explore*
> *what it means in daily living to believe and to adore.*[1]

What is the relationship between our daily lives, our daily prayer, and our gathering at the Lord's Table? In the hymn stanza just quoted, Fred Pratt Green proposes one relationship, that as we come to the welcome table we find the place in which "to explore what it means in daily living to believe and to adore." He assumes, therefore, that there is a connection between what we do in worship and our daily lives. But, if I read him correctly, he is saying more than this because he seems to be challenging the way many in our churches think about the relationship between daily living and our gathering at the Lord's Table. That is, we tend to think that it is our daily living and often our personal prayer and piety that not only informs but, more, establishes the meaning of what we find at the Lord's Table. We seem to be saying that *my* seeking, *my* hunger, *my* desire, *my* need establishes the meaning and importance of what we do at the Table. As I will explore later, the Eucharist becomes a kind of "device" for the dispensing of grace and to make Christ available at our disposal.[2] Consequently we assume that any relationship between eucharistic praying and a life of prayer begins with us, moves from our lives to the Eucharist, and back again. More broadly, we assume that

---

1   Fred Pratt Green, "The Church of Christ," in *The Hymns and Ballads of Fred Pratt Green* (Carol Stream, IL: Hope, 1982), 92; also as "God Is Here," st. 3 in *The United Methodist Hymnal* (Nashville: United Methodist Publishing House, 1989), 660.

2   As Lieven Boeve argues, "Christ is not at our disposal. Encountering him only occurs in and through an event of the symbolic mediation of the church, itself resulting from the dynamic interrelation of Scriptures, sacrament, and ethics. Only a Christ who is not turned into an object . . . can be symbolically mediated." Lieven Boeve, "Theology in a Postmodern Context and the Hermeneutical Project of Louis-Marie Chauvet," in *Sacrament: Revelation and the Humanity of God*, ed. Phillippe Bordeyne and Bruce T. Morrill (Collegeville, MN: Liturgical Press, 2008), 14.

personal private prayer as well as individual experience provides the template for the prayer of the Christian community.

In contrast to such an understanding, Pratt Green's hymn invites us to consider how our coming to the Table should inform and shape all of our meals and relationships—"as bread and wine are taken . . . [we] explore what it means in daily living to believe and to adore." In other words, he proposes a eucharistic *spirituality* that moves from our prayer and participation at the Lord's Table into our prayer and participation at all tables, in all forms of prayer, and through all our days. It is a spirituality that finds its center at the table and radiates into all of life from that center. Pratt Green's hymn further invites us to consider how this communal, public, ritualized event establishes *the* framework for our daily living that orients our patterns of believing, our patterns of praying, and our patterns of living (for example, ethics). Therefore, rather than thinking of the Eucharist as the ritualization of daily life, we need to think of daily life as the embodiment, the living out, of what is given in the Eucharist. The relationship between eucharistic prayer and practice and our lives of prayer begins, rather than ends, at the communal table and moves from it into daily life—and back again.

It is this movement from eucharistic prayer and practice into personal prayer and life that I intend to explore here. To do so, I want to propose three possible ways to think about this relationship: first, that the Eucharist is a "paradigmatic means of grace," second, that our eucharistic praying and practice is a "focal practice" of the church, and third, that the Eucharist provides a canon or rule for Christian life.[3] Each of these frameworks interact, even overlap, with the other, but each also emphasizes slightly different practical consequences for the life of prayer.

A Paradigmatic Means of Grace

In mainline/oldline Protestant traditions such as my own United Methodist

---

3   Here I am obviously playing with the much used (and sometimes misused) axiom *lex orandi lex credendi*—the law of prayer [establishes] the law of belief. While Michael Church and others have taken liturgists to task for our inaccurate use of the axiom, it continues to provide for me a shorthand with which to explore the relationship between worship and belief in the Christian community as well as a means to begin exploring the functional theology of particular Christian communities. See Michael G. L. Church, "The Law of Begging: Prosper at the End of the Day," *Worship* 73.5 (September 1999), 442–53. For a fuller contextual reading of Prosper, see Paul de Clerck, "'Lex orandi, lex credendi': The Original Sense and Historical Avatars of an Equivocal Adage," *Studia Liturgica* 24.2 (1994), 178–200.

Church, much current discussion about church renewal has focused on institutional reorganization, redeployment of resources, and diminishing financial support, as if such concerns defined the church and its mission. In the Wesleys' attempts to renew the church, however, they focused their attention on the renewal of Christian life and the reorientation of personal and communal life around central practices—the "ordinary means of grace." They gave their primary attention to creating communities in which the means of grace were practiced and sustained, to whom individuals could be accountable for their practice, and which had as their end personal and social holiness. Organization and deployment of resources, including personnel, flowed from these foci. Recent United Methodist statements on the meaning and practice of baptism and Holy Communion have attempted to reclaim these Wesleyan emphases, yet the ecclesial implications of these documents as well as the implications for personal piety remain largely ignored or unexplored.[4] I believe that attending to, explaining, and practicing more fully and faithfully these ordinary means of grace can provide primary strategic practices of the renewal the church is seeking. More, I believe there will be no evangelical renewal without sacramental renewal, at the heart of which is a recovery of the Eucharist as the paradigmatic means of grace for the church.

Such an understanding of the Eucharist is evident in the Wesleys' writings. In a helpful article on Wesleyan spirituality, David Trickett explores the Wesleyan focus on the means of grace and, particularly, on the Eucharist. He argues that John Wesley's "understanding of the [cooperative] relationship between God and human beings led Wesley to see the Eucharist as paradigmatic of all the means of grace, and therefore to urge 'constant communion' to his people." Pressing the link between Eucharist and spiritual disciplines and anticipating my third claim that the Eucharist is "canonical," Trickett emphasizes Wesley's claim about this paradigmatic means of grace: "Thus, the 'true rule' that is to guide one's spiritual discipline is this: 'so often are we to receive [the Eucharist] as God gives us opportunity.'"[5]

---

4   Dan Benedict's work on congregations centered on the means of grace provides one exception. See "Ordering Congregational Life around the Means of Grace," in *Worship Matters*, vol. 1, ed. E. Byron Anderson (Nashville: Discipleship Resources, 1999), 43–50; and *Come to the Waters: Baptism and our Ministry of Welcoming Seekers and Making Disciples* (Nashville: Discipleship Resources, 1996).

5   David Trickett, "Spiritual Vision and Discipline in the Early Wesleyan Movement," in *Christian Spirituality: Post-reformation and Modern*, ed. Louis Dupre and Don E. Saliers (New York: Crossroad, 1989), 365. Trickett is quoting Wesley's "On the Duty of Constant Communion" as found in Albert Outler, ed., *John Wesley* (New York: Oxford, 1964), 336. Outler makes a similar claim about the paradigmatic character of the Eucharist in his introduction to "On the Duty of Constant Communion."

That Wesley needed to advocate for "constant communion" reflected a context in which infrequent reception (often only annually) was more common than not. But his motivation in writing "The Duty of Constant Communion" also reflected the challenges he encountered from "quietism" and "enthusiasm." To the quietists who argued that the Christian need do nothing but wait in stillness on God, John (and Charles) Wesley made a case for the necessity of the means of grace as the most appropriate instruments for actively waiting on and participating in God. To the enthusiasts "whose spontaneous experiences of grace were so much more vivid than their usual experiences of its ordinances and means,"[6] they made the case that the Lord's Supper was "the chief actual means of actual grace" (that is, not a mere "sign" of grace), paradigmatic of all the means of grace, and therefore "literally indispensable in the Christian life."[7] Wesley also reminded both quietists and enthusiasts that "constant communion" was both a command of God and an act of God's mercy. To disobey the command was, in effect, to renounce one's baptismal vows; to neglect God's offer of mercy was to reject whatever God had on offer to us "according to our several necessities."[8]

Many in our churches today still do not receive the Eucharist as often as it is offered (though, admittedly, the frequency with which it is offered continues to be a problem). While the forms of "quietism" and "enthusiasm" that challenged the Wesleys are no longer the reasons for our neglect, we are confronted, on the one hand, with those who claim to be "spiritual but not religious" and therefore have no need for the church or, on the other hand, with those who are on a never-ending quest for "peak experiences" and who are easily bored by Christian sacramental practice. Increasingly, however, it seems that our relative neglect of this "paradigmatic means of grace" may be less because of these concerns and more because Christian people see it as simply irrelevant to their daily lives. Such "paradigmatic failure" may be because the people are not, in Wesley's words, "rightly prepared" to participate in this paradigmatic means of grace or because they do not "rightly receive [it], trusting in God."[9] But such failure also may

---

6   John Wesley, "The Means of Grace," in *The Works of John Wesley: Sermons*, vol. 1, ed. Albert Outler (Nashville: Abingdon Press, 1984), 157. See also E. Byron Anderson, "The Power of Godliness to Know: Charles Wesley and the Means of Grace," *Wesleyan Theological Journal* 43.2 (Fall 2008): 7–27.

7   Albert Outler, *John Wesley* (Oxford: Oxford University Press, 1980), 333.

8   Wesley, "The Duty of Constant Communion," *The Works of John Wesley*, vol. 1, ed. Outler, 427–39, and John Wesley, "June 28, 1740," *The Works of John Wesley: Journals and Diaries*, vol. 19, ed. W. Reginald Ward and Richard Heitzenrater (Nashville: Abingdon, 1990), 159.

9   Wesley, "The Duty of Constant Communion," *The Works of John Wesley*, vol. 3, ed. Outler, 438.

be because of the form in which it is presented (the dull reading of the prayer, the lack of grace in presiding), the "faulty" use of it in celebration ("drop-in" or "serve-yourself" Communion, truncating the eucharistic prayer), because the church and its leaders do not seem to care one way or the other whether we celebrate the Eucharist or not and, perhaps, because we simply do not expect anything from it.[10] As Christopher Kiesling reminds us, in order for something to be paradigmatic, it must be "public, recognized by the community as paradigmatic."[11] One more potential reason for "paradigm failure" then is the increasing separation between what the church believes at the "official" communal level, as represented in official denominational and ecumenical documents, and what is believed and practiced at the local communal and personal level. Without actual practice, without paradigmatic *use*, the paradigm is undermined and eventually replaced.[12] Given these concerns with practice and formation, it is not surprising that frequent reception of the Lord's Supper and its central place in the Christian life still requires our advocacy today.

Wesley provided another response that is suggestive for our task here. To those "quietists" who argued that "worship in spirit and truth" (that is, without outward practices other than the practice of stillness) is enough and that attention "to outward things clog the soul," preventing it from "soaring aloft in holy contemplation," Wesley wrote,

> One branch of worshiping God in spirit and truth is the keeping his outward commandments. To glorify him therefore with our bodies as well as our spirits, to go through outward work with hearts uplifted to him, to make our daily employment a sacrifice to God, to buy and sell, to eat and drink to his glory: this is worshiping God in spirit and truth as much as praying to him in a wilderness.[13]

All of the images Wesley uses here—glorifying God, uplifted hearts, a daily sacrifice, eating and drinking to God's glory—are eucharistic, drawing on the eucharistic prayer in the 1662 Book of Common Prayer. The Eucharist is

---

10   For this description of sacramental failure, I am drawing on Christopher Kiesling, "Paradigms of Sacramentality," *Worship* 44.7 (August–September 1970): 431.

11   Ibid., 430.

12   Lee C. Barrett argues that "paradigmatic use . . . gives significance to the rule" in "Theology as Grammar: Regulative Principles as Paradigms and Practices," *Modern Theology* 4.2 (January 1988): 165. While Barrett's focus is on Christian doctrine rather than sacramental practice, the connection is easily made between them, particularly in light of his claim that "many doctrines are paradigmatic instantiations of the standardized usage of a Christian concept" (161).

13   Wesley, "Upon our Lord's Sermon on the Mount, IV (Matthew 5.13-16)," *Works of John Wesley*, vol. 1, ed. Outler, 543.

directly connected to the character of one's daily life and to the keeping of God's commandments. And, while this quotation suggests that the Eucharist's paradigmatic status rests primarily on its being a command of God and therefore our "bounden duty," Wesley shows us the consequences of that paradigm in the shaping of our daily lives. But he also goes beyond this emphasis on divine command to call our attention to the ways in which the Eucharist is a means of "actual grace." Through the Eucharist, God acts in a distinctive way to forgive sins, to strengthen and refresh our souls, to provide a continual remembrance of the death of Christ. It is paradigmatic, therefore, not because of what we bring to the table—as if we were somehow in a position to negotiate terms—but because of what God offers to us and because of what we receive. "We come to the table," Wesley writes, "not to give [God] anything but to receive whatever [God] sees best for us."[14] The way in which it works may be "unfathomable" but it is "sure and real" nonetheless.[15]

In what ways, then, is the Eucharist paradigmatic? Of course it is paradigmatic for and provides the exemplary model for how we gather for meals and how we receive the gifts of food. But if we are to move from eucharistic prayer to daily prayer and life, if we are to pray and live eucharistically, then the model Wesley describes also includes glorifying God with our bodies—regardless of age, nation, race, gender, sexual orientation—working with uplifted hearts, seeing our work as a sacrifice to God, and letting all our eating and drinking be to God's glory. Also, praying and living eucharistically is to live each day knowing that God in Christ is with us and active in all of our praying, rather than absent from us waiting to be summoned; that our prayer is always a dialogue between God and the world, rather than a monologue about our fears and desires; that thanksgiving is first and foremost for what God has done and is doing in the world through Christ and the Spirit, rather than for our personal benefit; that all our praying is animated by the Holy Spirit, rather than by our personal desire; that our praying always seeks communion with God and neighbor, rather than a moment of personal privilege before the throne of God; that though we are many, we are one in Christ, whose body we share, rather than diverse and disconnected solitaries. As Kevin Seasoltz writes, "The Eucharist is contaminated if it does not serve as a paradigm for honest, just, loving relationships outside the celebration. Eucharistic celebrations which

---

14   Wesley, "June 28, 1740," *The Works of John Wesley: Journals and Diaries*, vol. 19, ed. Ward and Heitzenrater, 159.

15   See Charles Wesley, "O the depth of love divine," *Hymns on the Lord's Supper* (Bristol: Felix Farley, 1745), 41.

do not correspond to the world view of Christ readily become corrupting agents in the lives of the celebrating persons and communities."[16] As divine command and means of "actual" grace, the Eucharist "lays out a series of verbal and nonverbal symbols and puts us through a series of actions that are meant to shape our attitudes toward God, toward ourselves, toward one another and toward the world." Through our eucharistic prayer and practice, God's reshaping, transformative work continues; through it, rather than through our own creativity, "persons and communities are being created in the image of God."[17]

As I have noted here, the Eucharist is paradigmatic, at least in part, because it is a divine command and a means of actual grace. I have also noted that paradigms require practice if they are to remain paradigmatic. Therefore, if the Eucharist is to be paradigmatic for Christian life, it needs to have central and focal place in Christian worship.

As a Focal Practice

To return to Pratt Green's text: "Here . . . children find a welcome," here we are sustained, here we explore what it means in daily living. Pratt Green's emphasis on a particular time and place—"here"—suggests a second way to think about the relationship between eucharistic praying and the life of prayer: as a "focal practice." Perhaps in more popular language, it suggests a way to "keep the main thing the main thing" because it is *here* and *not there*.

Philosopher Albert Borgmann is generally credited with developing the concepts of "focal things" and "focal practices." He introduced these concepts as a way to counter what he called the "device paradigm" of contemporary culture, a paradigm in which technology is seen as a device for delivering some commodity and, as such, draws us further into a consumerist approach to church and sacrament. (That his book on technology was published the same year as the introduction of Apple's Macintosh computer makes him seem prophetic in his reading of contemporary culture.) Devices, Borgmann argues, are intended to "make goods and services available" in the most convenient and least conspicuous way; they are available to "be enjoyed as a mere end unencumbered by means"; they make possible anonymity or, at the least, concealment of true identity; and they result in what Borgmann calls "disburdenment" from

---

16   Kevin Seasoltz, *God's Gift Giving: In Christ and through the Spirit* (New York: Continuum, 2007), 241.

17   Ibid., 232–33.

relationship in contrast to engagement with one another and the world.[18] (One church musician speaks of the "iPodization" of our experience of music—no longer is our music-making, much less our music-listening, a shared activity. We may find technological ways to share what we are listening to, but our experience of music is increasingly an individual and device-oriented activity. And, once unencumbered by the means of its production, we are free to engage in other activities—to multitask—while listening.[19] The device paradigm describes the "crucial force that more and more detaches us from the persons, things, and practices that used to engage and grace us in their own right."[20]

As Borgmann demonstrates, however, it is not the device itself but its paradigmatic use that is problematic: central heating is certainly more enjoyable than chopping wood and tending a fire, city water or integrated wells are preferable to fetching water by the bucket. But when we consider, as does Borgmann, the contrast between convenience foods and what he calls the "culture of the table" we begin to see the problem more clearly. Convenience foods permit isolation from others, are "grabbed to be eaten" often while our attention is elsewhere—the TV, the computer screen, while driving—are commodified for uniformity and easy consumption, and separate us from their source and from engagement with one another.[21] Fast food may provide a meal or temporarily satisfy some physical or emotional craving, but it is not "dinner." It neither requires our focused attention nor nourishes soul as well as body.

Eucharistic theologies and practices have sometimes succumbed to such device-oriented understandings as well—for example when we give in to various kinds of liturgical minimalism, which often grow out of a misplaced preoccupation with sacramental licitness or validity but more often from a lack of understanding of the church's prayer. The result is that we believe or act as if (not that the two are separable) the eucharistic prayer or the institution narrative or the *epiclesis* (the invocation of the Holy Spirit) is all that is necessary to "make" present Christ in such a way that we can receive/consume him. We give in to such a device-orientation when presiders abbreviate the eucharistic prayer for the sake of "efficiency" or when someone decides that only certain words in the

18   Albert Borgmann, *Technology and the Character of Contemporary Life* (Chicago: University of Chicago, 1984), 42, 44, 59.

19   See James L. Brauer, "The Challenge of the iPod Tribe to Liturgical Music," *Liturgy* 24.4 (October–December 2009), 16–23.

20   Borgmann, *Technology and the Character of Contemporary Life*, 76.

21   Borgmann introduces the "culture of the table" on p. 59 in *Technology and the Character of Conemporary Life* and returns to it throughout the book. This description of convenience foods is from 204–5.

prayer need be said by the ordained or when someone decides one can or should "preconsecrate" the bread and wine in the absence of a community (or an ordained presider) so that it can be taken (not given) on our own time and to fit our own schedules. We give in to such a device-orientation when the eucharistic table (or the baptismal font) disappears from its central place, brought forward or out of storage on those rare occasions when it is used. Our eucharistic celebration also takes on a device-like character when we treat it as some "Pez-like" dispenser of grace (even leading some entrepreneur to create a very "Pez-like" dispenser of eucharistic wafers) that provides us with regular inoculation against our sinfulness or as one more prepackaged item for consumption and disposal (one company sells such prepackaged "juice and wafer celebration cups" in quantities of 100, 250, and 500). Unfortunately, even our understanding of the Eucharist as "means of grace," especially when disconnected from its paradigmatic status, can drift toward a device or consumer model through which a seemingly absent God momentarily appears with the gift of grace or which we use to some other end.[22] As Borgmann notes, "a culture informed by the device paradigm is deeply inhospitable to grace and sacrament."[23]

In response to this device paradigm, Borgmann develops the concept of "focal things and practices." Focal things, like book, font, and table, Scripture, baptism, and Eucharist, operate in two directions: first, they gather together a set of relationships, the multivalence of meaning that we generally think of in terms of symbol. The table is a place for a meal, a place of hospitality, and a gathering of a family; in some families it is a workspace as well—children doing homework, parents sorting through bills, younger children with their coloring books. Should the table be not only the "dining table" but also the "kitchen table," it also serves as the workplace, or supplemental workplace, where the meal is prepared. Joined to these references is the additional reference of the table as "altar table," a place for a specific kind of holy action. Like a concave mirror, the focal thing that is the eucharistic table draws together all of these references and meanings.

But as a focal thing, the eucharistic table also operates in an outward direction, informing what surrounds it. Like a convex mirror it takes what

---

22   Ralph Keifer argues that our perception of the sacraments as "means of grace" has "for all practical purposes, including the mode of their enactment, eclipsed their function as signs and revelatory actions that disclose the action of God already present in the world and to the whole of life." "Liturgy and Ethics: Some Unresolved Dilemmas," in Kathleen Hughes and Mark R. Francis, ed., *Living No Longer for Ourselves* (Collegeville, MN: Liturgical Press, 1991), 73.

23   Albert Borgmann, "Technology and the Crisis of Contemporary Culture," *American Catholic Philosophical Quarterly* 70 (1996): 41.

seems to be but a single idea (holy Table) and reveals the diversity of its many parts (meal, work, home, family, hospitality). This constant work of reflection and refraction, of focusing and dispersal, helps center and orient our attention, our relationships, and our lives. Even the empty table is able to serve as a focal thing; its very presence is a reminder of the meal not celebrated, a signifier of what is absent, a question to us about our (lack of) practice.

A focal thing requires "focal practice"; it requires regular use or it loses both its meaning and its influence. Without focal practices, the focal thing would no longer have "centering and orienting force."[24] Devices can provide goods without their practices, ends without attention to the means of their production, but focal things require practices in order to prosper, just as paradigms require instantiations to remain true (ibid., 196). Focal practices are ways of "keeping the faith"—both in reference to the faith we profess and in relationship to the focal thing itself. Through focal practice, the focal thing is saved "for an opening in our lives" (ibid., 209). This may make it seem like little more than a kind of practical bookmark or placeholder, but the focal practice keeps us continually engaged. As Borgmann describes it, a focal practice "sponsors discipline and skill which are exercised in a unity of achievement and enjoyment, of mind, body, and the world, of myself and others, and in a social union" (ibid., 219). In addition, he writes, "Focal practices . . . bring us closer to that intensity of experience where the world engages one painfully in hunger, disease, and confinement. A focal practice also discloses fellow human beings more fully and may make us more sensitive to the plight of those persons whose integrity is violated or suppressed" (ibid., 225). Unlike "peak experiences" that seem to transcend our daily world, focal practices, he seems to suggest, intensify the reality of the world in which we live, drawing attention to that reality by means of focusing our attention through the thing and its practice.

The "great meal," Borgmann argues, is a "focal practice par excellence." Here "guests are thoughtfully invited, the table has been carefully set . . . food is the culmination of tradition, patience, and skill and the presence of the earth's most delectable textures and tastes . . . there is an invocation of divinity at the beginning and memorable conversation throughout." The great meal "gathers a scattered family around the table . . . recollects and presents a tradition . . . [and] brings into focus closer relations of national or regional customs." The great meal "is enacted in the discipline called table manners . . . the enactment of generosity and gratitude, the

---

24   Borgmann, *Technology and the Character of Contemporary Life*, 207.

affirmation of mutual and perhaps religious obligations" (ibid., 202, 204, 205). In the "culture of the table" that is the Eucharist, we are not offered "convenience food" but are drawn toward the "great meal"—even when what we physically receive is but a "token" of that great meal. At the great meal there is no number to call for delivery and no vending machine to distribute our soda. Pizza and coke may be "daily food" for some, but they are devices, not focal things or practices.

Perhaps the separation of the communal meal from Eucharist so long ago was our downfall—or perhaps it is the absence of so many (especially men) from the kitchen.[25] Preparing a meal, whether simple or extravagant, domestic or sacramental, calls us to attention—knives are sharp, pans are hot, over-salted or overcooked food is difficult to save, bread dries out, and unfermented juice begins to ferment. Where a focal thing says, "pay attention here," a focal practice is our work of repeatedly paying attention, of "constant communion." Because repetition often leads to ritualization, a focal practice is always at risk of degenerating "into an empty and perhaps deadening ritual."[26] At that point, the practice seems to collapse in upon itself. Correction to empty ritual comes, Borgmann argues, not by avoiding the focal practice, as has been the case for many Protestants, but by allowing the great thing "to re-emerge in all its splendor."[27] As he makes clear, when a focal thing "in all its splendor" draws our attention, it enables our attention to "radiate out" from this meal to other meals, from this community to a larger community, from this action of God to God's saving work in the world. As it does so, we begin to see how eucharistic prayer and practice is not only "focal" but also "paradigmatic." It also helps us see the connection between what we do and pray at the Lord's Table and what we do and pray at other tables.

If we understand how focal things require focal practices, we may also understand how the eucharistic Table requires eucharistic practice—praying the Great Thanksgiving, receiving and sharing bread and wine in the midst of community, and extending those gifts to those absent from the community. The connection between focal things and focal practices also helps us understand how our eucharistic praying is always action—the action of God's bestowal of grace, of our response in thanksgiving, of our being joined together in and through the Spirit. Unlike fast food, we cannot "have it our way"; it

---

25 See the connections Sara Miles makes between the eucharistic Table, the communal meal, and feeding the hungry in *Take This Bread: A Radical Conversion* (New York: Ballantine, 2008).

26 Borgmann, *Technology and the Character of Contemporary Life*, 209.

27 Ibid.

is not available on our own schedule and at our convenience; we do not invite ourselves to the table and we do not choose with whom or what we will eat. In eucharistic prayer and practice we see something of the world rightly ordered and experience a foretaste of the heavenly banquet. Here we are invited to consider the "radiating focus" of our prayer and the ways in which the eucharistic prayer makes clear that "it is right and a good and a joyful thing, always and everywhere to give thanks" to God. The generosity and communion we experience at the eucharistic table radiates out into daily prayer and practice, gives our daily praying and eating meaning; it focuses our attention on primary things—this community gathered, this loaf broken, this cup poured and shared, *here*. As Richard Gaillardetz writes, "Focal things and practices invite us to abandon a largely instrumental view of our world and its inhabitants in favor of an attitude of 'communion' that draws us into attentive, respectful engagement with the larger world."[28] The multiple "I's" that gather at the table are themselves "focused" as one, and that one moves again into the world as the body of Christ, an image Charles Wesley captured well in verse when he described the ideal Christian community as "concentered all, through Jesus' name, in perfect harmony."[29]

As a Canonical Practice or Rule of Faith

As we saw in our initial discussion of John Wesley, a significant emphasis in "The Duty of Constant Communion" was on our duty to obey God's command to "do this" even to the extent that it is to be the "true rule" of our spiritual discipline. Charles Wesley provides a similar emphasis in a number of his hymns, including the hymns "Because Thou Hast Said" and "And Shall I Let Him Go?" In the latter he writes, "Jesus hath spoke the word, / His will my reason is; / *Do this* in memory of thy Lord, / Jesus hath said, *Do this* . . . Because He saith, *Do this*, / This I will always do; Till Jesus come in glorious bliss, / I *thus* His death will *show*" [emphases are Wesley's].[30] For the Wesleys, then, what made eucharistic prayer and practice canonical as well as paradigmatic is that it is a dominical command.

But dominical commands do not seem to carry much weight today—in the church or in the world. What is more, any attempt to claim something as

---

28   Richard R. Gaillardetz, *Transforming Our Days* (New York: Crossroad, 2000), 26.
29   "All Praise to Our Redeeming Lord," in *The United Methodist Hymnal*, 554.
30   "Because Thou Has Said" was published as part of a tract against "quietism" in 1745. It is included in *The United Methodist Hymnal*, 635. "And Shall I Let Him Go?" in *Hymns on the Lord's Supper*, no. 73.

having "canonical" status—that is, serving as a normative or regulative rule and requiring universal obedience—in our postmodern context bumps up against critiques of the "canonical" as modernist, Western, and hegemonic; it brings to the fore what some have called the "canon wars" of North American culture.[31] Yet we only need undertake a quick Google search to discover lists of new "postmodern canons" in literature as well as in theology and to realize that, as we keep creating canons, we must have some need for them.

Liturgical theologians find themselves in conversations about canons in several different ways—in discussions of the canonical status of the Bible, in the claims we make through our use of the axiom *lex orandi lex credendi* (the rule of prayer [establishes] the rule of belief), in our varied attempts to articulate a common ecumenical liturgical pattern for the church, in the questions liturgical historians raise about the historical variety of liturgical practice, and in the challenges posed to us from free- and emerging-church communities about the missional need for the church to adapt its liturgical practices to the changing needs of our culture. What is often lacking in these discussions and critiques of canon is any awareness, as Charles Gutenson claims, that "the goal of engaging the canons of the church is not knowledge, per se, or certainty; rather, it is to be formed so as to live out a particular kind of life—namely, one that God intends humans to live."[32] More, it is to be able to know the "rules of the game" that is the Christian life. Indeed, to be "religious" rather than or as well as "spiritual" is less about knowing some *thing* and more about knowing ourselves as bound to some *one*, as is expressed in the hymn attributed to Saint Patrick: "I bind unto myself today the strong name of the Trinity, by invocation of the same, / the Three in One, and One in Three."[33]

Alexander Schmemann argued in his *Introduction to Liturgical Theology* that the church's "rule of prayer"—its canon—never required complete uniformity or adherence to one "particular 'historical' type of worship." Put another way, the theological and liturgical diversity of the church does not require setting aside the "rule of prayer." Rather, as liturgy continues to develop in particular times and places we need to be able to discern between

---

31 See, for example, Jonathan Z. Smith, "Canons, Catalogues and Classics," in *Canonization and Decanonization*, ed. A. Van der Kooij and K. Van der Toorn (Leiden: Brill, 1998), 295. Throughout this section I am also indebted to William Abraham's discussion of canon as means of grace in *Canon and Criterion in Christian Theology* (Oxford: Clarendon, 1998), 477–80.

32 Charles Gutenson, "The Canonical Heritage of the Church as a Means of Grace" in *Canonical Theism: A Proposal for Theology and the Church*, ed. William J. Abraham, Jason E. Vickers, and Natalie B. Van Kirk (Grand Rapids: Eerdmans, 2008), 253.

33 See http://www.hymnary.org/text/i_bind_unto_myself_today.

faithful expression and development of the church's "rule of prayer" and development that results from "just a series of more or less accidental metamorphoses";[34] we need to discern between what is (or should be) binding on the whole church and what is local custom; we need to discern between "ordinary" and "extra-ordinary" expressions of the means of grace.

Schmemann's approach to the rule of prayer, which he calls the *ordo*, helps us see that the problem of its canonicity is not a postmodern creation. It has been a problem, in some form, throughout the church's history and has generated a variety of responses. Schmemann describes two of these responses. One response tends toward blind obedience from a kind of "idolatry of the book" that believes any change to liturgical material or practice is a subversion of Orthodoxy—a kind of liturgical fundamentalism comparable to any biblical fundamentalism. Anthropologist Roy Rappaport describes this as the "oversanctification of the specific" arising from a "conflation, or confusion, of specific social and ritual practices with general social and religious doctrine." The result of this approach is the inability to make adaptive responses to changing historical circumstances.[35] Rules do change as a game develops over time, but the game remains recognizable as a particular game.

A second response, Schmemann suggests, is liturgical or sacramental indifference, which places the canon or *ordo* in the background, "allowing the most 'popular' moments of worship to stand out and be performed with maximum effect," making selections that either please or "can make an impression on the congregation"—perhaps a kind of liturgical subjectivism or enthusiasm.[36] We do something because we "like" it or because it makes us feel a certain way. Or, we let something happen because we (leaders or congregations) just do not care; we settle for a liturgical "whatever."

Such indifference suggests a third option, certainly more common as well as more possible in Protestant worship than in Orthodox or Roman Catholic liturgical practice: we simply set aside all notion of canon and

---

34 Alexander Schmemann, *Introduction to Liturgical Theology*, trans. Ashleigh Morehouse, 2nd ed. (New York: St. Vladimir's Seminary Press, 1975), 16. Schmemann develops his discussion of the rule of prayer as the theological and liturgical *ordo* of the church. Cyril Vogel makes clear the connection between "canon" and *ordo* with this definition: "the term *ordo* means an arrangement, disposition, grouping, composition or plan and is equivalent to the term *regular* or *canon*." See Cyril Vogel, *Medieval Liturgy: An Introduction to the Sources*, trans. William Storey and Niels Rasmussen (Washington, DC: Pastoral Press, 1986), 135.

35 Roy Rappaport, *Ritual and Religion in the Making of Humanity* (Cambridge: Cambridge University Press, 1999), 441, 442.

36 Schmemann, *Introduction to Liturgical Theology*, 30, 32, 33.

canonical practice, except perhaps of Scripture, though sometimes even that. If we are uncomfortable rejecting all rules of prayer, we might decide to make up our own rules; at best we create *my* rule in place of *our* rule. Those who claim no need for rules have either simply quit the liturgical game or are unaware or in denial of the tacit rules that shape worship in their particular places and traditions. But this option seems to be simply another form of "spirituality without religion," which as Barbara Newman observes can be initially liberating but easily devolves "into an eclectic past time or even a self-congratulating narcissism."[37] Where blind obedience makes *ordo* a "dead letter" and where indifference makes it lifeless, this third option seems to simply do away with any notion of canon or *ordo*. Without a rule of prayer, we are left without a framework within which to make meaning and without a foundation to which that framework is tied; we are easily blown away by passing storms.

Anscar Chupungco's work on liturgical inculturation suggests a fourth response to the canon or rule of prayer. He describes this response as a kind of liturgical creativity without reference to or without understanding of the tradition.[38] Such suggestions fail to see the ways in which the component parts are connected to one another—Word to Table, thanksgiving to generous sharing, the common table to our many tables. As a result we turn the whole of the church's liturgical tradition into a kind of library of "worship resources" from which we can pick and choose, depending on the theme or purpose or agenda we are seeking to emphasize. Rather than offering some version of the "great meal" we provide a liturgical cafeteria from which we can select what we like and reject what we dislike, all according to our particular tastes.

Given this range of potential responses and problems with claims of canonicity, how then might we talk about eucharistic prayer and practice as canonical, as a rule of faith and of prayer? First, we need to be aware that the Eucharist is not the only canon of the church, but that it interacts with the canons of Scripture, baptismal faith, and church governing structures, whether the Code of Canon Law of the Roman Catholic Church or *The Book of Discipline of the United Methodist Church*.[39] These canons, especially the baptismal and eucharistic canons, function as "rules of the game" which

---

37 Barbara Newman, "On Being Spiritual but Not (Yet? Ever?) Religious," *Spiritus* 10.2 (Fall 2010): 286. She then asks, "In the absence of tradition, authority, or recognized communal standards, are all spiritualities created equal?"

38 See his discussion of the impact of culture, technology, and ideology on liturgical creativity in *Liturgical Inculturation: Sacramentals, Religiosity, and Catechesis* (Collegeville, MN: Liturgical Press/Pueblo Books, 1992), 51–54.

39 See Aidan Kavanagh, *On Liturgical Theology* (New York: Pueblo, 1984), 139–41.

enable our liturgical play to take place. We see one example of this interaction in Paul's dealings with the church at Corinth (1 Cor 11), where he brings "what he received from the Lord"—a version of what we call the "institution narrative" from the upper room—to call the Corinthians to account for their inhospitality to the poor when they gather to celebrate the Lord's Supper.

Second, as rules of the game, the liturgical canons tend toward a certain kind of invariance although they may, and do, develop over time as the game continues to be played. Such development is reflected in the ways in which United Methodist and other mainline Protestant eucharistic prayers have been revised over the past generation in response to contemporary biblical and liturgical scholarship and ecumenical conversation. We also know, however, that disagreement about or focus on the rules usually brings the game to a halt. Our eucharistic practice has lost is centrality not only because of "paradigmatic failure" as described earlier, but because we cannot agree on or do not know the rules. We might call this a form of "canonical failure," a failure made evident in the brokenness of the church as it gathers around separate tables in celebration of the Eucharist, as well as in the ways in which some communities exclude baptized children and persons with developmental disabilities from participation. But more, when we enter into a particular liturgical game such as the Eucharist, we are entering into a "ruled" context that we "transmit" but do not encode. That is, when we come to the eucharistic table, we are not responsible for creating the rules; we receive and make use of the rules. These rules belong to the whole church, not to individual denominations, congregations, or pastors. Though sometimes misused, the point that this is "the Lord's Table" is central here. Canonicity limits variation, but it also leaves open some forms of variation, such as those variations created by diverse languages, cultural contexts and traditions, and musical and artistic traditions. As noted earlier, canonicity is not the same as uniformity. The canons of liturgical practice are always interacting with the actuality of our liturgical practices in particular times, places, and communities.[40] We might say that these canons are like a *cantus firmus*, the firm foundational melody upon and around which other melodies build and interweave, enter and depart. It both regulates what happens with those other melodies as it sets a tonal or harmonic framework and invites creativity within those melodies. (Johann Pachelbel's "Canon in D" provides one familiar example.)

---

40   The Open Source Liturgy Project, sponsored by the United Methodist Church, provides one example of this relationship between canonicity and creativity. See http://wikigbod.org/wiki/tiki-index.php.

For much of the church's eucharistic history, reference to the eucharistic canon has meant primarily the institution narrative. But, as recent scholarship has demonstrated, this is a misplaced identifier. To speak of the eucharistic canon as intended here is to speak of a theological ordering of our prayer at the Table and, thus, the whole prayer through which we give thanks for God's saving work with Israel, remember God's saving work in Jesus Christ, beseech the Holy Spirit to transform us and the gifts we offer, and are nourished for service in the world. These component parts show us a "rule of faith": as Christians our lives are to be characterized by giving thanks for God's saving work in Israel and the church, by our beseeching of the Holy Spirit, by the offerings of ourselves and our gifts, and by our service in the world, as well as by our remembering Christ's death and resurrection. And, in these component parts, we see one way in which the canons of Scripture and prayer interact; our praying is, in part, a summarizing, proclaiming, and rehearsing of that scriptural narrative. Kevin Seasoltz describes well the consequences of understanding the Eucharist as a canon or rule of faith as he writes,

> Christian people cannot really know what the Eucharistic prayer is meant to be in their lives until they experience it as expressive and constitutive of their faith on its deepest levels. That faith of course is not simply an intellectual response to God's presence set out in doctrinal formulas such as the texts of Eucharistic prayers; it is above all the response of body-persons and communities who are called back to God as the images of that God who has become incarnate for us in Jesus Christ so we might all become more and more like God.[41]

In this quotation, Seasoltz also helps concisely describe the interaction of the paradigmatic, focal, and canonical character of the Eucharist. It not only expresses our faith, but constitutes it "on its deepest levels." It not only constitutes our faith but also gives it focal direction: through it we are "called back to God." We are not called back to any or every god, but a specific God, "who has become incarnate for us in Jesus Christ." Finally, we see that our eucharistic practice is not an end in itself but seeks our transformation; it is a means through which we "become more and more like God." Our eucharistic celebration, of which our eucharistic praying is part, provides a paradigmatic pattern, focus, and rule for our lives as Christian people.

---

41   R. Kevin Seasoltz, "Non-verbal symbols and the Eucharistic Prayer," in *New Eucharistic Prayers*, ed. Frank Senn (New York: Paulist Press), 233.

Rule of Prayer and Rule of Life

In the preceding, I have pointed to some ways in which the broad shape of our eucharistic praying provides a pattern, focus, and rule for our lives as Christian people. Although the whole of prayer requires closer attention, let us look at just two parts of that prayer: the opening dialogue and the *epiclesis* or invocation of the Holy Spirit.

The opening dialogue. The opening dialogue to the Great Thanksgiving is not yet prayer but preliminary to the prayer. Yet it shapes our understanding of the prayer as the prayer of a gathered community.

> *The Lord be with you.*
> **And also with you.**
> *Lift up your hearts.*
> **We lift them up to the Lord.**
> *Let us give thanks to the Lord our God.*
> **It is right to give our thanks and praise.**

The first thing we can note about this opening sequence is that it is, in fact, a dialogue. The Great Thanksgiving is not simply a presider's prayer that can happen with or without a gathered community. This prayer requires a community gathered for prayer.

Second, note that this dialogue orients us in two directions—horizontally and vertically. Horizontally, "The Lord be with you. And also with you" is a theological statement about the character of this community. We are a community in which Jesus Christ is present in and with us by the Holy Spirit and in which we recognize this presence in each other. At the same time, the grammar of this exchange suggests that this presence, while recognized, is also something that is mutually bestowed on one another. We gift each other with the presence and grace of Jesus Christ. More, because this exchange occurs in relationship to the Lord's Table, it now focuses our attention on the Table. Then, the vertical orientation of the summons to "lift up our hearts" shifts our attention from one another to attention to, orientation to, God. Of course, it does not require that we think about God as "up there" and humanity as "down here"; it does require that we recognize that we are not God and that if we are to pray we need to turn our attention toward God.

In the third exchange, "Let us give thanks...", we return to the horizontal, now with the specific intention of offering our thanks and praise to God. One of the distinctive things about this exchange is that it has the effect of "giving permission" to the presider to continue to pray not in place of but in the name of and on behalf of the gathered community. It is *our* thanks and praise that we now offer, even if in the voice of the presider.

This opening dialogue calls us to focus our attention on the gathered community and God and suggests that the awareness as well as the presence of the gathered community is paradigmatic for Christian prayer and that a rule of prayer is to offer thanks and praise.

Epiclesis. The invocation of the Holy Spirit or *epiclesis* has a twofold orientation—on the gifts of bread and wine and, again, on the gathered community. We pray:

> *Pour out your Holy Spirit on us gathered here*
> *and on these gifts of bread and wine.*
> *Make them be for us the body and blood of Christ,*
> *that we may be for the world the body of Christ,*
> *redeemed by his blood.*
>
> *By your Spirit, make us one with Christ,*
> *one with each other,*
> *and one in ministry to all the world,*
> *until Christ comes in final victory*
> *and we feast at his heavenly banquet.*[42]

Through this invocation, we make explicit our request that consecration and Communion, so often focused on the individual recipient, benefit not only the individual but also the world. Our request that the Holy Spirit make the bread and wine be "for us the body and blood of Christ" is surrounded by, even completed by, "us gathered here" and the request "that we may be for the world the body of Christ, redeemed by his blood." Similarly, the request that the Holy Spirit "make us one with Christ and one with each other" is completed with "and one in ministry to all the world." The communion we seek is not only within this particular gathered community but also with the world (and beyond). That is, we do not simply ask for something for our own sake, but make our request with God's missional end in mind. Our eucharistic *epiclesis* is incomplete without the request that we be transformed and empowered by the Spirit for ministry in and to the world. The benefits we receive as participants in and partakers of the bread and wine are benefits to be shared, benefits not for our sake but for the life

---

42 *The United Methodist Hymnal*, 10.

of the world.[43] Having offered ourselves in praise and thanksgiving, we receive this offering back, transformed by the Holy Spirit, empowered to fulfill our vocation to love God and neighbor.

This portion of the Great Thanksgiving shifts our attention just slightly—from the Table to the gifts on the Table and from the meal in the upper room to the meal in this room. At the same time, it keeps our attention focused on the community gathered around the Table even as it begins to turn that attention toward a larger community in mission and ministry. What is paradigmatic here is that this prayer, this meal, this gathering, is not for ourselves but for the world. What is canonical is that, as is true of the whole of this prayer, our prayer is and must be empowered by the outpouring of the Holy Spirit.

As I argued at the beginning of this essay and as I have tried to demonstrate in these brief examples, our daily life as Christians is the embodiment, the living out, of what is given in the Eucharist. The relationship between eucharistic prayer and practice and our lives of prayer begins, rather than ends, at the communal table and moves from it into daily life—and back again. It is the Lord's Table, rather than our own tables, that serves as paradigm, focal practice, and rule of prayer. God takes bread and wine from our hands and they become the means for sustaining and transforming our lives; God takes the offering of ourselves and we become the means for sustaining and transforming the world; God takes our regret, sorrow, and despair and returns it to us as thanksgiving, joy, and hope. Moving from the Lord's Table to our many tables we discover not only a link between eucharistic prayer and our daily prayer but also a link between all of liturgy and our lives. What we receive at this Table is the paradigmatic model, the focal center, and the rule of faith for the community gathered about each table at home and workplace, day in and day out, until the next Lord's Day and until the Lord comes.

---

43   This paragraph draws on a much longer discussion of the eucharistic *epiclesis* I develop in E. Byron Anderson, "A Body in the Spirit for the World: Eucharist, Epiclesis, and Ethics," *Worship* 85.2 (March 2011): 98–116.

SEVENTEEN

Eucharist and Ecumenism

Karen B. Westerfield Tucker

Early Methodist "Ecumenism"

Methodism's origin as a "society" within the Church of England has given it a natural proclivity to define itself in relation to other church-ly communities. Such a comparative and evaluative orientation was also encouraged by John Wesley's instruction in 1784 to "follow the Scriptures and the primitive church"[1] in matters theological and liturgical. For Methodism thereby received a norm and authority that is shared with many ecclesiastical traditions, though interpretations and practices derived from those standards vary widely. Thus, from John Wesley onward, Methodists have considered themselves free to borrow the "best" practices and theological statements of other Christians from the past or from their own day. For example, the perceived spiritual effectiveness of the watch night and the love feast in apostolic times and among eighteenth-century Moravians inspired their use among the early Methodists. Conversely, the questionable practices and theologies of other communities have been avoided, countered, or actively denounced, such as (for a time) the formal practice of church building consecration. John Wesley had publicly critiqued his own Church of England's praxis that was not authorized by the Book of Common Prayer, arguing that it was a suspicious innovation sanctioned by neither divine nor national law.[2] By the 1840s, however, American Methodists reversed

---

1   John Wesley, Letter to "Our Brethren in America," September 10, 1784, *Letters of the Rev. John Wesley, A.M.*, vol. 7, ed. John Telford (London: Epworth Press, 1931), 239. In some instances, this letter was bound in with John Wesley's *The Sunday Service of the Methodists in North America* (1784). A facsimile edition of the *Sunday Service* that includes the letter was published as *John Wesley's Prayer Book: The Sunday Service of the Methodists in North America* (Akron, OH: OSL Publications, 1995).

2   John Wesley, "Thoughts on the Consecration of Churches and Burial-Grounds," *The Works of John Wesley*: The Methodist Societies, vol. 9, ed. Rupert E. Davies (Nashville: Abingdon Press, 1989), §6, 532. No order for consecration was found in the 1662 Book of Common Prayer or in any previous version. The bishop of each diocese had the authority to create a consecratory form as need arose.

Wesley's position and sought to produce dedicatory or consecratory rites in order to displace encroaching Masonic customs.[3]

Methodists have also always engaged in honest and fruitful conversation with Christians of other affiliations, striving to exercise a "catholic spirit" even on matters related to worship and sacraments.[4] Indeed, as early as 1742, Wesley proposed that the "character of a Methodist" could offer an example of a more generous alternative to the religious tensions of his day. Because Methodists, similarly to other Protestant Christians, believed Scripture to be "the only and the sufficient rule both of Christian faith and practice" and professed Christ to be "the Eternal Supreme God," Wesley judged Methodists to differ both from the Church of Rome and from the anti-trinitarian Socinians and Arians. But Methodists were not to be distinguishable from other "real Christians of whatsoever denomination they be" should those persons uphold the "common, fundamental principles of Christianity." In those "opinions which do not strike at the root of Christianity," Wesley posited that persons "think and let think," that the Protestant Christian community in England be "in no wise divided among ourselves" and that they should thus keep "the unity of the Spirit in the bond of peace."[5]

Early Eucharistic "Ecumenism"

Within the context of inter-Christian discourse, and in the borrowings or critique of the practices of others, Methodists have been able to find and articulate their own theological and liturgical identity. Such a comparative and relational approach certainly undergirded what emerged as the "official" theology, rite, and legislation of the Lord's Supper for the Methodist Episcopal Church at its creation in 1784.

Lex Credendi: *Developing a Theological Statement*

A theology for the Supper is laid out in four of the twenty-four Articles of Religion that John Wesley derived from the Church of England's Thirty-Nine Articles and included with his abridgment of the 1662 Book of Common Prayer that was published in 1784 as the Sunday Service.[6] The Thirty-Nine

---

3   See Karen B. Westerfield Tucker, *American Methodist Worship* (New York: Oxford University Press, 2001), 249–51.

4   See John Wesley's sermon "Catholic Spirit."

5   John Wesley, "The Character of a Methodist," in *The Works of John Wesley: The Methodist Societies*, vol. 9, ed. Davies. (9:32-42, §§1, 17, 18.)

6   See n. 1 above. A twenty-fifth Article was added appropriate to the American context: "Of the Rules of the United States of America."

Articles themselves had been hammered out in a climate of ecclesiastical comparison and critique, as evident by affinities in the document to the Lutheran Augsburg Confession and by the clear rejection of aspects of the praxis of Roman Catholics, Anabaptists, and others. So, in regard to the Lord's Supper, the Methodists inherited via Anglican Articles Twenty-five, Twenty-eight, Thirty, and Thirty-one (Methodist Articles Sixteen, Eighteen, Nineteen, and Twenty) a theology born from inter-church controversy that defined the sacrament in large part by what it is not: it is not to be regarded only as a token of Christian profession and a sign of Christian love for one another; it is not to be reserved, venerated, or gazed upon but, rather, used; it is not to be received unworthily and without faith; it is not to be understood or deemed effective by means of the theo-philosophy of transubstantiation; it is not to be denied to the laity in both kinds; and it is not to be understood as a new offering of Christ. More positively put, the Supper is, when received with faith, a "sacrament of our redemption by Christ's death" by which Christ enlivens, strengthens, and confirms that faith. Wesley's editorial pen did not touch the Anglican Article "Of the Lord's Supper," but it did make two small yet significant adjustments to "Of the Sacraments." The Article defined sacraments as "certain sure witnesses and effectual signs of grace, and God's good will towards us." But Wesley, perhaps sensitive to longstanding complaints (especially from the Puritan wing of the Church of England as well as from Presbyterians and Congregationalists) about the language of "sure effectiveness" lest it give more power to the rite than to God and concede (as Wesley believed Catholics did[7]) that the grace of the sacrament could be received objectively *ex opere operato*, deleted "sure witnesses and effectual," leaving the definition simply "certain signs of grace." In addition, Wesley softened "damnation" to "condemnation" in regard to the stated consequence received by those who partake unworthily (1 Cor 11:29), again possibly in recognition that matters of judgment belonged solely to God, and also conceivably owing simply to a different translation of the Greek word κρίμα. Anglican Article Twenty-nine, which employs "condemnation" in speaking "Of the wicked which do not eat the body of Christ, in the use of the Lord's Supper," did not find a place in Wesley's revised Articles. Wesley argued that faith even the size of a mustard seed is still faith, which contrasted with the

---

7   John Wesley, "A Roman Catechism. Faithfully Drawn Out of the allowed Writings of the Church of Rome. With a Reply Thereto," in *The Works of the Rev. John Wesley, A.M.*, ed. John Emory, vol. 5 (New York: J. Emory and B. Waugh, 1831), Section VI, Response to Question 54, 785.

Articles's insistence on "lively" faith and the view of the Moravian Philipp Heinrich Molther (with whom Wesley debated) that a full, undoubted assurance of faith was requisite for participation in the Supper.[8] Besides, the necessity of faith stressed in Anglican Article Twenty-nine was preserved sufficiently elsewhere in the articles that Wesley opted to retain.[9]

Lex Orandi: *Establishing Liturgy and Prayer*

"The Order for the Administration of the Lord's Supper" that Wesley provided in the Sunday Service bears obvious resemblance to its Church of England origins—more so than does the first authorized sacramental rite (1789) of the Protestant Episcopal Church in the United States which, thanks to ecclesiastical politics, incorporates substantial liturgical material from the Communion Office (1764) of the (Episcopal) Church of Scotland.[10] Under Wesley's hand the 1662 rite remained mostly intact, though in places he abbreviated parts of the liturgy in response to persistent concerns about its length and duplications— since in practice the Lord's Supper order commonly would have been preceded by Morning Prayer—and he adjusted the text and rubrics to what he understood to be the American situation, especially the reality of clergy itinerancy. A few of Wesley's deletions matched the complaints of Puritans and non-Anglicans, among them the dropping of the rite's use of the "non-Protestant" Apocrypha (though, strangely, a reading from Tobit survives at the offertory sentences) and the removal of the rubric about the reception of the sacrament by "meekly kneeling" (which could imply adoration of the elements). Wesley's willingness to reappropriate early Christian eucharistic practices, in keeping with the

---

8   John Wesley's sermon "The Means of Grace" was written during these debates that took place in the late 1730s and early 1740s at the Fetter Lane Society in London where Moravians and Methodists met together. For a study on the Wesleys' reactions to Molther's views, see my "Polemic against Stillness in the *Hymns on the Lord's Supper*," *Bulletin of the John Rylands University Library of Manchester* 88, no. 2 (2006): 101–19.

9   In 1808, the General Conference of the Methodist Episcopal Church approved a restrictive rule that barred the alteration of any of the Articles of Religion. In the twenty-first century, the Twenty-five Articles remain part of the doctrinal standards of the United Methodist Church, the African Methodist Episcopal Church, the African Methodist Episcopal Zion Church, and other Methodist/ Wesleyan bodies.

10 See Marion J. Hatchett, "The Colonies and States of America," in *The Oxford Guide to the Book of Common Prayer: A Worldwide Survey*, ed. Charles Hefling and Cynthia Shattuck (New York: Oxford University Press, 2006), 176–79.

trend of the time both inside and outside of Anglicanism,[11] is shown by his expectation of a weekly observance of the Lord's Supper that would have been unusual in his time among Protestants: not only did Wesley delete the final collect "to be said after the Offertory, when there is no Communion," he also specifically advised the Elders "to administer the supper of the Lord on every Lord's day."[12] Weekly reception was unlikely for most Methodist communities, but weekly presidency (in different locations) was certainly possible by the ordained Elders.

Wesley made few additions to the ritual text, but one of them is consistent with Methodist practice and the preference of many non-Anglicans: a rubric providing for extempore prayer. Surprisingly, another common Methodist practice—the singing of hymns during the sacrament—received no rubric in the text. Methodists were not the first to use hymns/poems on the topic of the Supper for personal devotion or to occupy the time in song during a lengthy distribution or after the Communion liturgy; English Baptists had already put the poetry of Joseph Stennett and Benjamin Keach to such purposes as had Congregationalists with the texts of Isaac Watts.[13] The Methodists recognized the spiritual and liturgical benefit of these practices (at the time, hymns were not permitted during the Anglican liturgy) and utilized their own repertoire by Charles Wesley, most notably from a hymn collection inspired by and linguistically indebted to the Anglican divine Daniel Brevint's treatise "On the Christian Sacrament and Sacrifice" (1672). The significance of Brevint's work for the Wesleys was such that an extract of Brevint's work by John Wesley appeared as the preface to the 166 hymns in *Hymns on the Lord's Supper* (1745). The hymns were polemical and apologetic as well as devotional and functioned as a compendium of sacramental theology for the people called Methodist. Through poetry the Wesleys broached the sticky theological issue of Supper and sacrifice,[14] spoke to the controversy

---

11   On the eighteenth-century interest in the recovery of apostolic practice, see my essay "John Wesley's Prayer Book Revision: The Text in Context," *Methodist History* 34 (1996): 230–47.

12   Wesley, "Our Brethren in America," September 10, 1784.

13   See my essay "'In Thankful Verse Proclaim': English Eucharistic Hymns of the Seventeenth and Eighteenth Centuries," *Studia Liturgica* 26 (1996): 237–52.

14   Two sections within the hymn collection take up the topic of sacrifice: "The Holy Eucharist as it implies a sacrifice" and "Concerning the sacrifice of our persons." It is notable that here the word *eucharist* is employed. See John Wesley and Charles Wesley, *Hymns on the Lord's Supper* (Bristol: Felix Farley, 1745; facsimile ed. Madison, NJ: The Charles Wesley Society, 1995), 98–131 (hymns 116–57).

It is on the subject of the relation of baptism and the Lord's Supper that Methodism's tendency to define its theology and practices by comparison with other churchly communities becomes quite clear. American Methodists were often in competition with Baptists of various stripes who insisted on submersion and believer baptism prior to admission to the Table, and who might also practice "close" Communion that restricted Table fellowship only to members of the local congregation in imitation of what was believed to be New Testament practice. Attempts by certain leaders of the Methodist Episcopal Church to legislate baptism as a prerequisite to the Supper during the mid-1800s failed in large part on account of the absence of previous limitations and the lack of an explicit biblical injunction delineating a requirement and also because of the fear of appearing to be as closed as the Baptists. The Virginian Leonidas Rosser, a clergy member of the Methodist Episcopal Church, South, laid out in a lengthy tome his arguments against the Baptists, and in particular criticized reception limited to the local membership that fractured the two basic principles he understood to be fundamental to the unity of the church: common faith and brotherly love. Answering no to his own question whether baptism is "indispensably prerequisite to sacramental communion," Rosser made the case for "open communion."[24] Almost twenty years later, a similar perspective was argued by another Methodist Episcopal Church, South, clergyman, Jacob Ditzler, in a staged and lengthy debate at Carrollton, Missouri, with the Baptist Landmarker and polemicist J. R. Graves; a published transcript records their discourse focused on the connection between the two sacraments.[25] The Baptists were not the only ecclesiastical community to challenge the Methodist reluctance to mandate the long-held and ecumenically practiced sequence of baptism to Supper, and with the rise of the ecumenical movement at the beginning of the twentieth century and the rediscovery of early Christian praxis with the liturgical movement, it became even more evident that Methodists were not of one mind regarding access to the Table.

---

confirmands, supplied the necessary connection: "What is required of them who come to the Lord's Supper? To examine themselves, whether they repent them truly of their former sins, stedfastly purposing to lead a new life; have a lively faith in God's mercy through Christ, with a thankful remembrance of his death; and be in charity with all men" (*The Book of Common Prayer* [1662] [Cambridge: John Baskerville, 1762], n.p.).

24   Leonidas Rosser, *Open Communion* (Richmond, VA: Author Published, 1858), 7–23.

25   J. R. Graves and Jacob Ditzler, *The Graves-Ditzler: Or, Great Carrollton Debate*, vol. 3: The Lord's Supper (Memphis, TN: Southern Baptist Publication Society, 1876).

Formal and Informal Ecumenical Sharing: The United Methodist Church

The United Methodist Church, itself the product of ecumenical sharing and dialogue between the Methodist Church and the Evangelical United Brethren Church, inherited at its creation in 1968 the doctrinal statements regarding the sacraments in the Twenty-five Articles and the Evangelical United Brethren Confession of Faith[26] as well as two Lord's Supper rites that exhibited kinship via the Book of Common Prayer.[27] The new denomination expressed in its constitution the ecumenical commitment to "seek, and work for, unity at all levels of church life," and to that end established within its structures committees to oversee ecumenical relations and ensured that United Methodists would be participants in bilateral and multilateral dialogues both nationally and internationally. Through formal and informal ecumenical conversations, and by evaluating its developing theology of the Supper and related rite in comparison with the eucharistic reflection and liturgies of other churches, The United Methodist Church has been able to articulate a fuller understanding of the sacrament than is found in the authorized documents of its ecclesiastical predecessors.

Although discussions for the merger to bring into being The United Methodist Church were well underway, the Methodist Church in 1964 nevertheless published a new *Book of Worship* (which subsequently became an authorized United Methodist book) with a Lord's Supper rite that showed little awareness of the sacramental renewal being discussed in ecumenical forums and formalized in new liturgical texts. This disconnect was obvious to United Methodists who had been active

---

26 Article 6 of the Confession of Faith on "The Sacraments" defines sacraments as "symbols and pledges," and the Lord's Supper as "a representation of our redemption, a memorial of the sufferings and death of Christ, and a token of love and union which Christians have with Christ and with one another" (*The Book of Discipline of The United Methodist Church 1968* [Nashville: The Methodist Publishing House, 1968], ¶94, 45–46). Both the Twenty-five Articles of Religion and the Confession of Faith remain authoritative standards for the denomination.

27 The Evangelical United Brethren Communion liturgy included at the "Consecration of the Elements" a prayer that petitioned: "Hear us, O merciful Father, and of thy almighty goodness grant to bless and sanctify with thy Word and Holy Spirit these gifts of bread and wine" (*The Discipline of the Evangelical United Brethren Church* [Dayton, OH: The Board of Publication of the Evangelical United Brethren Church, 1963], ¶2253, 394). This epicletic language is doubtless borrowed from the 1928 Book of Common Prayer of the Protestant Episcopal Church, which had incorporated the phrase from the Church of England's 1549 Prayer Book.

contributors to, and participants in, the ecumenical and liturgical movements—among them members of the Order of St. Luke (founded in 1946) who were committed to the faithful and informed practice of the sacrament—and also to their ecumenical partners engaged in similar labors. In a 1964 letter to Order of St. Luke member M. Lawrence Snow (who would be a principal drafter for the denomination's new wedding liturgy), Episcopal Church liturgical scholar and ecumenist Massey Shepherd wrote:

> I am sorry to see the Methodists being so traditional and conventional, instead of pioneering in the light of current liturgical developments—such as, e.g., the rite of South India or Taizé. . . . [M]y main concern is that the revision seems to be made too narrowly within the compass of the Prayer Book tradition, and is not sufficiently oriented towards the ecumenical dimensions of liturgical revision that now are so important.[28]

Thus the Alternate Rituals Committee that began its work in 1970 on a "united" liturgy for the denomination was keenly aware of the need to produce rites that resonated with the best efforts toward theological and liturgical renewal in the other churches, including the Roman Catholic Church in the aftermath of the Second Vatican Council. Adoption of the liturgical movement's ideal of early Christian theology and forms, and imitation of the historic Antiochene pattern for the construction of contemporary Communion prayer (with a prayer in the Apostolic Tradition [ca. 3rd to 4th century], the often-consulted model) was in keeping, the Lord's Supper drafting committee believed, with Wesley's injunction for the Methodists to "follow the Scriptures and the primitive church." The *Sacrament of the Lord's Supper: An Alternate Text*, first used officially at the 1972 General Conference, was a liturgy of Word and sacrament following the early church's paradigm: the Lord's Supper on the Lord's Day was designated as the ritual and theological norm, which embraced both contemporary ecumenical schemes and Wesley's own preference specified in 1784. Though a clear departure from Prayer Book precedents, the alternate text was favorably received and the drafting committee continued to make further refinements, many of them based on the writings of liturgical scholars from several Christian traditions (for example, *The Shape of the Liturgy* by the Anglican Benedictine Gregory Dix) and the input of

---

28 Massey Shepherd to Lawrence Snow, March 15, 1964, Order of St. Luke Collection, Drew University Library, Madison, NJ.

(formal and informal) ecumenical consultants.[29]

Ecumenical sources, theological and ritual, were also consulted during the process of liturgical revision. Reports from the Faith and Order Committee of the World Council of Churches were studied, notably among them *Ways of Worship* published in 1951[30] and the convergence text *Baptism, Eucharist, and Ministry* (BEM) approved in 1982. Each of the five aspects of the meaning of the eucharist proposed by BEM—thanksgiving to the Father [eucharistic], anamnesis or memorial of Christ [anamnetic], invocation of the Spirit [epicletic], communion of the faithful [koinonetic], and meal of the kingdom [eschatological][31]—would ultimately find expression in the final version of the United Methodist rite. Of course, many of these aspects had been poetically addressed in the *Hymns on the Lord's Supper*, which was known well by the drafters. In addition, the consensus reached or the places requiring more conversation were noted from the reports that issued from international bilateral dialogues, especially those involving the World Methodist Council. National multilateral and bilateral theological statements were also examined, especially the work of the Consultation on Church Union (COCU), which published a basic shape for the Sunday liturgy as well as eucharistic prayers. "Eucharistic Prayer II" in the COCU document *Word, Bread, Cup* contributed the inspiration for the phraseology "Make them be for us the body and blood of Christ, that we may be for the world the body of Christ redeemed by his blood" that would appear in the final version of the United Methodist text; the majority of the original sentence had been composed for the Consultation document by a United Methodist.[32] The main United Methodist memorial acclamation ("Christ

29   For accounts of the process that created the eucharistic text, see Robert Brian Peiffer, "How Contemporary Liturgies Evolve: The Revision of United Methodist Liturgical Texts (1968–1988)," PhD diss., University of Notre Dame, 1993; and Hoyt L. Hickman, "Word and Table: The Process of Liturgical Revision in the United Methodist Church, 1964-1992," in *The Sunday Service of the Methodists: Twentieth-Century Worship in Worldwide Methodism*, ed. Karen B. Westerfield Tucker (Nashville: Abingdon Press [Kingswood Books], 1996), 117–35.

30   Pehr Edwall, Eric Hayman, and William D. Maxwell, eds., *Ways of Worship: The Report of a Theological Commission of Faith and Order* (London: SCM, 1951).

31   *Baptism, Eucharist, and Ministry*, Faith and Order Paper no. 111 (Geneva: World Council of Churches, 1982), ¶¶2-26, pp. 10–15.

32   The text from "Eucharistic Prayer II" reads: "Loving God, pour out your Holy Spirit upon us and upon these gifts, that they may be for us the body and blood of our Savior Jesus Christ. Grant that we may be for the world the body of Christ, redeemed through his blood, serving and reconciling all people to you" (Commission on Worship, Consultation on Church Union, *Word, Bread, Cup* [Cincinnati, Ohio: Forward Movement Publications, 1978], 26–27); see also Hickman, "Word and Table," 367, n. 13.

understanding of the structural parts of the eucharistic celebration is not always the same in the two churches, especially when considered on the level of popular piety and liturgical practice."

Questions arising from the structural parts were the familiar sticking points in Roman Catholic conversation with many Protestants: understandings about the presence and sacrifice of Christ as well as the matter of faith in relation to the sacrament. On the latter, the document continues:

> Roman Catholic teaching avoids the "receptionist doctrine" that sacramental reality is a matter of personal faith-experience only. United Methodists, in devotional piety, emphasize experience, especially the need to experience the presence of Christ. However, the language of their new texts makes clear that faith is located both in the church as community by the operation of the Holy Spirit and in the hearts of the believers. For United Methodists, faith is not located solely in the individual believer's response. It is the faith of the church which is the ongoing context of "the word rightly preached and the sacraments duly celebrated."

The dialogue participants concluded their document by admitting that their work together had caused them to "respect more deeply our differences and our similarities" and to view them as a "call to deeper sharing."

After thirty years of conversation, an overview of the progress of the United Methodist and Catholic dialogues was published in which the continuing controversial areas of presence and sacrifice were highlighted and joined with a third subject: the question of eligibility to preside at the Lord's table.[39] Yet when the decision was taken for the Eucharist to be the subject for the seventh round of the national dialogue beginning in 2008, it was determined that these problematic topics would not be addressed, but rather a pressing theological and ethical challenge facing the present age and around which both bodies could form a consensus: the Eucharist and the stewardship of God's creation. Since by this time The United Methodist Church via the World Methodist Council had signed on to the Joint Declaration on the Doctrine of Justification between the Catholic Church and the Lutheran

---

39   The text "Methodist–Catholic Dialogues: Thirty Years of Mission and Witness" may be found at: http://www.usccb.org/beliefs-and-teachings/ecumenical-and-interreligious/ecumenical/methodist/upload/Methodist-Catholic-Dialogues-Thirty-Years.pdf. See especially 19–23.

World Federation,[40] the seventh round was to consider the implications of that affiliation and so speak with a common voice: "We seek to move from justification to justice, from the solid ground of our common baptismal faith to a prophetic witness that shows our obedience to the divine Creator and our gratitude for the divine handiwork that finds apt expression in the celebration of the Eucharist."[41] In the document "Heaven and Earth are Full of Your Glory," finalized in 2012, the dialogue team affirmed together that "in the Eucharist we experience the unity of the mystery of divine salvation which encompasses creation, redemption, and consummation" (¶4) and that the "theology that underlies our celebration of the Eucharist is integrally related to our ecological stewardship of the earth" (¶5). To illustrate the claim that "in the Eucharist, Christians encounter the whole of the Christian story, the reconciliation of all creatures which is the fruit and promise of the Paschal Mystery," the common shape of the churches' eucharistic liturgies was employed, expressed in the general framework of "the gathering of the people of God, the proclamation and reception of the word, our communion with the Lord, and the sending in the Spirit" (¶14). In concluding the document, the team issued three calls to their own and to the others' churches: "to participate more deeply in the Eucharist by recognizing its intrinsic connection with the renewal of creation" (¶33); "to attend more carefully to the production of the sacramental bread and wine both in itself and as a sign of the interconnection of worship, economy and nature" (¶34); and "to practice stewardship of creation in a manner that insists on the relation between the church's *lex orandi* and *lex vivendi*—its way of praying and its way of living" (¶35).

Addressing the Sticking Points on the Eucharist: The World Methodist Council and the Roman Catholic Church

In the processes that led to the establishment of United Methodist eucharistic texts and theological statements on the sacrament, and in the

---

40   For the original Catholic/Lutheran document, see: http://www.vatican.va/
     roman_curia/pontifical_councils/chrstuni/documents/rc_pc_chrstuni_
     doc_31101999_cath-luth-joint-declaration_en.html.   The   World   Methodist
     Council's statement of association can be read at: http://www.vatican.va/ro-
     man_curia/pontifical_councils/chrstuni/meth-council-docs/rc_pc_chrstuni_
     doc_20060723_text-association_en.html.
41   "Heaven and Earth Are Full of Your Glory: A United Methodist and Roman
     Catholic Statement on the Eucharist and Ecology," ¶2. The text may be viewed at:
     http://www.usccb.org/beliefs-and-teachings/ecumenical-and-interreligious/
     ecumenical/methodist/upload/Heaven-and-Earth-are-Full-of-Your-Glory-
     Methodist-Catholic-Dialogue-Agreed-Statement-Round-Seven.pdf.

work of dialogue between the United Methodist Church and the United States Conference of Catholic Bishops, the reports of the international bilateral dialogue between the World Methodist Council and the Roman Catholic Church were regularly consulted. Starting with the initial Denver Report of 1971 (the quinquennial reports are often referenced by the place and year of their presentation to the World Methodist Council), points of agreement or difference regarding the eucharist were indicated (to greater or lesser extent) in each succeeding document.[42] A synthesis document "Together to Holiness" was prepared by members of the international commission in 2010 that drew together the accomplishments of eight rounds of the dialogue (through 2006), with thirteen paragraphs addressing the subject of the Eucharist.[43] At approximately the same time, Cardinal Walter Kasper, then president of the Pontifical Council for Promoting Christian Unity, published his own summarized collation of the fruits of the World Methodist and other dialogues and included a section on the Eucharist with observations similar to those in "Together to Holiness."[44]

In addition to other Eucharist-related subjects, "Together to Holiness" identified what could be affirmed and the differences that remained around the issues of Christ's presence and sacrifice.[45] Given the need for a fuller examination of these sticking points (with the persistent nervousness about transubstantiation and sacrifice possibly grounding some Methodists consciously or unconsciously in their own Articles of Religion), the ninth round of the international dialogue took them up in what would be the third chapter of the Durban

---

42 The other reports are Dublin (1976); Honolulu (1981), "The Holy Spirit"; Nairobi (1986), "Towards a Statement on the Church"; Singapore (1991), "The Apostolic Tradition"; Rio (1996), "The Word of Life"; Brighton (2001), "Speaking the Truth in Love"; Seoul (2006), "The Grace given you in Christ"; and Durban (2011), "Encountering Christ the Saviour: Church and Sacraments."

43 The International Commission for Dialogue between the Roman Catholic Church and the World Methodist Council, "Synthesis: Together to Holiness. Forty Years of Methodist/Roman Catholic Dialogue." For the text, see: http://worldmethodistcouncil.org/wp-content/uploads/2012/02/Roman-Catholic-Dialogue-Synthesis-Report.pdf. The document "Together to Holiness" was formally received by the World Methodist Council at its meeting in Durban, South Africa, in 2011; the Vatican has yet to issue a formal acceptance.

44 See his synthesis of the Methodist–Catholic work on the Eucharist that is embedded among his comments on other dialogues in Cardinal Walter Kasper, *Harvesting the Fruits: Basic Aspects of Christian Faith in Ecumenical Dialogue* (New York: Continuum, 2009), 176–90.

45 See "Synthesis: Together to Holiness," especially ¶¶ 100–104.

Report (2011).[46] Drawing upon the poetical theology in the *Hymns on the Lord's Supper*, Methodist/Wesleyan eucharistic texts and theological statements (for example, "This Holy Mystery" and the British Methodist "His Presence Makes the Feast" [2003]), and Catholic liturgy and magisterial teachings, the committee pressed toward greater convergence. Regarding Christ's presence, which both affirmed is a gift he gives to the church in various ways to be discerned by, though not dependent upon, the eyes of faith (¶¶79–80), Catholic and Methodists are also said to agree "not only that 'Christ is present and active, in various ways, in the entire eucharistic celebration,' but also that his presence is mediated through the elements of bread and wine and these become the 'sign par excellence of Christ's redeeming presence to his people'" (¶81). "The bread and wine, while remaining to all outward appearances bread and wine, sacramentally become through Christ's words and the Holy Spirit's power the body and blood of Christ and are able to convey the gift of his grace. The one through whom all things were made and who makes all things new (John 1:3; Rev 21:5) utilizes elements of his own creation to give himself to that creation. The eucharistic bread and wine are thus efficacious signs whereby the faithful are invited to 'feast on the Incarnate God'" (¶82). "Feast on the Incarnate God" is a direct reference to Hymn 71, st. 2, in *Hymns on the Lord's Supper*. The document does not deny that differences remain on this subject— Catholics identify Christ's presence in the Eucharist as a "substantial" presence (¶83) while Methodists prefer to speak of Christ's presence in a "spiritual sense" (¶84)—but it states that both together can affirm the "real presence of Christ" in the sacrament (¶88).

Christ is specified to be the one who "presides at and offers the Eucharist," and there he meets the faithful to unite them with himself "each personally and within the communion of the baptized" (¶91). Both partners affirm that the "Eucharist is the celebration of Christ's full, perfect and sufficient sacrifice, offered once and for all, for the whole world. It is a memorial which is not a mere calling to mind of a past event or of its significance, but the church's effectual proclamation of God's act in Christ" (¶93). Catholics, the document states, believe with Methodists that there can be "no repetition of or addition to" Christ's singular sacrifice for sins (¶97). Following upon the observation that Catholics speak of "offering" Christ's sacrifice and Methodists sometimes speak (particularly via the Wesley hymns) of "pleading" that

---

46   "Encountering Christ the Saviour: Church and Sacraments" (Lake Junaluska, NC: World Methodist Council, 2011), ¶¶73-134, 47–72; also at http://worldmeth-odistcouncil.org/wp-content/uploads/2012/10/final-version-dialogue-book-from-Clark.pdf.

CPSIA information can be obtained
at www.ICGtesting.com
Printed in the USA
FFOW02n0043201016
28590FF